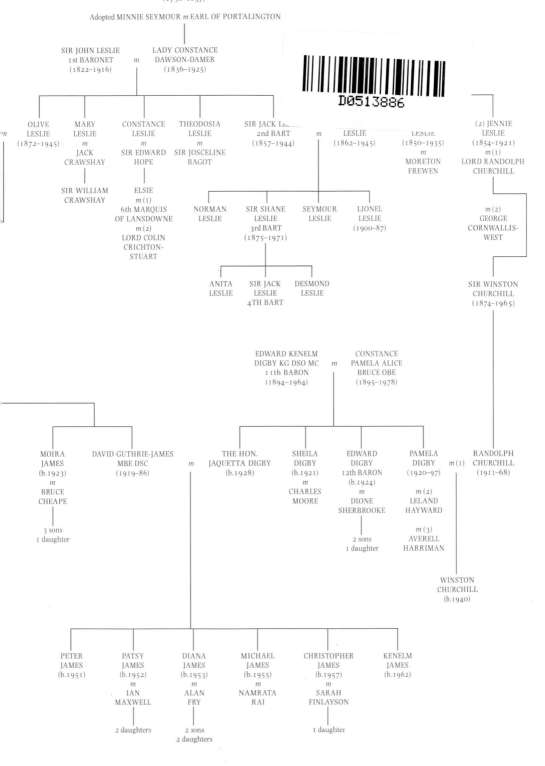

MRS FITZHERBERT
Morganatic wife of King George IV
(1756–1837)

Adopted MINNIE SEYMOUR *m* EARL OF PORTALINGTON

SIR JOHN LESLIE
1st BARONET
(1822–1916) *m* LADY CONSTANCE
DAWSON-DAMER
(1836–1925)

D0513886

OLIVE
LESLIE
(1872–1945)

MARY
LESLIE
m
JACK
CRAWSHAY

CONSTANCE
LESLIE
m
SIR EDWARD
HOPE

THEODOSIA
LESLIE
m
SIR JOSCELINE
BAGOT

SIR JACK L...
2nd BART
(1857–1944) *m*

LESLIE
(1862–1945)

LESLIE
(1850–1935)
m
MORETON
FREWEN

(2) JENNIE
LESLIE
(1854–1921)
m(1)
LORD RANDOLPH
CHURCHILL

SIR WILLIAM
CRAWSHAY

ELSIE
m(1)
6th MARQUIS
OF LANSDOWNE
m(2)
LORD COLIN
CRICHTON-
STUART

NORMAN
LESLIE

SIR SHANE
LESLIE
3rd BART
(1875–1971)

SEYMOUR
LESLIE

LIONEL
LESLIE
(1900–87)

m(2)
GEORGE
CORNWALLIS-
WEST

ANITA
LESLIE

SIR JACK
LESLIE
4TH BART

DESMOND
LESLIE

SIR WINSTON
CHURCHILL
(1874–1965)

EDWARD KENELM
DIGBY KG DSO MC
11th BARON
(1894–1964) *m*

CONSTANCE
PAMELA ALICE
BRUCE OBE
(1895–1978)

MOIRA
JAMES
(b.1923)
m
BRUCE
CHEAPE

DAVID GUTHRIE-JAMES
MBE DSC
(1919–86) *m*

THE HON.
JAQUETTA DIGBY
(b.1928)

SHEILA
DIGBY
(b.1921)
m
CHARLES
MOORE

EDWARD
DIGBY
12th BARON
(b.1924)
m
DIONE
SHERBROOKE

PAMELA
DIGBY
(1920–97) *m*(1)

RANDOLPH
CHURCHILL
(1911–68)

3 sons
1 daughter

2 sons
1 daughter

m(2)
LELAND
HAYWARD

m(3)
AVERELL
HARRIMAN

WINSTON
CHURCHILL
(b.1940)

PETER
JAMES
(b.1951)

PATSY
JAMES
(b.1952)
m
IAN
MAXWELL

DIANA
JAMES
(b.1953)
m
ALAN
FRY

MICHAEL
JAMES
(b.1955)
m
NAMRATA
RAI

CHRISTOPHER
JAMES
(b.1957)
m
SARAH
FINLAYSON

KENELM
JAMES
(b.1962)

2 daughters

2 sons
2 daughters

1 daughter

JOHN ROBSON

ONE MAN IN HIS TIME

And one man in his time plays many parts,
His acts being seven ages. – AS YOU LIKE IT

JOHN ROBSON

ONE MAN IN HIS TIME

The biography of David James,
Laird of Torosay Castle,
traveller, wartime escaper, and
Member of Parliament

SPELLMOUNT
Staplehurst

© John Robson, 1998

British Library Cataloguing in Publication Data:
A catalogue record for this book is available
from the British Library

ISBN 1-86227-036-8

Published in the UK in 1998 by
Spellmount Limited
The Old Rectory
Staplehurst
Kent TN12 0AZ

1 3 5 7 9 8 6 4 2

Set in Photina
Designed and produced by Pardoe Blacker Publishing Limited
Lingfield · Surrey

Printed in Hong Kong by
Midas Printing Ltd

Contents

Foreword

by Nicholas Witchell

THIS IS THE STORY of a remarkable man. David James was an adventurer, explorer, writer and politician. In many ways he was a man born out of his time. Yet he made the most of the time that he did have; seeing much, doing more and inspiring many. His is the story of a style of life which can now only be imagined and which can never be repeated. This was a man born a year after the end of the First World War, into a world facing change, but into a family which was part of the old establishment.

His father was a Conservative MP. There were homes in London and Sussex. Education was at an exclusive preparatory school and Eton. And there was a Castle in Scotland. David James was made in the establishment mould and would always be close to it. Yet, in his way, he rebelled against it; eschewing the route marked out for young men of his background to make his own way in life. Thus, aged 17, he left Eton not to take up the offered place at Oxford but for an experience in which he had to prove himself for what he was, as an apprentice aboard a sailing ship which took him on voyages to the far corners of the globe.

This was young David, the restless adventurer, always in search of something. It was how he remained for the remainder of his remarkable life. He went to the Spanish Civil War in search of knowledge. A few years later he found himself in a Nazi prisoner-of-war camp and began a celebrated, and eventually successful, search for freedom. Later still he explored the frozen wastes of Antarctica; braved the treacherous corridors of Westminster as an MP, restored Torosay Castle on his beloved island of Mull with his wife Jaquetta, and even went off in search of unidentified creatures in Loch Ness.

We need lives like that of David James. We need them to add colour, to induce wonder or, indeed, to spark argument. We need them because they are such a contrast to the ordinary, the routine, the mediocre and the humdrum. How dull it would be without such characters. Read, in John Robson's acute and thoughtful biography, of the places he visited: the sights he witnessed, the adventures he had.

Can one sum up such a life? His Housemaster at Eton came close to it at an early stage when, in 1937, as David embarked on his life of adventure, he wrote (with remarkable prescience):

> David is a complex creature, so muddle-headed and untidy, so full of ideas that cannot be expressed, so eager and sometimes so idle. One feels there are such great birth pains going on that in the end something tremendous may emerge.

Something tremendous did indeed emerge, and I hope you will enjoy sharing his adventures, searches and upsets as they are chronicled in the pages that follow.

Nicholas Critchley

Preface

HAVING WRITTEN SEVERAL ARTICLES and books recounting his early experiences, David James, after his retirement from politics and on his return to Torosay, intended to write his autobiography linked with his family history. He prepared a lot of early material, but in the event he was overtaken by illness and the project lay fallow.

In 1992 Jaquetta James, looking for someone to take on David's biography approached Elspeth Huxley, who was in the middle of writing Sir Peter Scott's biography. She declined on the grounds of age saying 'I shall be 85 this summer and with Peter Scott shall definitely have shot my bolt. The Peter Scott biography is full of interest – so would a biography of your husband be. It would make a marvellous tale.'

Having co-authored a biography of another valued friend, Jaquetta allowed me to look through David's papers and unpublished material and encouraged me to venture into this task – a daunting challenge as runner up to Elspeth Huxley.

After acknowledging each other on the hunting field, David and I broke the ice, during the unattractive circumstances of commuting, on the Haywards Heath platform. We soon found things in common. We both had to earn our living in London, but I had pigs to sell and he bought pigs. We shared the same passions for hunting, stalking and fishing and it was not long before he was generously sharing his sporting life in Mull with me. Every month or so we commiserated over our fate in London with a much anticipated lunch at Rules (steak, kidney and oyster pudding) or at the Cavalry Club (lobster bisque and lamb chops) which maddeningly he failed to consume, albeit well washed down with sherry. We found each other's company easy and drew humour from the inanities of some of his fellow MPs or from the pomposity of some of the sporting establishment. Deep down I came to share his passion for the hills and waters of Mull and respect for their denizens.

In presenting this biography I will be ever grateful for the help and encouragement I found among friends old and new in scrutinising drafts, offering suggestions and corrections or allowing reproductions of their pictures. First and foremost must be the family, the most prominent being, of course, Jaquetta and Christopher, Bruce and Bunny Cheape and Joan Hirsch. From his wide circle of friends and colleagues the following were especially helpful: Kevin Ney, Adrian Head, John Dent, Ron Topson, Michael

Mates, 'Junie' Clarke, Victor Russell, Richard Fitter, Susan Grinling, Julian Taylor, Hugh Cotton and Barry Penrose. For giving permission to reproduce their paintings or photographs to enlighten the book, I must thank Sancho Carlos, Sylvia Macartney, Tom Wells, Ian Orchardson, Robin Don, Peter Hodge, Jarrolds through Vivienne Buckingham and the British Antarctic Survey through the good offices of Ken Richard and Joanna Rae.

Of the publications to which I referred I would like particularly to recognise the information I gleaned from Eric Silver's *Victor Feather, TUC*, Tom Burn's *Use of Memory* and Robert Hichen's *We Fought Them in Gunboats*. I would have progressed little without the excellent and willing service provided by the East Grinstead branch of the West Sussex C.C. Library Service.

Finally the book could never have been produced without the good tempered typing skills of Ana-Marie Blunt, and Elwyn Blacker working miracles with his fine editorial hand and the design skills, dedicated application and patience of his staff.

JOHN ROBSON

I

TOROSAY: THE BEGINNINGS

Prehistory *to* 1865

Islands of wild enchantment
Riding the Western seas
Stark to the grey Atlantic
Windblown, the Hebrides

Names with an ancient meaning
Rhyme with the sound of the sea
Washing against them forever
Mull and Iona, Tiree.

LIONEL LESLIE (1900–1987)

LYING OFF THE WEST COAST of Scotland, at the end of the rift of the Great Glen, lies the magical isle of Mull. An eagle soaring away from Fort William over Loch Linnhe, past the enticing limestone greenery of the island of Lismore, pauses over the Table of Lorn above Morven's cliffs and the Sound of Mull, whose coasts were once guarded by eight sentinel castles with warning beacons visible to each other, stretching from Duart to Mingary. Over the Sound – through which the weather passes in an endless procession of light and shade, sun and showers, storm and calm – stands the forbidding profile of the Mulleach hills: Ben Meon, Dun-da Gu and Mainnir nam Fiadh, and the corries of Scallastle and Garmony. These are lit from time to time as on a stage by staggering shafts of sunlight, green in the spring, golden red in the autumn, white and black in the winter. To the north of Dun-da Gu's 2512ft summit opposite, the hills slope gently past the little harbour town of Salen, towards the distant wooded cliffs of the principal port of Tobermory, where a Spanish galleon lies hidden in the deep. To the south the hills tumble steeply to the sea at Craignure and the castle on Duart point, which looks menacingly over the Firth of Lorne and the Viking stronghold of Kerrera, behind which shelters Oban, the coastal hub of the Western Highlands. Tucked away, and cushioned by trees in a bay of its very own, Camas Mor, beyond Craignure lies Torosay Castle, one of the main characters in our story.

The geological map of Mull, psychedelic in its colouring, gives a clue to the volcanic island's violent beginnings, before the great ice sheets moulded and smoothed it into its present shape. Out of sight beyond the guardian ridge of Dun-da Gu lie the corries, hills and glens culminating in the massif of Ben More – at 3169ft the highest lump of basalt in the British Isles –

whose far slopes dive steeply to the western cliffs, sea lochs and inlets of Mull. From these, sticking out like a great finger, runs the Ross of Mull, a gentle undulating boss of red granite – some of which was filched to build the Albert Memorial and Holborn Viaduct – whose surface is scarified by unforgiving winds so that the few trees lie pointing eastwards. At the end of the Ross, alone and serene, are the islands of Iona and Erraid. Erraid, attached to Mull only at low tide, is familiar as the shipwreck site of Davie Balfour, soon after the start of his adventures in Robert Louis Stevenson's *Kidnapped*. The choice of this island as the site of the shipwreck was probably because Stevenson's uncle was responsible for the light there, as consulting engineer to the Northern Lighthouse Board and went on, in 1853, to build the 'Stevenson' Pier, which still stands at Craignure; it was used to ship in the stone to rebuild the house at Torosay in 1858.

Iona's fame is truly steeped in history. On the northern shore of the Ross are found the hexagon outcrops of basalt which emerge in their glory on the Isle of Staffa some five miles northwards out to sea and continue their submarine journey till emerging as the Giant's Causeway in Ireland. In AD 563 Ireland, in return, sent St Columba to Iona whence he set off the spark of Christianity across Northern Europe. It was the religious mysticism of Iona that attracted first the Scots of Dalraida and then the Picts to bury their kings there, followed by the Norsemen who held violent sway over the north and west coasts of Scotland during the ninth and tenth centuries.

Let us then retrace Davie Balfour's steps for some 30 miles to Torosay, starting across the windswept Ross and hoping not to fall in with the 'blind catechist' of the tale. The great sea loch, Loch Scridain, is on our left and was formed when St Columba won an argument with the Devil whom he pushed over a precipice on Ben More. The Devil, bouncing over a ledge, landed at the bottom of the mountain creating a cleft into which rushed the sea.

Over this loch looms the promontary of Burg, rising to over 1200 feet, at the foot of which stands a 40ft-high fossil tree in the inaccessible cliffs so aptly called The Wilderness. Also there lies the entrance of McKinnon's cave into which the renowned piper and his dog fled from their enemies. The dog emerged hairless, having struggled through to a small hole on the far side of Burg, but McKinnon has remained there ever since and his pipes are sometimes heard today.

Continuing our journey we pass Bunnessan, a little fishing village on the loch, round which the activities on the Ross centre, and which was brought into the twentieth century by the Royal Navy during the last war. On the opposite shore can be seen Tavool and Tiroran. Tavool was the home of the indomitable seaman, Lord Tweeddale who declined Her Majesty's command to swap his Albert Medal, awarded for bravery at sea, with the newly created George Medal. Further up the loch Tiroran was the erstwhile home of the Ismay Cheapes, whose story included serving the country as cavalry and highland soldiers. One of the family, Bruce Ismay, Chairman of the White

Star Line when the *Titanic* sunk, was on board at the time and took to a lifeboat when no more response to 'women and children' was heard. He was thus a survivor, but lived on only to die of anguish as the magnitude of the disaster overwhelmed him.

Leaving Loch Scridain near one of the Viking forts on the lochside we divert from Davie Balfour's route for a moment to take the road from Pennyghael which descends sharply over the lump of the Ross to the south coast of the island at Carsaig Bay. At the steepest and narrowest point of this descent stands in isolation a red telephone box, erected so that the lonely wartime RAF outpost could maintain communication with the folks at home, but was made entirely inoperative by the roar of the adjacent waterfall. At Carsaig we arrive at the site of the herb garden of the Beaton's, once hereditary physicians to the Lords of the Isles, who learned their skills from the Iona monks. As the years have rolled by it has changed its character, through chicken rearing and fish farming, to end up as an artists' colony.

After this little excursion, returning to the loch at the mouth of the River Coiladair, where otters work the tide and seals and seabirds make their living, we resume Davie Balfour's route and are led over the flats to the croft at Craig, perched on a jumble of rocks on the edge of a basin. This glacial

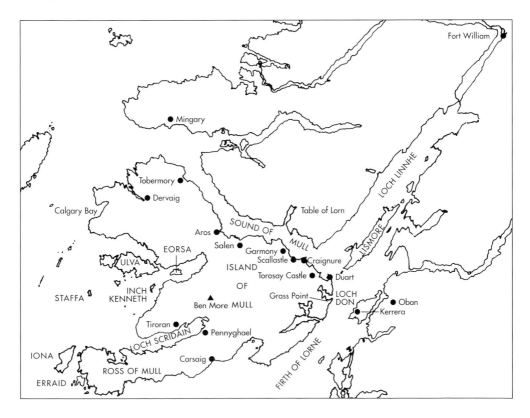

debris is a reminder of the ice-age through which the young river picks its way. All the while the mass of Ben More looms on our left as we climb steadily to the watershed. All that is left of the old road now are the disused bridges each side of what is effectively a one-lane motorway which cuts through the glen without twisting through the bogs and burns.

Over the top of the watershed to the right is the vista of the Ishriff lochs and the glen – the one time home of Siegried Sassoon – leading through the hills to the shores of Loch Buie, the former seat of the Maclaines of Loch Buie. Trudging on downhill towards the source of the River Lussa as it issues from Loch Squabain, named after a local giant, we pass the site of a clan battle in 1527 in which 'Ewan of the Littlehead' literally lost his and the headless body galloped into the distance. His father, the Maclaine of Loch Buie, was then seized by the Maclean of Duart and imprisoned on the Treshnish Islands so that he could not perpetuate his line. To ensure this he was put in charge of the ugliest woman in the district – who nevertheless produced an heir and went into hiding with him. Maclaine and seven loyal Loch Buie supporters fled to hide in Glen More, only to be found and slaughtered by the Duart Maclean. Even after this, as the years rolled by, the remaining Maclaines of Loch Buie were troubled by a rider on a black horse who appeared and galloped toward the graveyard to herald a death or disaster, until the last Maclaine to inhabit Loch Buie died. Loch Buie, which means yellow loch, is a broad sandy bay nearly a mile wide at its head with the massif of Ben Buie to the north-west and the cliffs of Laggan to the southeast. It is part of the Great Glen fault which runs from Inverness through Loch Ness, Loch Oich, Loch Lochy, past Fort William down Loch Linnhe, between Torosay and Duart Point and down Loch Spelve to Loch Buie where it disappears from view to re-appear in Loch Foyle in Ireland.

The road which follows the Lussa turns right to Torness, the old shepherd's hut which marks the Torosay march, and makes its way through the forest with the Torosay hills on the left and Ardura and Ben Glass to the right. By now we are at sea-level and the Lussa disgorges itself through the sea-pool into Loch Spelve, close by the monument to the poet composer of the Mull song, *An t'Eilean Muileach*. Crossing the flats, with Johnson's Glen rising four miles up to Sgurr Dearg on our left, we see the scattered rocks at the foot of the valley and wonder what terrors caused the crofters from the coastline to drive their cattle up there and persuade an old woman to turn them into stone. A burn emanating from Johnson's Glen is now crossed by a modern concrete structure which, nevertheless, is still called the 'Witches Bridge'. Still trudging the route of Davie Balfour we pass the road leading by Auchnacraig to the Grass Point ferry, the nearest point from Mull to the mainland, and the drovers' inn where the cattle were rested before being taken to Oban on their long trek from the north of Mull and the outer isles, to the market at Falkirk. Leaving the sea loch, Loch Don, with its rafts of water fowl in the season, we follow the coast near Craignure and soon come to the woods which hide and house Torosay in its discreet bay. From it are views of Duart Castle and away beyond to the hills on the mainland.

Having soared over Torosay with the eagle and returned on foot with the ghost of Davie Balfour, we enter the Torosay domain to discover how it cast a spell over the Guthrie family and became the inspiration for David James.

*   *   *

When Davie Balfour completed his journey through the glen in the summer of 1751 he would have entered the parish of Torosay, as described by its Gaelic name 'Torr Raseach' – the hill covered in shrubs – to find low ridges and hillocks sparsely covered by whins and birch and with views to the hills or to the sea. During his journey he passed a greater number of people than is found in Mull today. They were mostly broken and dejected, grubbing for a living and forced to forsake their customary highland dress for the uncomfortable trousers and coats of the lowland Scots, as a result of the decrees following the 1745 uprisings. Torosay, once part of the living of the Abbots of Iona, became part of the clan lands of the Macleans of Duart, but as a result of the running feud between the clans Maclean and Campbell – accentuated by the greater political rivalries of the Stuarts and Hanovers – their lands had all become forfeit to the Campbells, Dukes of Argyll, at the end of the seventeenth century. Davie, hesitating for a moment to glance over the bay of Camas Mhor to Duart Point, would have seen the skeleton of Duart Castle, reduced to a ruin by a garrison of redcoats which had recently evacuated it. It was not to return to Maclean ownership until early in the twentieth century. On his way to the inn and the ferryboat where the village and pier of Craignure is found today, Davie would have passed the crofts and buildings at Achnacroish, to become the site of the farm attached to the new Campbell dwelling. Davie fell in with a well-educated – soon to be a well-inebriated – Maclean inn-keeper and we leave him there to catch the ferry to Loch Aline the following morning.

During the early part of the eighteenth century the Campbells, having acquired the Maclean lands, ignored the ruins of Duart and instead built a comfortable house of the current early English Georgian style and named it Achnacroish, on the site of what was to become Torosay Castle. Up the burn behind the house the farm steadings were built, the farm square and tower remaining today; in front of the house, before reaching the bay of Camas Mhor, a walled garden was made. However, by the 1820s the Campbells were selling off some of their outlying properties and, presumably, the unco-operative nature of the remaining Macleans and the lack of fertility in the soil encouraged them to part with the parish to Lt.-Col. Charles MacQuarie of Glenforsa. At the time his illustrious relation Lachlan MacQuarie of the 73rd Highlanders was serving as Governor of New South Wales with such success that he became known as the 'Father of Australia'. He was to return to England in 1821 after an exhausting eleven-year stint, to die disillusioned in London in 1824. His body was conveyed to Mull and laid to rest in a mausoleum at Salen where the MacQuaries had put down their roots, having sold the Torosay estate back to some Campbells in 1825.

Colonel Campbell of Possil Park – now in the centre of Glasgow – a distant relative of the Campbells, the Dukes of Argyll, was from a family who had made their way through service in the Army and trade to become well established in Glasgow. They clearly wanted to stretch their fortunes by repossessing old Campbell territory and building up an estate, and to become known as the Campbells of Possil and Torosay. By 1850 their future was so well established that they demolished the existing house and commissioned David Bryce to build something more in line with their ambitions. Bryce, who lived from 1803 to 1876, was the unquestioned leader of the 'Scottish Baronial' school with all its accompanying pastiche. In the case of Torosay he combined it with the unmistakeable influence of a French château on the south side. It was most fortunate for him that his work attracted clients from the nobility and institutional world at the peak of Victorian prosperity. Many commissions came his way in the shape of public buildings – such as Fettes College, the Royal College of Physicians and the New Club in Edinburgh – and many commercial and banking establishments. In addition the practice renovated or repaired some thirty churches in Scotland, Ireland, England and Gothenburg, not to mention the mausoleum at Hamilton Palace, a feature on the motorway approach to Glasgow from the south. But the mass of his work came from the private sphere and numbered among his commissions were Armadale Castle, Skye, for Lord McDonald, additions to Blair Castle for the Duke of Atholl and the large mansion at Castle Milk, Lockerbie for Sir Robert Jardine. Other patrons included the Earl of Seafield, the Earl of Airlee, and Baron Panmure; his office became one of the major teaching centres of the day. Alas, almost all of his country houses have become victims of two world wars and economic depression.

🌑 *Miraculously, Torosay stands virtually alone and intact as a monumental reminder of Bryce and a most prosperous age.*

When the house was completed in 1858 the Campbells appropriated the name of the ruin which had been the Maclean stronghold across the bay, and named it Duart House. During their ownership of the estate they worked assiduously to improve the commercial prospects by planting trees and the aesthetic aspects by landscaping the park and surrounds with work such as realigning and pitching the burns with stones. On one particular wooded knoll they created a mausoleum for the Campbells, which stands pathetically today among the brambles, rent aside by tree roots; three of the headstones bear inscriptions but two remain empty. It seems that Alexander Campbell, who bought the property, died at Craigie Hall on the mainland in 1847, aged 63. His son John, who continued with the Campbell aspirations

Achnacroish, *the Georgian house built by the Campbells on the site of what was to become Torosay Castle, overlooking the bay of Camas Mhor. This watercolour by an unknown artist also shows across the bay the ruined Duart Castle.*

by employing Bryce, sadly lost a wife aged 33 in 1849 and a second wife aged 34 in 1851. Nevertheless, he still continued to create a prestigious Scottish estate and bravely held on to the family dream – until he could last no longer when trade suffered during the American Civil War and sugar prices crashed. Bryce's creation, sitting on such a choice site, with so much care and attention put into the planning and the landscape, was a witness to the hopes and ideals of the Campbells of Possil.

The Castle was not to be neglected. It was acquired by the Guthries, who were to guard and look after the property and its soul, much as a ship's company look upon a ship in which they are serving. Torosay became the home which nurtured future generations of the family and the Guthries, in their turn, were to make many sacrifices in order to keep Torosay as their heritage – a treasure for many people to share with them.

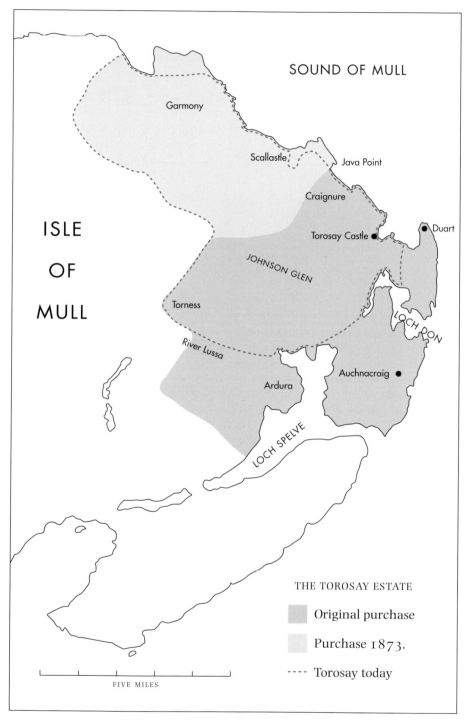

SOUND OF MULL

Garmony

Scallastle

Java Point

Craignure

ISLE

OF

MULL

Torosay Castle

Duart

JOHNSON GLEN

Torness

LOCH DON

River Lussa

Auchnacraig

Ardura

LOCH SPELVE

THE TOROSAY ESTATE

Original purchase

Purchase 1873.

---- Torosay today

FIVE MILES

2

THE ARRIVAL OF
THE GUTHRIES

1865 *to* 1919

Voice of clear and silvery sweetness
Breaks the silence of the hills.
Mountain streams all check their fleetness,
Creeping hushed in little rills.
Trees arrest their careless swinging,
Island creatures hold their breath.
As those pure notes to heaven are winging,
The very sea lies still as death.

Poem by MARY CRAWSHAY, to mark
Nellie Melba's visit to Torosay.

THE GUTHRIES sprang from an ancient line found in the Vale of Strathmore, near Forfar in the east of Scotland. An early Guthrie was known to be falconer to King Malcolm Kenmore in 1093. The Guthries who bought Torosay trace their lineage back some eighteen generations to Alexander Guthrie, whose son and grandson both fell at the Field of Flodden in 1515. Thereafter the family survived several vicissitudes by making sure that their interests always leant to the prevailing wind, like the Vicar of Bray, and in spite of the Reformation, civil war, Jacobite rebellions and other major disturbances they survived with their lands intact to emerge as respectable lairds, ministers or merchants in the east of Scotland.

Such a man was David Charles Guthrie of Craigie who lived from 1788 to 1859. With his friend, Patrick Chalmers, they set up as merchant adventurers in Dundee as Chalmers Guthrie and by 1810 the income from their joint 'trading adventures' had added £71,000 to the steadily growing capital of the firm. Shares of a ship's cargo were purchased in the hope they would reach port safely – there to be sold and goods bought for the return voyage. They soon became a recognised merchant bank in the City of London at No. 9 Idol Lane, just by the Tower of London, diversifying later into underwriting and insurance broking. David produced two sons; the first, James Alexander, was born in 1823 and the second, Arbuthnot, in 1825. The business continued to expand until 1840 when the Mauritian sugar-based economy nearly collapsed and the partners found themselves severely overexposed in sugar plantations. This was, therefore, a good chance for James, the elder son, to be tested in the firing line. Having recently come down from

Oxford, he was sent out to foreclose on a number of properties. Soon both the sons were fully engaged in the business but, unfortunately, became attracted to the same girl, Ellinor, the daughter of Admiral Sir James Stirling, the founder of Perth in Western Australia. The older brother won the girl but the younger one, Arbuthnot, in a fit of pique went off and bought Torosay in 1865. In those days a 14,000 acre estate, he paid the huge sum of £90,000 with cash which was found from the improvement in the fortunes of the properties on which they had foreclosed in Mauritius some twenty-five years before.

Thus Torosay made its first tenuous and gentle embrace on the Guthrie family.

No sooner had Arbuthnot completed the purchase than he got cold feet about the enormity of what he had done and put it straight on the market again. This did not suit the older brother James at all; he felt that his young sibling would always be looking over his shoulder at his beautiful bride, without something else to occupy his mind. James, therefore, in the autumn of 1865, went on an inspection to see what his brother had bought and was appalled by the price paid. He consoled himself with the thought that once the railway had gone through to Oban, ferry services from Oban to Mull would soon follow and the estate would clearly rise in value.

It had been a major operation for him to get to Torosay from London and necessitated a train journey to Inverness in the east and then taking the 'swift boat' through Loch Ness and the Caledonian Canal to Oban. Here they had to charter a small cutter to take them to Salen, where they found a dog cart which took them the five miles down the coast to Craignure – only to find that the inn was too small to take the party they had brought with them. However they soon arranged to have some rooms prepared for them at the castle which they found were 'as good as any man could wish'. The grounds were in good order and in James' opinion required no more money to be laid out. The sporting potential was seen to be about 10 brace of grouse a day at the beginning of the season and 10 brace of black game in the woods, while in the winter no end of duck and woodcock could be accounted for. There were only about 50 head of deer on the estate, which information came from a fellow called MacLaine who was said to be 'about the only dangerous man on the place and that sometimes he ate deer flesh'. The full list of servants comprised the gamekeeper, £45 a year; forester, £40 a year; ploughman, £24; gardener, £36 – but negotiating for a further £8; two apprentices, £5 each; a fisherman, a sawman and staff. The sawman had an additional duty to attend the gasometer which was used for lighting and which consumed 14 tonnes of coal a year at £1 a ton, in addition to the 45 tonnes of domestic coal at 12s a ton. This coal would have been landed on the beach by a 'puffer' at low tide in the little bay of Camas Mhor. James was unamused by his return journey, particularly having to wait for an hour on the old stone 'Stevenson' pier to get conveyed out in a small boat to

A 'puffer' *unloading coal at Torosay, painted by Ian Orchardson. Coal would have been landed in this way until the beginning of the Second World War.*

a passing steamer. He made it quite clear that an early priority should be the lengthening of the pier so that such steamers could come alongside. It was over 90 years before this came about.

Nevertheless, he persuaded his young brother not to sell the estate and so Arbuthnot, having acquired a plain and rather dreary wife Anne, settled down to 32 uneventful years of ownership. The couple remained there childless, but never let up entertaining friends and relations particularly in the summer when, with the aid of the yacht anchored in the bay, frequent fishing trips and picnics were taken. Arbuthnot used his wealth to collect objets d'art and was prepared to pay thousands of pounds for a piece of furniture including bidding spiritedly to secure two commodes from Hamilton Palace at £10,000 a piece. He then strained the goodwill of his guests and relatives, on returning from the sortie, by the niggardly economy of making two grouse furnish an adequate repast for a room full of hopeful diners. For all this mean streak his nephews and nieces enjoyed their visits and were prepared to put up with the unexciting Anne, whose waist became notice-ably absent, as did her hair as the years went by. The only bit of brightness she provided was a sapphire so large it was known as the Mediterranean Sea, which was permanently pinned to the ruche round her sagging neck. She was the sister of Field Marshal Sir Neville Chamberlain, who had been Lord Roberts' Commanding Officer in the Indian Mutiny. While she served her purpose as a companion to Arbuthnot, she was thought to be little consolation to him for his adored sister-in-law Ellinor, whom he never brought himself to meet again, except once after his brother's early death at the age of 50.

However in 1867, two years after Torosay had been acquired, Chalmers Guthrie ran into further trouble when Lyal Still & Company failed in Hong Kong, owing the partners nearly £575,000 – of which something over £134,000 had ultimately to be written off. This led the partners to turn their attention to pastures new in Central America where they enjoyed considerable success for some years. Arbuthnot put some of his improved fortune to adding some 10,000 acres to the estate, including the farms of Scallastle and Garmony in 1873.

Arbuthnot died in 1897, worth around £960,000 (well over £35 million today) and having made due provision for the dreary Anne, who retreated to her own London house with the contents of Torosay which he had left to her, including the Hamilton Palace commodes. The rest went in equal portions to his three nephews and six nieces, the children of James. Murray, James' third son got as his share, the castle, empty apart from the dining room sideboard – the only thing that Anne had left in the house, being too large to remove and which still remains there to this day – the estate, a steam yacht, two houses on the sea front at Oban and shares in the Oban &

The front elevation *of Torosay Castle in 1897.*

Callander Railway Company. But there was no supporting cash for the estate. In spite of being an extremely rich young man he was appalled at this additional burden and promptly asked Edwin Fox and Bousfield of Token House Yard to put the property on the market. The description of the property, as expressed by the agents, gives an idea of the state of this windfall after Arbuthnot's 32 years of occupation. The estate now comprised over 24,000 acres including Duart Castle and

> whether for beauty of situation, varied enjoyment, accessibility or extent compares favourably with any that have ever been offered to competition. There is a substantial and commodious mansion adapted for a family of rank occupying a choice position commanding views which cannot be surpassed for beauty. Seated on the hillside on the sloping lawn and having appropriate out-offices, numerous cottages, a shooting lodge and a dower house on the lovely knoll rising from the sound. The mansion is in the Scottish baronial style erected about 40 years ago from the designs and under the superintendence of the eminent architect David Bryce of Edinburgh. The sporting characteristics are varied and unique ... offering to the CAPITALIST (sic) and LOVER OF SPORT an almost unparalleled opportunity of indulging his energetic proclivities. Great attention has been paid to the sanitation and drainage, the water supply is perfect, being from a large reservoir on the side of the hillside, supplied also from springs, the running water by natural gravitation to the large cisterns in the tower and on the roof, thus avoiding the trouble and inconvenience experienced in so many country houses by pumping being avoided.

The particulars listed 16 principal and secondary bedrooms, 3 of which had marble chimney pieces, the laird's set of apartments, 7 servant's bedrooms, 2 lifts, 7 WCs, 2 bathrooms, 4 reception rooms, 1 billiard room, 2 entrance and staircase halls, 3 smoking/business and gun rooms, 3 staircases and a conservatory and domestic offices. It went on to describe the garden, rhododendron walk, lime avenue, rabbit warren and fruit gardens (the gardens being two acres in extent) and listed the fine orchard house, gardener's cottage, a carriage drive a mile and a quarter long, the drive through the shrubbery to the pier in Duart Bay and the nearby boat-house and storehouse for coal; not to mention a secluded cove with ladies bathing house, with the walls lined with pitch pine. The out-offices comprised; a stable yard, a coach house for 8 carriages, harness room, wash-house, stable of 3 stalls and 2 loose-boxes attached to the coachmans cottage of 3 rooms.

🌑 *Thus, once again, Torosay looked like slipping from the grip of the family it had so firmly embraced in 1865.*

Murray Guthrie was born a fortunate young man in 1869. He was graced with stunning good looks and an immense amount of charm which carried him easily through Eton and Trinity College, Cambridge, where he was bone idle in all respects other than founding and editing *The Granta*. He came down from Cambridge in 1892 and was immediately accepted as a partner in Chalmers Guthrie, by then the biggest importer of coffee into the United Kingdom through its Central American connections. Very soon, in 1895, he married Olive, the beautiful youngest daughter of Sir John Leslie Bt. of Glaslough, County Monahan who had just given up being a Member of Parliament. Finding his London home surplus to requirements he gave it to his third daughter as her dowry. This house was Stratford House*, just north of Oxford Street and Murray, considering this wedding present rather over generous paid Sir John £16,000 towards its cost. The cheque was found unpresented among Sir John's papers after he died in 1916.

Murray immediately set about improving the house by installing drainage and raising the two wings of the house by a further floor, in order to add further bedrooms. Not content with that he turned his attentions to the partners' offices in Idol Lane, which had originally been built by Sir Christopher Wren for his own occupation while he was building St Pauls Cathedral. Here he installed oak panelling through the hall and stairs and in his own offices. Thus a wealthy, good-looking young man started a comfortable married life in a superb house with all in front of him and produced his family. In 1895 Patrick was born, followed in 1898 by his first daughter Bridget. In 1901 his second son David came on the scene, to be followed in 1903 by Violet.

The couple's backgrounds and wealth, coupled with their natural vivacity and charm put them near the top rung of the social ladder. They were launched into a world of entertainment on a lavish scale, conducted with much grandeur. Part of their success was due to Olive's sister-in-law, Jennie, Lady Randolph Churchill, recommending Rosa Lewis, a freelance cockney cook, to them – or more likely persuading Rosa to take them on her books. She had started her career in service and became an agency cook before going on her own and becoming a byword, in great demand by the nobility. She was particularly in demand if royalty were to be entertained, as was the case when the Prince of Wales and Princess Alexandra dined at Stratford House. She later became the chatelaine of the Cavendish Hotel in Jermyn Street and held sway there until she died in 1952.

One of the highlights of their social life was to be among the 700 guests to be invited to the Duchess of Devonshire's Ball, the 'Ball of the Century' to mark the Diamond Jubilee of Queen Victoria in July 1897. It was a costume ball, each guest to come as a pre-1815 historical or allegorical character. Jennie Churchill shone as the Empress Theodora, Murray was attired as Cassio and Olive as 'La Belle after Titian'. Those members of society not receiving an invitation, found some reason to leave London for the time being.

* Stratford House was built by the 2nd Earl of Aldborough in 1776. Untouched until Murray's alterations in 1894 which 'did not improve the artistic symmetry of the original building', it is now the Oriental Club.

Olive Guthrie of Torosay, *by Sir Edward Poynter* PRA, *1889.*

After only two years of marriage, this successful social existance in London was momentarily disrupted by the unheralded inheritance of Torosay. The immediate reaction to sell it was soon thrown into doubt by second thoughts, and in the event Murray and Olive went to look at the place in the spring to find the hills and glens behind the 15 miles of coastline at their loveliest, so promptly took it off the market.

Once again Torosay strengthened its embrace on the family and prevented them slipping from its grasp.

Murray quickly had a vision of the setting he wanted for Torosay, and it is thought that he consulted Sir Robert Lorimer to help him effect his scheme for linking the house to the original walled garden, which lay some 120 yards away, by creating three levels of Italianate terraces. As these terraces did not lie true with the alignment of the house, a Statue Walk was laid out to connect the whole. This work was well under way by 1900 and on a visit to Italy he found a derelict villa on the outskirts of Padua, in whose garden were nineteen life-size limestone statues representing artisan figures such as gardeners, gamekeepers, serving maids and fisherman by Antonio Bonazza (1698–1763), which he acquired for a song. They came back as ballast in a tramp steamer from Genoa but the expense really began to tell when they had to be brought up from the Clyde by 'puffer' and hauled by farm cart into position on their plinths, as each weighed three-quarters of a ton. Thus this most important collection of eighteenth-century secular Italian sculpture came to rest in the Inner Hebrides.

The Statue Walk *in the gardens of Torosay.*

In 1899 Murray was returned as Conservative MP for Bow and Bromley in a by-election and six months later was joined in the House by his distant family connection, Winston Churchill. Olive's older brother Jack had married Leonie, the youngest of the three Jerome sisters, the second, Jennie, being Winston's mother Lady Randolph Churchill. The third Jerome sister married a somewhat profligate character, Moreton Frewen*, commonly known as 'Mortal Ruin', as all his schemes failed. Murray burnt his fingers on one of them, the Sulphide Trust, which predictably came to nought.

Then came ten golden summers at Torosay as the visitors' book makes clear by illustrating so vividly the wide and varied circle of friends who made the journey

Murray Guthrie – *a charcoal sketch by John Singer Sargent* RA, 1909.

to stay. Jennie Churchill was there when she received letters from her son, Winston, from Khartoum describing his part in the charge of the 21st Lancers at Omdurman. As always in those more leisurely days there was ample time for correspondence and she copied out the letters to send to her family and friends, including the Prince of Wales and her brother-in-law Jack Leslie, telling him 'This is the most delightful place I have been in – too lovely'. The main tenor of this letter was about spraining her ankle. This came about because her latest beau, George Cornwallis-West, was staying at Torosay and taking every opportunity to shed his duties with the Scots Guards to press his suite. Tactfully he encouraged Jennie's 12-year-old nephew, Shane Leslie, to help him land a record trout before setting out with the stalker and a ghillie for a day on the hill. Jennie, donning her stoutest – but not stout enough – footwear, cajoled her nephew to set off up the hill with her to meet them coming home, when her ankle turned and she hobbled painfully the four miles back. This story got back to elderly Leslie aunts in Ireland whose reaction was: 'chasing George – determined to get him – ruining the man's sport – serve her right'. Eventually she caught him – or vice versa – and they were married in 1900.

In September 1899 the couple were back at Torosay and were joined by Winston who shot his first stag there. He was about to set off for South

* *Mr Frewen of England* by Anita Leslie

Africa as a war correspondent and Murray tried to interest him in a bio-graph (a primitive cine camera) to record his stories. But the equipment was far too bulky and the idea was rejected.

In under a year Murray and Olive were to 'follow the flag' to South Africa themselves. Taking up the mood of the time, both felt that they should do more than being seen to support the patriotic cause. Murray, as an MP, was able to arrange a passage in February 1900 to Cape Town in SS *Norman* under the auspices of the War Office. Rail passes were issued – OHMS as requested – and the Remount Depot provided horses, to be reimbursed by the Army Pay Office. A nice touch was a chit issued by the Assistant Military Governor of Bloemfontein:

> Billeting
> Distribution of Military Comforts. Mr Murray Guthrie is
> allowed to occupy provisionally Mrs Bartman's House.

He was later allowed 8s 6d a day for his stay in the Bloemfontein Club.

Murray was accredited as secretary to an American field hospital and the Van Allan ambulance, with Olive to render what help she could to sick and wounded. Under this umbrella they did what they could towards the comfort and well-being of the troops. Soon after arriving in Bloemfontein they came across serious administrative dereliction in the movement and care of the wounded. A large number of seriously ill and wounded men had been left on the platform unattended for at least 24 hours, and Murray reported indig-nantly to the Press that he could not believe that 'the Principal Medical Officer had not even arranged to have a supply of Bovril on hand for the ben-efit of the sick and wounded'. While her husband pursued the medical inade-quacies, Olive got a canteen underway at the station. Eventually she became much more involved when an attack of enteric flu hit the area. The local Press praised Olive in their jingoistic journalism but managed to get it wrong:

> Lady Mary Guthrie of Craigie. I don't know if I am correct in giving her this title, but you take the word of a Tommy she is well worthy of it. Lady Guthrie with a few more ladies visited the hospital and found the nurses working a 16-hour day and thoroughly done up. What did they do! Write to the papers. No! They took off their coats and buckled to.

Lord Roberts, the Commander-in-Chief, whose biography David James was to write some 50 years later, got hold of Murray and asked him to organise the distribution of creature comforts. These had been sent out to the troops by friends from home, and were lying about in railway sidings between Cape Town and Bloemfontein. He detailed a sergeant and ten privates to help. Among other things Murray discovered 10,000lb of tobacco, which had been sent out for free distribution, held up, waiting Customs clearance. He cleared the tobacco at 1s 4d a lb, costing him over £650.

They returned home in July to a rousing welcome from the Bow and

Bromley Conservative Association and a safe re-election to the seat in October. Meanwhile he gave evidence to the Royal Commission on Military Hospitals, subjecting the administration to fierce criticism, while praising some individual hospitals and, in particular, the nurses. His conclusion read, 'Had the RAMC had at Head Quarters some man of capacity and determination there would be no occasion for a Royal Commission.'

Meanwhile the run of guests to Torosay during the summer was unabated. Among the distinguished visitors were F.C. Selous, the great South African explorer, naturalist and big-game hunter, who had led Rhodes's column to Mashonaland; Dame Nellie Melba, the Australian soprano, who was propelled by guests and ghillies up through the woods to view the hills, the sight of which caused her spontaneously to burst into song; Jeanne Langtry, daughter of the actress Lily Langtry, the 'Jersey Lily', an intimate friend of King Edward VII; Sir Edward Poynter, the artist and director of the National Gallery; A.E.W. Mason, a journalist who covered the war in the Sudan, from which stemmed his novel, *The Four Feathers*; the actress Faith Cellie; the talented Swedish doctor, Dr Axel Munthe who wrote his biography as *The Story of San Michele*; and Vice-Admiral Prince Louis of Battenburg, the First Sea Lord in 1912, and the father of Earl Mountbatten. Admiral Lord Charles Beresford, Olive's cousin, brought his whole command, the Channel Squadron, into Duart Bay when he was invited for two days shooting.

Duart Castle – *the view across the bay from Torosay. The castle was returned to the Macleans in 1912.*

Torosay found its walls humming during the summer season and the Guthries becoming more deeply enmeshed in its walls.

The end of the first decade of the twentieth century found Chalmers Guthrie's business imperceptibly sliding the wrong way. Problems in central America, both physical, such as the Valparaiso earthquake and the collapse of the guano trade, and political, such as the Spanish/American war, created instability leading to a currency collapse. This deprived them of their principal export market so that they were unable to finance their main activity of importing coffee. By 1907 things were in such a state that Murray, to provide working capital for the partnership, mortgaged Torosay for £58,000 and saved the day. Three years later a mortgagee tried to foreclose on him. His health was failing rapidly at the time but luckily his personal standing in the City still stood high and he approached his friend, the banker Sir Ernest Cassel, who made an arrangement to help ride out the crisis. While fighting to save his business, diabetes, then incurable, was diagnosed and a fruitless series of trips to spas abroad took place. He had been forced to give up being a Member of Parliament in 1906, and conceded his seat to his old opponent George Lansbury who set off on his path to become Leader of the Labour party with the comment to Murray that 'if there were more like you, there would be fewer like me'.

Murray's resignation as an Alderman of the City of London followed swiftly and sadly dashed his hopes of becoming the youngest Lord Mayor of London. To cap it all Stratford House had to be sold to Lord Derby.

The gloom was momentarily relieved in 1909 when Olive found herself at a dinner party next to John Singer Sargent RA, the American portrait painter then at the height of his fame. He enquired why she was so silent and, having been told the reason, reacted with no more than one of his notoriously gruff snorts; however, as she was leaving, he came up to her and asked if a picture would help. She said of course but she could not possibly afford to come to him. He replied curtly that all he wanted to know was how long Murray could sit for him and on being told about half an hour, announced that he would be over at about 10 o'clock the following morning. The result, a charcoal sketch, hangs in Torosay and shows the fragile good looks of a young man who had achieved and sparkled so much in a short life that was so clearly near its end.

Murray's mind was active to the last. He sold the ruin of Duart Castle to Sir Fitzroy Maclean, 10th Baronet and Chief of the Clan Maclean, and thus restored to the Macleans their heritage after 200 years. Nevertheless the deal was quite shrewd as it took place in two tranches. The first involved the ruin and about 10 acres of the policies which fetched £10,000, while the second made over about 300 acres of farm land for only £1,000. The proceeds were immediately put to acquiring the eighth motor car in Mull – a 1911 15hp Darrocq-Landaullette, number 5B310, coloured a beautiful blue with a white line – and installing an electricity generating plant. Sir Fitzroy, then 77 years old, was to restore the ruin painstakingly and live there for another quarter of a century until he was 102. At a gathering at Duart Castle on 24th August 1912, the Chief, Sir Fitzroy received a letter from Olive Guthrie. The letter was read to the assembled clan:

My Dear Sir Fitzroy.

As the day draws near for you to formally hoist your banner on the Castle of Duart, so long the property of your ancestors, I feel strongly that I ought to change the name of my house and estate to what I believe it was formerly called i.e. TOROSAY. I wish to leave the name of Duart to you alone, who certainly have the senior right to it. My husband and I loved the old buildings, and have been proud to act as guardians for the past fifteen years. Now it remains for me to wish you long life and all happiness in its possession and to express the sincere hope that as long as the tides meet and swirl round the Lady's Rock, Duart Castle will remain in the keeping of the Chief of Macleans.

Believe me,

Yours very sincerely,

Olive Guthrie

At this point, of course, Torosay gave up calling itself Duart and resumed the name of the parish in which it lay.

Sadly, in April 1911 Murray's sight failed; he lapsed into a deep coma and died peacefully, cut short at the age of 41. Had he lived but another eight years insulin would have come to his rescue and saved his beloved wife a long widowhood. He was buried on the point beyond the slipway where a cross was erected cementing the partnership between Torosay and the Guthries. Olive had a simple plaque set into the fountain terrace reading: NIHIL TETIGIT QOD NON ORNAVIT ('He touched nothing he did not adorn'). A friend was to write of him, 'there was nothing commonplace about this last year, the scene was changed from that London element in which he had moved so smoothly and so surely to his home on the Island of Mull where the last stand was made and the final triumph achieved.'

After ten years of social Edwardian glitter and living in the glow of promise and achievement, with the trappings of two substantial establishments in London and Scotland, Olive Guthrie found herself in very shortened circumstances with an uneconomic pile in Mull and four young children to bring up. This came after a fraught period of nursing her ailing husband through illness and his financial problems. She nailed her colours to the Torosay mast and valiantly looked to the future, which after 17 years of marriage was to lead to 32 years of widowhood. It was interrupted only by a brief marriage to Jack Stirling from 1917 to 1919 which did not work out. But in years to

come Jack Stirling's widowed daughter-in-law was to marry Archie James, after he and David's mother had divorced in 1936. Olive was elected as a director of Chalmers Guthrie in 1912 and became the first woman chairman of a London banking company in 1925, as well as being a JP.

☺ *She relied on the familiarity and friendship of Torosay and its surroundings to succour her, and in return held the estate together as an entity, keeping the staff, establishment and fabric in as fine fettle as was possible.*

Her background and beginnings must largely explain this obstinate and courageous stance. Olive was understandably proud of being only five generations removed from John Leslie (1571–1671) the 'Fighting Bishop', a colourful character who died but six weeks short of his hundredth birthday. A grandson of King James VI's falconer, he was born in Aberdeen and consecrated Bishop of the Scottish Isles in 1628. His fortified palace was on the Island of Lismore within sight of Torosay. From there he was translated to Raphoe, Co. Donegal, in 1633, and eight years later, at the age of 70 he married a girl of 18, who bore him ten children. In the same year he raised a Company of Foot to support King Charles I against the Roundheads. He was the only Episcopalian Bishop in Ireland to remain at his post throughout the interregnum and in 1661, when nearly 90, he rode from Chester to London in 24 hours to do homage to Charles II at his Coronation. For this he was promoted to the see of Clogher and the Irish Parliament voted him a sum of money which he used to buy the property of Glaslough, where Olive was born.

Her other great source of pride was that her mother, Lady Constance Leslie (1836–1925), known as 'Granny Boo', was the daughter of 'Minnie' Seymour, the adopted daughter of Mrs Fitzherbert, the morganatic wife of the Prince Regent, later King George IV. There has been much speculation as to whether she may or may not have been the King's daughter. The late Sir Shane Leslie's view was that Mrs Fitzherbert was such a devout Catholic that, while she would have honourably brought up an adopted child as a Protestant, she would never have done so for a child of her own body.

Olive was very proud too, of her old father, Sir John Leslie, 1st Baronet who inherited much of the Fighting Bishop's longevity, being born in 1822 and living until 1916. The span of years was such that in his childhood he met Sir Walter Scott in a stage-coach and in old age saw the first Zeppelin

OPPOSITE

(TOP) **The Dining Room at Torosay** *showing the large painting by Sir John Leslie of a monk preaching to peasants. The small painting hanging beneath the antlers of an Irish elk (extinct for 10,000 years) is also by Sir John and is of his daughter, Olive, at the age of 4.*

(BOTTOM) **The Drawing Room** *contains a large painting by Frederick Whiting* RP, *of the Guthrie children: from left to right, David (12), Violet (10), Bridget (15) and Patrick (18). It was painted in 1913.*

air-raids. Soldier, sportsman, MP, man-about-town, landlord and, above all, artist, he had a huge collection of friends ranging from prize-fighters (he witnessed the Heenan v. Sayers fight) to people such as the Duke of Wellington, Carlyle, Tennyson, Ruskin, Thackeray, Dickens, Landseer, Rossini, Chopin, and Mendelssohn. On the sporting front, he was one of the original 25 members who formed the renowned cricket club, I Zingari. In his political days he evidently took a somewhat cross-bench view since he played cards with Gladstone and entertained Disraeli at Stratford House. By all accounts he had that indefinable touchstone – charm.

It was his painting, though, that he took most seriously. Over the sideboard at Torosay hangs his *Roman Campagna*, an 8ft by 4ft 6in canvas, in classical style, of a Franciscan friar teaching country children. Their beautiful peasant faces do not quite fit in to any definable school which is perhaps understandable, being painted by an individualistic Scots/Irishman who studied in Italy under a German. The painting was exhibited in the Royal Academy in 1855, the same year that he won the Grand Military Steeplechase – surely a unique double. In 1858 he painted a large portrait of his bride – which also hangs in the dining room at Torosay, having also been exhibited at the Royal Academy. In the next decade he painted many other society portraits but thereafter his work fell off, probably because he had so many other interests. He was MP for Monaghan from 1870 to 1879, following in the footsteps of his elder brother and father, who between them clocked up nearly 80 years of continuous service in Parliament. He also had to administer the affairs of a 130,000 acre estate. In 1906 most of this was bought by Government under the Wyndham Act of 1903*, from which he received over £1 million in compensation. On the advice of Sir Ernest Cassel, financial adviser to Edward VIII, as well as Murray Guthrie, this was invested almost exclusively in Russian Government Bonds which only too soon became valueless.

Olive's rearguard action was fought with the disadvantage of being chronically short of capital and having two sons who were to be of no practical help to her. The first, Patrick, was a very sweet natured fellow much liked by everyone, but was fatefully weak both in body and resolution. He was absurdly generous and whenever he managed to lay hands on some of Olive's money it was immediately lavished on presents to all around him. He was a mental casualty of the First World War who never got over his experience; unable to give Chalmers Guthrie a lead, he saw the firm wilt away as he was to do himself. Having sold his Purdey guns, the only valuable possession he had, he idled his life away in Paris and died suddenly, on his own, in a restaurant, aged 37, in 1933.

There were then two sons who died in infancy, before Bridget was born in 1898 to be followed by David and Violet; she married Bertie de Klee, who

* The Act reformed landholding in Ireland; the Government advanced money to landlords on sales to tenants.

was to command the Royal Horse Guards. David, the younger one, also had no liking for work and always managed to fall on his feet but proved to be no help to his mother in holding the establishment together. He had a heart attack at about the age of six and was not expected to reach maturity. Nevertheless he went to Eton at the outbreak of the First World War and grew to be 6ft 4in. Still the recipient of sympathy and oozing charm he went up to Oxford and disposed of a very nice legacy of £5,000 (today worth £100,000) in four terms. His bank manger informed him at the beginning of his second year that there was only £1 0s 8d to the credit of his account. He replied 'Dear Sir, Thank you for your letter. Please give the one pound and eight pence to a deserving charity of your choice and continue to pay the standing orders as instructed.' On being summoned to the bank, within five minutes he was discussing racing with the manager. He concluded the interview by offering the manager a lift to his lunch date; he was somewhat taken aback to find a chauffeur-driven limousine outside. The conversation went, 'Mr Guthrie how do you manage a car like this in your present financial position?' To which David replied, 'Simple, I pay by cheque'.

This concluded the Oxford career but there were attempts at gainful employment in the next ten years. First Rolls Royce took him on as a salesman in Paris, but there was never time enough in the day to attend the showroom. The job came to a quick end, as did his two-day career as a reporter on the *Daily Express*, where he considered he was equally available on the telephone in his club as in the newsroom. There was a burst of activity in 1931 when he decided to fight his father's old seat at Bow and Bromley, but even the landslide of that year failed to propel him into Parliament.

He continued to irritate Olive incessantly as he lounged about Torosay, often half drunk by eleven o'clock and with an infuriating whistle. On being sent off for the day with the stalker in driving rain to get a stag, he turned up three-quarters of an hour later, having shot the heaviest stag ever in the forest at the deer fence gate. In desperation he was told to leave the next morning with only 5s in his pocket. The fare to Oban was 1s 3d; the cost of a rude telegram to his mother from the station was 3s 9d – which accounted for the 5s. Yet within 48 hours another telegram arrived from Cannes announcing he was about to embark on a six-week cruise of the Mediterranean, by courtesy of an old girlfriend he had run into at Oban station. Thereafter his month in Mull was spent with friends, and included raids on his mother's cellar when she was out.

When the war broke out he joined the RAF; his health and age precluded flying duties but he was engaged on various station duties, eventually being uprooted from his luxurious London flat to Canada. He kissed every girl in sight on his way to embarkation and was lost to sight and sound for a month or so. Then a telegram arrived from New York: 'All my dreams come true. Am marrying my darling Emeline'. The family sighed with relief when it was disclosed that Emeline was the daughter of Eugene Grace, the President of the Bethlehem Steel Corporation. His future was assured and the pressure was off.

Meanwhile, Olive, not lacking in courage, managed surprisingly well. Although there was not a great deal of ready money there was still quite a lot of surplus fat and she sold 6,000 acres of the low ground, including three of the farms, to the Forestry Commission for 15s an acre. This, at least, supported the estate the way she expected; in her view anybody connected with the estate could expect a job, although at a small wage. For example the wife of McKechnie, the shepherd, bore him thirteen children who were all found jobs somewhere in one capacity or another. At one time three of them were employed at once in and around the garage, even though the total complement of vehicles had been reduced to one carriage, one car and a truck. Deer stalking and fishing were let to help the estate pay its way during August and September. Luckily there was the dower house – called Java Lodge by its builder, a Maclaine of Lochbuie who had made a fortune out East – for the family to move into it for a few weeks each summer as Torosay itself was part of the let. But some of the fishing was kept back for herself and there were always a few days stalking for the family at the beginning and end of the season.

If Olive's lot was difficult, the state of the island as a whole was even worse and remained so well into the 1930s. Hill sheep farming rapidly became uneconomic and the tenanted farms found themselves with summer visitors as their only cash crop. In 1928 even the home farm had to be let. So, apart from the minister, the doctor, the shop, the innkeeper, the schoolteacher and the postman, everyone was dependent on subsistence crofting and/or the estate to keep them going.

If the overall picture was depressing the detail was far worse, since most of the seventy-odd farms, crofts and cottages that comprised the estate, were two-roomed, stone-built buildings with small windows and flag-stoned floors. None of them, except those in the farm square, had running water or sanitation, while electricity was still thirty years away. The main house graduated to its own battery diesel-driven supply, which supplanted the previous gasometer. But this did not have the capacity to do all the farm as well, though a 30-watt bulb was put in for old Mrs MacLeod, a widow living in a 'bothy'; this was considered very generous.

In these primitive homes people raised large families and the stench, on entry, was naturally appalling. But in those days the smell of unwashed bodies and overcrowding was not a shocking matter. When Murray was given Stratford House as a wedding present, the first thing he did was to instal main drainage since his old in-laws liked 'good country smells' and had an open sewer under the entrance hall.

The farm children used to wear clothes redolent of the Irish potato famine and none wore shoes except, perhaps, on Sundays. They walked barefoot four miles each way on gravel roads to school in Loch Don, yet one of them ended up as Professor of Surgery at a North American university. These good people lived at least in windproof and waterproof houses with no shortage of food. Their grandparents – or even parents – had been brought up in 'black houses', as in Davie Balfour's day, which had dry-stone walls, turf roofs, no chimneys and earthen floors. They shared their single room with their livestock for warmth, and frequently were near starvation in winter.

The lives of the children in the Castle were not all that different, except for access to a bathroom and a few more sticks of furniture. They were brought up in the attics opposite the rooms shared by two or three housemaids apiece, where the beds had to be positioned carefully to avoid the drips from the ceiling. They were only promoted to the main bedrooms, and the dining room – other than on special occasions – on either engagement for girls, or on obtaining a commission or a university degree for boys.

Basically, people lacked neither for food nor warmth, but everyone did far more for themselves, such as cutting peat, which was free, for fuel. They grew their own vegetables, and nearly all crofters kept a cow. It was not unusual to see the 'wee minister' rowing the fat bundle of a district nurse round the bay sea-fishing in the evenings. This was not because they were ardent sportsmen but because 'cuddy' (saithe) and mackerel were there for the catching and formed a staple element in the diet, being salted down, or smoked, for the winter.

It could be said that the only respect in which there has been an undeniable improvement both in standards and in human happiness is in the field of health, primarily because of the eradication of the scourge, T.B. This was kept alive by the mistaken, but thrifty, practice of passing on clothes of the victims to younger members of the family, instead of burning them. Medical care was basic with Doctor Reg, whose main line of treatment was to tell you to go to bed and stay there till he came back – which he did not do until either you felt better and got up yourself or died, when he came back to write out the death certificate!

Mull was not living in the 1920s or 30s but much nearer the 1880s. For climactic gulf-stream reasons, the ruling philosophy was nearly Mediterranean. 'When God made time he made plenty of it', and only a highlander on being asked to give the Gaelic equivalent of *mānana*, could say there was nothing in the language to indicate such a desperate state of emergency.

◉ *This was the background into which Olive's grandson, David, appeared in 1919 – which was to mean that the future of the Castle and its estate was assured until the end of the century.*

3

THE YOUNG DAVID JAMES

1919 *to* 1927

The Earth is the Lord's, and all that it contains,
except for the Islands and they are MacBraynes.

IN THE MIDDLE of Olive's solitary rule, David should have been born at Torosay but his mother Bridget had to go up to London for an induction, and he made his appearance there on Christmas day, 1919. It was realised that he would be deprived of a double whack of presents, so, like the monarch, his 'official', known as his 'bogus' birthday was celebrated on June 25th. The custom held until he went to boarding school and his Great Aunt Isabel James continued to send him a 10s note every year until she died, when he was nearly 50.

Great Aunt Isabel was born in the middle of Queen Victoria's reign. Her father died when she was a child and she devoted the first half of her long life to looking after her mother who lived to be 90. She lived through the Boer War and two world wars – without any discernible change in her lifestyle – in London north of Hyde Park until the outbreak of the First World War, when she went to stay with her sister-in-law in Sussex. On returning, the lease north of the Park had run out, so she had to settle for Knightsbridge, but continued to keep the car in Bayswater 'because that's where my dear father kept his horses'. The car did less than 500 miles a year but was kept on to occupy the chauffeur. She lived on her investments which in the main were those left her by her father, a partner in Barings, in 1872, and remained unchanged. The years rolled by until she took to her bed with a chill at the age of 94. One day she announced she was getting up for her lunch, but was told that her clothes needed airing. This was the final straw; she just faced the wall and died. She never displayed the slightest interest in marriage, but few people can have been so kindly treated by the Fates; nearly a century of turbulent history passed her by without visibly touching her at any point.

Between 1922 and 1926 David's father, Archibald James, did two tours of duty with the Royal Air Force in India. David and his sister Moira, known as Bunny, who was born in 1923 in London, divided their time between their grandparents but were mainly with the James's who lived at Herstmonceux Place in Sussex – a charming Samuel Wyatt house near the Castle, some time the home of the Royal Observatory. Even as late as 1913 his grandfather Henry James had slapped on an extra wing with a new kitchen and six extra servants' bedrooms. Little did that generation know what was in store for them. The staff consisted of ten in the house, four in the garden, four or five on the farm, a keeper, a chauffeur and a groom, whose charge was two woolly ponies and occasionally David's father's horse. Even so they were considered only fairly comfortably off – in no way rivalling the great houses of the county – and it was the world which David was brought up to take for granted.

The cawing of rooks and the sweet smell of new-mown grass with a pony, plodding up and down towing a gang mower and wearing canvas boots so as not to mark the lawn, were among David's earliest recollections. But soon sharper and far less sweet memories impinged. It was the custom in that well-regulated household for Nanny to bring David down from the nursery to the drawing-room at 10 a.m. and 5 p.m. daily to see his grandparents. One morning, shortly after his third birthday, he was smitten by agonising pain, which Grandmother tried to alleviate by pulling crude little toys round the table by string. But the pain grew worse and he was carried upstairs screaming, to remember nothing for several days.

Dr Bott arrived on the scene in his open Trojan with solid tyres, and diagnosed appendicitis, advising an immediate operation. Efforts were made to get 'the best man' down from London but to no avail because the telephone was temperamental. So, in desperation, the car was sent to Eastbourne to bring out the local surgeon, who operated at once on the kitchen table. The appendix had just burst, but peritonitis had not had time to set in and David recalled subsequent agonising probing around the septic stitches. With his father's timely return from his Indian posting, bearing a painted balloon, snatches of normal life began to reach his consciousness.

He remembered the General Strike with soldiers in Hyde Park, his mother working in a soup-kitchen, and being evacuated to Herstmonceux in a train driven by a amateur engine driver, who had three bosh shots at Hellingly Station; in the end he and his Nanny had to jump down on to the track.

The tempo of the changing world had not yet gathered pace. Porter, the cowman, a grave, dignified figure, made his daily visit to the house in a Sussex smock. He brought two pails of milk on a yoke for the milk-maid who had a churn, in which she made the day's butter, while Porter returned to his wider duties.

The foreman, Reg Post, kept a daily log of who did what – hedging, fencing, ditching, ploughing and the like. While the rest had some element of variety, Porter had none, other than a little overtime hay-making at 8d an hour. Day after day, year in, year out, he 'tended stock'. He had Sundays, Christmas Day and Good Friday off but otherwise his routine was invariably the same. Twice he had two days off on full pay with a cold, once he had a fortnight off work with flu on 15s a week sick-pay, which was then considered very enlightened – but otherwise he 'tended stock'. Only twice in eighteen years did he have any other break; once a full day off for a family wedding, and once a half-day for undisclosed reasons. But the incredible thing was that throughout this period, wage rates were actually falling. They were paid fortnightly and in October 1920 he was receiving £4 15s 2d per week. By March 1921 this had fallen to £3 19s 2d per week and, after further successive decreases, by 1932 it was down to £3 12s 6d per week. Yet he seemed a contented and greatly respected man, who was secretary of the local branch of the Conservative Party for many years. There can be little doubt that all the servants were acutely aware of the depression and were delighted to be insulated from it by the protective shadow of the 'big house'. Practices which had not yet died out included the duty of Menzies, the butler, to iron the daily papers, and for a man to bicycle for five miles out from Hailsham to wind the clocks every Wednesday.

By 1926 when David's parents had finally returned from India they bought a house in London which meant less time in Sussex but recollections and snapshots of his life keep emerging.

His grandmother's presence remained pervading, if only for her passion for measuring the heights of the family on the gunroom door. As well as the children, this included the adults, their father and three aunts.

Helen, the eldest aunt, devoted herself to good works throughout a long life, being diddled right, left and centre in the process. She was mainly remembered because her car had oil headlights that had to be lit by match – leading to frequent ill-lit journeys as no one ever seemed to have a box of matches.

Audrey inherited her mother's practical intellect and, as so often happens, married one of the most intelligent men of her generation. Sir Karl Parker, was trilingual, got a double-first in chemistry and Greek at Zurich University and went on to become Keeper of the Ashmolean Museum for twenty-five years and then a Trustee of the National Gallery for a further nine. Yet he never mastered the art of driving a car because he could not remember how to switch on the ignition, nor could he ever buy his own cigarettes since he never understood any currency. In old age he devoted himself to his pekingeses, which he adored, and to watching all-in wrestling on the 'telly'. Aunt Auds was obviously the ideal foil for this massive unworldly mind and, with her sense of fun and scandal, greatly enlivened David's year at Oxford. Her contribution to academic life stopped at 'Why did Dr Craster* not get on faster? Because of Mrs Craster, blast her'.

Finally there was the irrepressible Dorothy, known as Doot, who was one of the first women to make a parachute drop and who spent the whole of Hitler's war as an ambulance driver in Dolphin Square, seeing much active service. Her best story was of pulling an aged general out of a bomb-destroyed house and asking him what he wanted. 'Champagne, morphia and the Last Sacraments', the old warrior replied, which happily she was able to arrange before he expired.

Life pursued its placid un-ruffled course at Herstmonceux with Grand-

* Dr (later Sir Edmund) Craster was a Fellow of All Souls and also the Bodleian Librarian.

father James killing hours playing patience in between his weekly visits to
the Bench, while Grandmother anxiously counted the pillowcases or sheets.

In 1890 he had made one great combined business-cum-sporting trip to
Colorado with his friend Walter B. Devereux, a New York lawyer. Within a
week he had shot a mule deer and a pronghorn, both of which were to win
first prize at Goering's big game exhibition at Munich in 1938 and which
are now on display at Torosay. Otherwise his only contact with the outside
world became the six o'clock news, listened to on a cat's whisker wireless
through headphones, until his asthma and hayfever became so bad that he
had to take a house in London for August. But this was convenient for the
Daimler, the only car he ever had and which lasted for more than twenty-
five years, since during this period it was able to have its annual overhaul. In
those days you did not buy a car but a chassis on which to attach the body
of your choice, so in alternate years it went to the engine manufacturer and

Three generations of James's: *David, Henry and Archibald in the 1920s.*

the coach-builder. When he finally died it still looked as though it had come straight out of the showroom. It fetched £30, which must still have been a good buy, since it had never been permitted to be driven at more than 30 m.p.h.

Eventually osteomyelitis caught up with him and his legs became more bowed till he could only go round the farm on a twelve-hand pony and shoot off a shooting-stick. By Easter 1932 he had to be carried up and down stairs by the butler and footman in a sedan chair, though his morale remained unaffected. But this was the end. He was buried in the little graveyard overlooking Pevensey Marsh in the presence of all the farmworkers, who were his pall-bearers, wearing their Sussex smocks – save Porter, who was 'tending stock'.

As Grandfather James' health declined, rather than spending August in London, David was to start spending more of his summers in Mull with the other grandparent, the formidable Granny Olive Guthrie at Torosay – known as Gran'Ol. Unlike the well-placed James she was relatively impoverished but still maintained an even larger retinue than the one at Herstmonceux.

The six-year-old David understood this, partly through the sharp contrast with Sussex but mainly because Olive, who was both egocentric and lonely, seemed to find a little boy good company when taking him with her on her rounds and expiated on her own and the estate's problems. It was probably already in her mind that Uncle Pat, who was charming but weak and ran up colossal bills at the Savoy, and Uncle David, were never going to be able to take things on and was grooming her daughters Bridget and Violet – and to a certain extent David – for the succession.

This became apparent to David on New Year's Day, 1927. On a visit to see the farmhouse at Auchnacraig, which had been burnt to the ground while the tenants were all at the Hogmanay dance in the office, Olive announced that Auchnacraig was destined for Violet as the younger sister, and his mother, Bridget was to get Torosay. David realised even then that he wanted it, but was far too young to know why.

Olive was totally self-centred and talked incessantly about herself, her forbears and of her possessions, which last were always used in conjunction with the adjective 'lovely'. This became a standing joke with the rest of the family: 'Archie, would you like to go out stalking tomorrow to get one of my lovely stags?' 'Bridget, dear, would you like to take David to Glennan for some of my lovely trout? And don't be too long because Jean Massereene's coming to tea and I'd like you to show her round my lovely garden', and so on.

She talked but little about her husband, Murray Guthrie, as the subject still pained her; but when she did it was always with the prefix 'dear'. Indeed, until David learnt to read the inscription on the beautiful Celtic cross which surmounts his grave and faces up Loch Linnhe, he always thought his name was 'Dearmurray'. But when she did talk of him she so surrounded him with light that its brilliance obscured the talented, tragic, yet infinitely brave, man he must have been.

David's earlier recollections embrace his first encounter with dt's when

Agnes Champion, *always known as 'Agg', joined the family as Nanny before Bridget was born. Always cheerful, she was a great favourite with David and his sister.*

still very small. Java, the dower house, was let on a long lease to a couple who had both taken to the bottle. When the weather was bad they used to take to their beds, surrounded by booze, and stay there for days. David was puzzled to call and find the husband picking flowers off the carpet, being much troubled by green horses that were stranded on the top of trees, and thousands of finches that attacked them when they walked down to the Point.

Although David spent two or three months a year at Torosay, usually with his mother, his early recollections of the place were far less clear than those of Herstmonceux. This was probably because he was nearly always there in winter with short hours of daylight and frequently days on end with rain. The nurseries were up in the attic where the wind sighed and moaned round the spires and turrets – which to a small boy seemed most romantic.

Constrained by the weather then, it is not surprising that David's allies (or adversaries, according to his behaviour!) were the old retainers. First and foremost there was Agg, who joined the family as Nanny before Bridget was born, then brought up David and his sister and finally played an elder states-man's role with his children. She was always loyal and cheerful, yet it was clear that being born in Brixton in the early eighties had been tough in the extreme. How loyalty was generated out of her background circumstances it is hard to tell. She died peacefully and happily at Torosay in 1955 in her 81st year. David, who had been carried in her arms as a baby, was proud in his turn to be pall-bearer at her funeral.

Next there came the long-suffering 'Fletch' (Miss Fletcher), Olive's lady's maid who used to have David on her bed for his afternoon rest and read the Golliwog books to him. She, unhappily, died of cancer just before the war after being with Olive for more than thirty years. In spite of the fact that she never earned more than £40 a year – a reasonable wage in those days – her will actually got into the papers because she left more than £4,000. Evidently she had never spent a penny on herself but, being privy to all Olive's correspon-dence, had picked up stockbroker's tips and invested shrewdly.

Then there was Florrie, the cook, who hailed from Sandringham and ulti-mately married Archie McColl, the gamekeeper. They stayed on in Mull after Olive's death in a 'grace-and-favour' cottage, and when Archie, her hus-band, died, Florrie continued to help out all and sundry to complete her golden jubilee on the island. So far as she was concerned, David was either the apple of her eye – with the freedom of the raisin tin or sweet condensed milk whenever he asked – or was *persona non grata*, as when he and his cousin William Crawshay dropped a horseshoe down one of the chimneys in the tower which, by ill-fortune, landed in her best game soup.

John Bill was the butler and in more than forty years never lost his cock-ney accent. David and his cousin, Jackie Leslie, got into his bad books when they spread butter over the dining-room parquet floor, and he went for six bringing in the joint at a large dinner party, but neither boy could under-stand why none of the absurd grown-ups found it funny. But John had a nice dry cockney wit. Once, on an unusually foul day, he brought the tea into the drawing room and was asked what he'd do if he won the Irish Sweep. His reply, peering through the rain at the barely visible bay, was that 'I'd go to the seaside for a nice 'oliday and change'. He had a terrible smoker's cough, which was quickly picked up by the pantry parrot, so that the basement was rarely silent. There was always a puckish grin on his face whenever the parrot, in his name, summoned the dogs for 'dinners' or 'walkies'. Among the male guests shove ha'penny in the pantry with John was always a popular pastime, not least because there always seemed to be plenty of port 'left-over'. Olive did not mind since it cost only 2s 6d a bottle – and the family did not mind because there was that much less for the old girl to tuck into!

Others came and went but these four stalwarts were immutable. While today it sounds a bit feudal, in those days they were looked upon more as friends and 'confidantes' than servants. They, for their part, felt themselves to be members of the family and regarded Torosay as being their home, where they could expect to stay until death.

*   *   *

The journey to Mull today is of little account as evidenced by the hordes of day-trippers, back-packers and tourists who visit the island during the summer months. But in David's childhood a visit was a prolonged and measured adventure which engendered a thrill of anticipation on every occasion. The old L.M.S. (London, Midland and Scottish Railway) ran directly from Euston to Oban via Stirling, leaving at 11 p.m. There was never any question of travelling in a first-class sleeper and third-class sleepers were not introduced until some time later. All they could do was to hope for a compartment to themselves and then his mother and Agg slept across the seats with their middles supported by suitcases, while David and his sister slept full length on the residual areas of seats between them. The only prolonged stop was at Crewe, where the wheeltapper struck the wheels with a hammer to make sure there were no cracks in the cast wheels, an elementary but effective safety procedure of the day.

The train was split at Stirling and the back portion was shunted into a siding until two engines, together with a dining car, arrived to take it to Oban. At this point breakfast was provided, consisting of porridge, haddock or kipper, followed by bacon and eggs, rolls and marmalade, toast and coffee at the cost of 4s each. The scenery got steadily wilder as the west coast was approached and such a litany of romantic station names paraded by – Bridge of Allan, Callander, Strathyre, Balquidder (of Rob Roy fame), Lochearnhead, Killin Junction, and Crianlarich. Here there were two stations, Upper, which was on the L.N.E.R. (London and North Eastern Railway) line to Fort William and Mallaig, and Lower from which the journey was continued through Tyndrum and Dalmally, Lochawe and the gloomy pass of Brander to Taynuilt and Connel Ferry. There, weather permitting, they would have their first glimpse of the sea and Mull beyond. The train arrived at Oban at 12.30 p.m. after a thirteen-and-a-half-hour, and 500-mile, journey which can now be done very easily in nine hours by car.

At Oban, then the focal point for all travel to the Isles, meeting the train were about a dozen elderly porters with large four-wheeled barrows. They were there to push the luggage 400 yards round the quay to the North Pier, where the *Lochinvar* waited. It was important that the porters did not muddle up the passengers' luggage because going north up the Sound of Mull, the *Lochinvar* called first at Craignure on Mull to port, then at Lochaline on the mainland to starboard, followed by Salen (port) Drimmin (starboard) and finally on to Tobermory, where she spent the night. So an immensely stout sailor with the words 'Passengers Luggage' emblazoned on his jersey had to ensure that everything was the appropriate side of the ship and in the right pile for unloading.

One day a new errand boy arrived on board to leave a parcel which he put down beside the gangplank. 'Where's yon going to, laddie?' asked 'Passengers Luggage'. 'To Craignure' the boy replied. 'Well take it over to the other side of the deck' he was told 'that side of the boat doesn't stop at Craignure'.

But the North Pier was to see many tricky problems when the time came to load the three cars that *Lochinvar* could carry as deck cargo for discharge at Salen or Tobermory. At low water this was particularly unnerving since the driver had literally to 'walk the plank', or rather two planks. These were put out at right angles and, with nothing other than a rather frayed bit of rope attached to the rear bumper and taken round a lamp-post, he had to edge his way until the planks tilted forward, sometimes at a terrifying angle. The rope would groan as it took the strain and the driver was eased down on deck. By this time he was keen to partake of the liquid refreshment which was plentiful on board – and always necessary after such an ordeal.

As soon as she sailed, a splendidly dressed steward would come up waving a menu fit to grace the Savoy and would say 'What will ye take?' On being asked 'what was on?' the reply, for over more than fifty years, never varied from 'mince or corned beef'. By the time this had been finished, followed by prunes – 'rice or custard, sir?' – Craignure itself was in sight.

The 'Stevenson' pier at Craignure had been built as famine relief work at the time of the Irish potato famine, which hit Scotland equally hard. But it was nothing like long enough for anything other than a 'puffer' to come alongside: indeed, at low water, even the end of the pier was left high and dry at spring tides. Therefore, in almost any wind and weather, a large open barge was rowed out by the brothers Donald and Alan to come alongside *Lochinvar*'s lower deck, where passengers, luggage, livestock and bicycles were piled in willy-nilly by 'Passengers Luggage' and his band of seamen. In view of the fact that there could be upwards of thirty passengers, that the baggage could be piled eight feet high and that there were frequently sheep, leaving only a few inches of freeboard, it is almost miraculous to think that with two calls a day, six days a week for more than one hundred years, there was no loss of passenger life – though on a number of occasions some very wet and frightened travellers ended up soaked on the beach.

Although the much-loved *Lochinvar* was a twin-screwed steel motor vessel, which served for more than half a century, most of the MacBrayne ships were paddle-steamers, built of iron. There was the *Fusilier*, built in 1888 and destined to survive until 1934, the twin-funnelled *Iona* on the round-the-island cruise, (billed by MacBraynes as 'sailing daily from Oban to Oban'), built as early as 1864 and lasting until 1936 and the *Gondolier*, which ran until the outbreak of war. But tragedy struck the *Grenadier*, which was burnt down to the water's edge alongside the North Pier in September 1927, with heavy loss of life. Small wonder is it that MacBrayne's ships with their red and black funnels have played such a large part in the lives of all at Torosay.

Certainly the modern fast ferries with six sailings daily, capacity for 1,000 passengers and eighty roll-on-roll-off cars are infinitely more convenient but, sadly, much of the old atmosphere has been lost, in exactly the same way as the diesel-electric engine lacks the attraction of the steam engine.

In his early days, David was traipsed round the dozen or so estates on the island, to be shown off by his grandmother. This gave him a good feel for the island, while Olive filled his mind with tales and legends while they processed.

Mull might be likened to a figure of eight with the squeezed-in waist at Salen and with Tobermory and Dervaig in the northern half and Torosay and the Benmore massif in the southern, with a long tail running down a

MacBrayne's continuity *portrayed by Ian Orchardson.* Loch Earn *(Lochinvar's successor) hands over to* Columba *at Craignure in 1964. This was the first step towards bringing over 300 cars a day to Mull, instead of 5 or 6. The* Loch Earn *was retired to the Greek islands while* Columba *has been converted to a prestigious cruise ship, the* Highland Princess, *still plying to her old haunts.*

further twenty miles to Iona at the bottom. The roads were all unmetalled and on hills and braes it was not unusual for the passengers to have to get out and push. On the way to Salen David remembered the car being stopped just outside so that his grandmother could have a gossip with Archie Cattenach, the stalker on Glenforsa, their nearest neighbour. David was shattered by his bright red wig. From the age of six he had been allowed to come for an hour to the New Year's Eve party in the office and hilarious occasions these turned out to be. They started sedately enough with the men sitting on one side and the ladies sitting on the other until the Castle party, in full evening dress, arrived at about 11 p.m. when the ice thawed. It was on such an occasion that Archie sported a black wig.

On one of these New Year's Eve parties, customarily given by Olive – ostensibly for the staff and ghillies – she had invited some of her Leslie relations from Ireland to stay. Neighbouring lairds and families were invited to dine in the Castle beforehand, and those from the far ends of Mull put up for the night. Quite which of the servants, for whose benefit the ceilidh was being held, cooked and served the dinner has not been ascertained. However, it got under way and after the first sets of reels and country dances were over, the mood changed to a waltz. Young Jack Leslie, aged 12, who had been pressed into service to keep up the coal fires, was far from shy and asked the tall, dark and awesome Lady Massereene – clad in a backless evening dress with her back powdered white – to waltz with him. When it was over to the joy of the staff and the guests, he bowed gracefully and withdrew, leaving a coal black imprint of a hand on her spine. The comparison between Olive's entertaining at Torosay with that of her early days at Stratford House could not be more marked, but for all the drop in grandeur it attracted as many people from different walks of life. The elegance may have gone but the spirit had not.

The abbey at Iona made the deepest impression on the young David in the days before it was restored. For the rest of his life he confessed to a prejudice here because he felt that the restoration had in some indefinable way deprived the place of its original atmosphere which was one of centuries of peace. Nor can this feeling be explained away by the absence of tourists, since, although coaches did not start to roll down the glen until the arrival of the new ferry in 1964, there was a daily paddle-steamer round Mull calling at Iona and Staffa in the summer months as early as 1845.

The way back from Iona led them past the road to Ardura and its charming white farmhouse overlooking the River Lussa. For a long time this had been part of the Torosay Estate, being on the road that branched off south from the Great Glen road down to Loch Buie. Murray had five very tall and beautiful sisters and one short misshapen one, David's great-aunt Maggie. Murray adored her and had generously given her Ardura. The locals held that her mother must have been frightened by a seal because she had very short legs and arms and flippers in lieu of hands. Yet she must have been a very courageous woman, since she qualified as a doctor in the 1890s when it was not the usual thing and, moreover, could drive a pony and trap. She also married and had two perfectly normal children. After her death, they erected a stone bench at the crest of the hill, inscribed to her memory: 'As the refreshment of water is to the weary traveller so her kindness and courage to the wayfarers of life'. Immediately alongside this bench is the Well of the Heads into which wayfarers dropped coins while expressing a wish. These coins were never taken out by tramps or tinkers because it would have brought them bad luck. From the hill behind Ardura the road descends to sea level alongside Loch Spelve which is headed by a freshwater loch, Uisg. It then bursts through some marvellous hardwoods to Loch Buie itself – assuredly one of the most beautiful places in the world.

After more than twenty generations of continuous occupation Kenny MacLaine of Loch Buie – who had gone on the music-hall boards in an attempt to retrieve the family fortunes – had been forced to sell up in 1919. But, until the turn of the century, his father also still owned Java Lodge in Craignure Bay and there his three old aunts lived. It is averred that before the death of the first two sisters, the sound of Ewan of the Littlehead's horse was heard nearby. David's grandfather, Murray, bought Java in 1902 when the third sister was moved to Loch Don; there she died as the locals heard the horse go by.

🌹 *Thus, at his grandmother's feet, David's attachment to Torosay and Mull was formed. The bonding was to become stronger as the years rolled by during school holidays, college vacations, service leaves, business breaks and parliamentary recesses, until it became his main 'maison d'être'.*

4

SCHOOL DAYS AND HOLIDAYS

1926 *to* 1937

*David is a complex creature, so muddle-headed and
untidy, so full of ideas that cannot be expressed, so
eager and sometimes so idle. One feels there are
great birth pains going on that in the end something
tremendous may emerge – David's final school report, 1937*

IN 1926, at the age of six, David's childhood consciousness widened when
his parents returned from two tours of service life in India so that his father
could resign his commission on his adoption as prospective Conservative
candidate for Wellingborough. His mother, Bridget, at the young and
impressionable age of 19, had been pushed by her mother – taking the
opportunity to get her off her hands – into marrying Archie James. He had
fallen for her when she was 14 and he was an undergraduate. Surprisingly,
he had survived the war. In 1914 he was serving in the 3rd Hussars and
was awarded the Military Cross; later he became a regular officer in the
Royal Air Force.

They bought a house in Gloucester Place in London where the faithful
Agg guided, supervised and enlarged the horizons of both David and his sister Bunny. Traits which were to remain with David all his life started to
appear, one of which was the strain of having to eat all the food put in front
of him, particularly fat. Agg tussled with this problem and strangely never
seemed to awaken to the fat slipped under the carpet when he was sent to
his bedroom to 'finish up'. The children's new horizons stretched from St
John's Wood in the north to the Albert Memorial in the south, which
seemed, in those days, as far apart as the North and South Poles, but it was
in that compass that their playmates resided. The nastiest war of all time
was over and London was slowly pulling itself out of the Edwardian and
Victorian eras – still the place of pea-soup fogs, the bell-ringing muffin men,
open-topped buses and half the traffic still horse-drawn. But signs of change
were in the air with the demolition of the great London mansions,
Dorchester House and Grosvenor House, to make room for hotels, which was
evidence of the move out of the nineteenth and into the twentieth century.
In this scenario David and his sister moved through a succession of day
schools – including the deliciously named 'Bernie and Flukeys' – finishing at
Dr Gibb's 'well known establishment' in Sloane Street where his reports

were obviously intended to relieve anxious parents rather than reflect the truth. Coming ninth out of nine in French received the comment 'tres bon travail', and coming one from bottom in writing he was considered 'to have taken pains'.

David got his first introduction to the motor car during these years, through his father's rich friend Mark Patrick who acquired the latest sports car to ease his visits to fish on the Test. On a local 'run out' for fun they would set off, wearing goggles in the open car, navigating the growing traffic nightmare at Hammersmith Broadway, where even then the jams were becoming horrific before the disciplines of roundabouts and lights. They soon burst out on to the Great West Road – now boringly known as the A40 – and actually reached 60 m.p.h. Bridget had also joined the motoring fad and acquired a car of lesser status – the renowned bull-nosed Morris, which could go at nearly 40 m.p.h. This did not inhibit her, with small son aboard, from slipping through an unguarded entrance on to the famous Brooklands circuit and doing a couple of turns round the steeply embanked track, managing not to topple inwards at this far too modest speed. So much for David's claim in his adult years to have driven round Brooklands!

During these early years it was not surprising for David to see his parents set out fully clad for a day's hunting from London by rail, to meet their mounts at the station the other end and to hack on to the meet. Other people who kept their horses in London, sent them in a train with a horse-box which would be detached at the destination and re-attached for the return. They could be seen exercising on Rotten Row on non-hunting days.

After a couple of years, Archie and Bridget set up a modest establishment of five or six hunters and ponies for David and his sister in the sleepy Northampton village of Silverstone. Bridget had decided that the Grafton was the sort of hunt she aspired to, attracted in all probability by Baily's Hunting Directory's description. 'It is a strongly fenced country; there is a good deal of grass. It is a moderate scenting country; the stout foxes show rare sport. There is no wire. A well bred horse is necessary, and he must be a fine performer'. It was from here that, in the autumn of 1928, the dreaded deed was done of packing young David off to board at Summer Fields, near Oxford.

*   *   *

Summer Fields was a prep school, founded in 1864, which retained a regime of cold baths and scholarship under the head-mastership of the Reverend Cyril Williams – known to the boys as 'Willie' – who was the grandson of Mrs McLaren, the founder. There was a record of long-serving teaching staff and retainers and in David's day he fell in with John Evans who had started as a master in 1914 and stayed there, apart from the war, to become Headmaster from 1939 to 1956. The man who taught the scholarship class for twenty-five years was there from 1919 to 1960, the last four years as Headmaster; the younger boys were taught by sisters, the Misses Hills, who were there from 1903 to 1946. All these were put in the shade by Charlie Feathers, the groundsman, who did sixty years.

David, one of fifteen new boys, arrived and looked forward to the future with eagerness while his mother, predictably, drove away in tears. The very next day he was issued with Kennedy's *Latin Primer* and education began with '*amo, amas, amat*'. He survived the first term without incident. The second term nearly everyone went down with flu and sadly one boy died – the first time that most of the boys had come so close to death. Everything was muted at a special assembly to announce that Frampton had died of pneumonia and when his father came and took away his toy tractor. Immediately afterwards David himself was invalided and sent with a governess to Herne Bay. The third term he fell in with Billy Reece-Davis – even at that age a renowned demon bowler and who in years to come had Bradman missed in the slips when a Cambridge freshman. Unfortunately his promise was cut short by losing his bowling arm in the war. He ended up a colleague of David's in the House of Commons.

Discipline was strict and the cane was in common use, but rarely to excess. The more common punishment was to be noted in the Black Book. A series of points dictated the severity of the punishment, which started with memorising lines, standing in the corner, etc., but a third offence produced the cane. 'Willie' effected a parsonical and theatrical stance and took Holy Orders as a headmaster's status symbol rather than through devout convictions. In fact, if caught unawares, he was invariably found reading the racing news. While the discipline may have seemed strict by today's standards it was no more than firm by the practice of the time. In fact Summer Fields was avant-garde in that when David arrived all were addressed by their surnames, to be distinguished in seniority by the suffix Major, Minor, Minimus or even Quart. This was done away with during his time there, and before he left the use of christian names was common practice. One master, Cecil Barnes, stoked David's ambition to become an explorer when teaching geography, by concentrating on the influence of weather almost to the exclusion of all else. It turned out to be a good start for someone who was to go to sea in sail not very many years ahead and later to spend eighteen months in the Antarctic.

On the less attractive facets of life, the loos left a lasting impression – not because they were known as the vinery, vin for short, since the original constructions were against the south-facing wall where Mrs McLaren had some glass house vines – but because they consisted of a continuous open sewer over which were approximately twenty partitioned seats; the sewer was flushed from east to west at ten-minute intervals. A well-timed release of an ignited bunch of newspaper at the beginning of a flush quickly created a mass evacuation. There was also in those days a morbid interest in murder trials which became great national events as, in the days of capital punishment, the outcome was final. David was to go up in everyone's estimation because luckily he had a tenuous link with two of the most notorious cases of his day. The first was the cherubic-looking Sydney Harry Fox – who happened to be his grandmother's page at some stage – and subsequently brained his mother with a club and set a hotel on fire after insuring her life. He was found guilty and hanged without expressing any remorse, nor even bothering to appeal. The next was Alfred Arthur Russ who, in a plot to disappear, gave a tramp a lift in his lorry, hit him on the head and then set the lorry on fire. Unfortunately for him he was seen sneaking away from the blaze. This dastardly deed was done in his father's constituency and at half term David actually saw the remains of the burnt-out lorry. Obviously on his return to school he was considered an expert on the subject and his views were eagerly sought. Russ, needless to say, was found guilty, with the terminal outcome.

This stimulated the school authorities to set up a lecture on 'Execution' which concentrated on showing how great the advances had been over the years from killing as painfully as possible to as quickly as possible. It dwelt through the whole gamut from crucifixion, disembowelling, poisoning, decapitation – where there was often a bodged shot – and hanging, which was slow unless a friend came and hung on the victim's legs. It concluded that enlightenment was spearheaded by Dr Guillotine who designed an engine for executing people 'quickly and mercifully', only marginally preceded by Derrick who ascertained that a drop of eight feet would sever the spinal column and thereby cause instant death. This, predictably, did little to add to the morbid interest of the normal prep-school boy, but it sowed the seeds for David later in his political life to become an abolitionist, even for terrorist offences in Northern Ireland.

A practice which also had a beneficial effect on David's later life was that senior boys had the ordeal of saying long Latin graces. This taught them to speak loudly and clearly, and was to be of benefit later on in the House of Commons. At the ensuing meal there was a fashion for consuming sausages with chunky marmalade, a gastronomic delight which stayed with David throughout his life, but was messy and inappropriate when produced from his pocket out of a plastic bag and consumed as his 'piece' on the hill while stalking on Mull.

A deeper and more significant influence on his future life, the germ of which was not to reach fruition until the enforced inactivity of a prisoner-of-war camp, was the impression made by the steadfastness of a fellow pupil, who throughout the hurly burly of prep school life, was never deflected from saying his prayers nightly. Unknown to him at the time this was the first step on the road to Catholicism.

David's main joy at Summer Fields was rugger. Hopeless at cricket and soccer, he enjoyed his position as a 'spoiling' wing forward, always keen to nip round and manhandle the opposing scrum-half. He made the XV team at the age of 11 and became captain in his last term in 1933. The ages of 11 to 13 represent a vintage period in a boy's life. Not trammelled by the com-

The 1933 Summer Fields first fifteen *which David (in the centre) captained.*

plications of puberty, he is a ball of undiluted energy and David used to revel in going straight from a hard fought rugger match to play nine holes of golf and then look forward to a game of 'fives', time and light permitting.

The time came for him to move on from Summer Fields which had certainly gone a long way to developing his character and attitude to life. While still there, in the landslide of 1931, Archie James was returned as MP for Wellingborough, wiping out the shadow of the General Strike and promising young David a life of ever-expanding prospects and prosperity ahead.

The calibre of the school can be judged by a glance at the list of its alumni. They include: a Viceroy of India, Field Marshal Lord Wavell; two Foreign Secretaries, the Honourable Oliver Stanley and Harold Macmillan; two Chancellors of the Exchequer, Hugh Dalton and Harold Macmillan; a Prime Minister of Southern Rhodesia, Sir Edgar Whitehead; two Governors of New Zealand, Lord Norrie and Lord Cobham; a C-in-C of the Home Fleet, Sir William Davis and an England cricket captain, G.O. Allen. In addition there was Monsignor Ronnie Knox and his elder brother Dillwin, the wartime code-cracker; Harry Crookshank, the 1951 leader of the House of Commons under Sir Winston Churchill; Lord Runciman, ship owner, Director-General of BOAC and Chairman of the National Maritime Museum and Sir Olaf Caroe, the last British Governor of the North West Frontier Province of India before partition. The various admirals and generals included two holders of the Victoria Cross. Among David's vintage, apart from the twenty-three boys killed in the war, Bickersteth became a bishop, and Thickness an Archdeacon, while Christopher Lee and Patrick MacNee went on the stage. Henderson became H.M. Ambassador in Paris and came out of retirement to become 'our man in Washington'; Barclay, whose family had eschewed banking for foxhunting, became an MFH, as were his father and grandfather; Howard 'quart' inherited Castle Howard – familiar to most through *Brideshead Revisited* – and engaged in a career of public service, ending as Chairman of the BBC; Julian Amery, who read *The Times* from cover to cover at the age of 8, remained only interested in politics and came within a hair's breadth of a Cabinet post.

So the time came for the final evening chapel with the familiar hymn, *Lord dismiss us with your Blessing* – usually so welcome but this time rendered poignant by its finality. He left with the accolades, 'always a keen worker and ready to take abuse in the right spirit': 'he can write well when he likes': and from Willie 'good luck to David at Eton. He has always been a *persona grata* here and during his last term he has accentuated his good qualities of leadership and his inspiring enthusiasm. Not only the rugger side will miss him but every department of the school'. Thus David negotiated the first big fence in life.

*   *   *

Equally important in forming David's character were his experiences during the holidays. In the early days the order of things was fairly standard: with his parents at Silverstone and the hunting background during the Christmas holidays; at Herstmonceux with his paternal grandfather, adding to his egg and butterfly collections, at Easter and the eight-week summer break with his maternal grandmother at Torosay. This smooth routine ended abruptly with his grandfather's death in 1932 at the age of 76. He had lived at Herstmonceux for thirty-two years and left an estate worth nearly £127,000. It was the sale of Herstmonceux that prompted David's father, Archie, to sell Silverstone and buy a 250-acre farm at Brackley, also in Northamptonshire.

While this was being altered the winter was spent in considerable discomfort in the Plough, the Brackley 'local', where Bridget acquired the then almost unheard of luxury of a radiogram. This miraculous instrument not only did not need winding but the record was amplified through the wireless and relayed through an in-built speaker – technology beyond belief – which stimulated David's interest in music. Emulating his mother's penchant for Wagner he nightly drove his unfortunate father insane by playing *The Ride of the Valkyries* and the *Meistersinger* overture loudly and incessantly.

The main purpose of these holidays was hunting and David loved it. With agriculture at a low ebb, little land under plough and barbed wire still being somewhat of a rarity, the Grafton attracted huge fields, all beautifully turned

out on first-rate hunters. Most of the men wore pink coats with the hunt but-
ton and top hats and most ladies becomingly riding side-saddle, also in top
hats with veils. In addition there would be a large phalanx of second-horse
men, dressed in the accepted livery and keeping in touch with proceedings by
road, ready to change the tired horses for fresh ones half way through the
day. This presented a great challenge to a small boy on a woolly pony to get
away to a good start if he were to see anything of the hunt, rather than trail-
ing along miles behind. He was also egged on by his mother whose total lack
of apprehension, combined with a complete lack of judgement, let alone fear,
caused her to take on obstacles that even the well-mounted hunt servants
would not have dreamed of tackling. Time after time she took a crashing fall,
always getting up unscathed, and David, learning to scrub along behind her,
realised he had the advantage of a broken rail or a gap in the hedge to retain
his place in the hunt. David's love of hunting was always to stay with him
and the excitement of the chase took hold at this stage of his life. His riding
capabilities were honed up because, at the age of 10, the War Office encouraged the local Pony Clubs to make use of their facilities at the nearby School
of Equitation at Weedon. The Pony Club members received regular lessons
there during the Christmas holidays for 2s an hour, under the expert tuition
of the best riding masters in the country. David, who was never short of confidence from then until the end of his hunting days would not accept that any
fence in front of him was insurmountable.

However, the schooled army horses at Weedon were a completely different kettle of fish to the series of ponies which David was graced with at
home. One of the most fiendish he had to deal with belonged to an 11th
Hussar subaltern, Geoffrey Miller, who was starting to make his mark on the
family – and Bridget in particular. He played golf with her, while David had
lessons with the 'pro', and met her once or twice a week in the hunting field.
In subsequent years he claimed the meetings were usually jumping a fence
going in opposite directions because of Bridget's complete lack of a bump for
locality. The Millers, his mother and sisters, had taken a house at Brackley
while he was on the two-year Equitation Course at Weedon, where hunting
was part of the curriculum. He kept two hunters for himself and a pony
called Nigger for his sister, Anne, who on her first day out soon lost control.
David, exalted by his Weedon-induced superiority, offered to swap with her
and let her ride his properly schooled pony. This proved completely disasterous. Nigger, with a mouth of iron, put his head down and deposited him on
the Northampton soil some dozen times. The reins became more and more
slippery, until David called it quits through a mouth full of mud, and lost
considerable face. His father took the situation in hand and saw to it that he
was properly mounted from then on.

The constant companion during ten years of David's school life was his
cousin, William Crawshay, who was brought up in London by his grandmother, Olive Leslie's older sister. In the winter holidays William's pony was

kept with David's and they went to Mull together in the summer. While they were inseparable in those days, curiously their paths rarely crossed after the war. William got a DSO in France and later a knighthood as Chairman of the Welsh Arts Council. In Northampton he rode his grey pony with great abandon, rather than horsemanship, and found that the easiest way to stop it was to run into the hindquarters of any horse in front.

Once Herstmonceux had been sold the Easter holidays were spent in Torosay which began to take on the mantle of home and so the holidays that meant anything took place up there – apart from the exciting month's hunting around Christmas. The love of hunting had been deeply instilled in Northamptonshire but the wider range of field-sports were nurtured on the hills, lochs and rivers of Mull, led by stalking. It is not surprising that the Mull stalkers were to become not only his frequent companions but also his greatest friends. Before David went to school, the stalker at Torosay was one James Young and David's love of stalking stemmed from the only time he went on the hill with James before he was eight. James gave up while he was still under 60 because his eyesight, the achilles heel of any stalker, started to fail him and it was clear that the deer were seeing him before he saw them. He was suceeeded by Gavin, who impressed all the young. A dapper and garulous chap with an endless fund of stories he was the best company in the world. Gavin was suceeded by Archie McColl who was promoted from being Olive's chauffeur in the garage to the keeper's cottage. Unlike the slap-happy James, Archie was a painstaking stalker, which might have been tedious by comparison at David's age, but was undoubtedly far sounder and led him into a much deeper understanding of what went on on the hill. It was through Archie that David was to have encounters with golden eagles at close quarters. On a trip to try and photograph them in their eyries Archie saved David from being swept off a steep cliff face when a disturbed female took to the air and nearly knocked him flying with her vast wings. Luckily Archie managed to get a grip on him. The following year on a rabbit-catching round they found a full grown eagle that had got its leg caught in one of the gin-traps which have since been abolished. They managed to release it, miraculously unharmed, and equally miraculously without doing any damage to either the eagle or themselves.

These, in retrospect, endless summer holidays at Torosay seem to circulate round Olive Guthrie's regular stream of annual visitors. The most notable of these was King George II of Greece, who originally came to Mull – because it was so reminiscent of the islands of his own country – when he was in exile from 1923 to 1935. Olive struck up a warm friendship with him which meant that, accompanied by his equerry Captain Ledidis, he came every summer. He was an unpretentious man who entered into the spirit of everyday life in Mull, such as when a car had to be pushed over the brae, a standard event in the course of a journey, he was the first to jump out and start pushing. He only brought his queen, Elizabeth, once. She was the sister of the unsavoury King Carol of Rumania and was far more regal and demanding. Her only contribution to that visit seemed to be to use her expertise on edible mushrooms to concoct some excellent dishes – which sadly never got repeated. After he got his throne back the King remained a regular and faithful correspondent with Olive, addressing her as 'Auntie Ole' and signing himself 'Roy'.

Olive's Irish background was to produce a noteworthy frequent visitor, Jem Barlow, who was presumably called such as she used to wander round the foreshore picking up crystals. Taking them back to Ireland, she had them cut and set, making several hundred pounds a year by selling the results to her friends. She claimed to have second sight but refused to look at anyone's palm or look into her crystal ball because she claimed she had foreseen too many tragedies and disasters. But she was always prepared to tell people's fortunes by cards as a party trick because she said she got nothing from them. Her claims to see into the future were not known to stand up to examination.

Olive's most popular annual visitor was a contemporary friend of Bridget and Violet called Dodo West. Her great wide-open china blue eyes could be depended on to believe anything she was told – provided it was with a straight face. She returned from her first sea-fishing trip and announced that she had caught five species of fish and a lobster which included a sun-fish, a moonfish and a starfish – so even originality was not called for to take her in. When challenged she produced a box which contained about a dozen identical looking mackerel and a lobster which was bright red, having been cooked earlier in the day and attached to her line when she was not looking. In the dining-room hang today the antlers of a long extinct Irish elk which were brought by Olive from her home in County Monaghan. She was easily persuaded that these were the 'horns of a dilemma' and a couple of weeks later when she was staying elsewhere and this phrase was used she said, 'Oh, that's most interesting. They've got one at Torosay but they don't shoot them any longer as they are becoming very rare'. Probably her finest moment was when she denied being ignorant on the grounds that she had won a scripture prize at school, so the impish David tested her knowledge by asking her what was stronger than the lion and sweeter than honey. After a momentary silence as her mind went into gear she said, 'That's very difficult. Oh, I know, the loins of John the Baptist'. This produced such an outbreak of hilarity that Sir William Tyrell, then Ambassador in Paris, who was also staying in the house, fell off his chair with laughter.

In the early thirties Jack Crawshay, cousin William's father – partly because of its availability and partly to help out Olive – took the stalking both on Torosay and the neighbouring estate, Glenforsa. This gave him more stalking than his house-party could manage and most generously he gave several days back to the family. The first time that David went over the tops to see how serious stalking was done the sport and what it meant in the context of the Mull hills, started to get an even deeper hold.

In 1932 another visitor to Mull was Hugh Ruttledge, of the Indian Civil Service, who was preparing to lead his 1933 Everest expedition. He became a neighbour and used to have members of the team and climbers to stay with him. Many of them, of course, were household names to a young schoolboy who used to go down to Craignure daily to see who would get off the boat. In the event the 1933 expedition reached within a thousand feet of the top – an incredible feat.

An annual holiday outing was to Calgary, a house overlooking the most perfect silver sand bay imaginable and the home of Hugh MacKenzie who so enjoyed his boyhood birthday parties that he continued them throughout his long life. He bred ponies so that all the children spent the afternoon riding and picnicking and it was always a much awaited day out. Calgary in Alberta, on the MacKenzie River, was named after this place and few of its 670,000 odd inhabitants will be aware of this heavenly backwater on Mull, with a population of less than 100, whose attractive name is the Gaelic for 'clear running water'.

Travel round the island for young David was no problem. From the age of 15 he drove his mother's famous bull-nosed Morris – with neither licence nor insurance since they regarded the public highway which ran for sixteen miles round the perimeter of the estate as being their property. In any event the nearest police station was eleven miles away. This meant that he was always able to go fishing early in the morning at a time when no one else was willing to take him. As he grew older the thrills and skills of fishing for salmon and sea trout became as magnetic to him as sea fishing had been in his earlier days.

The southern march of the estate was the River Lussa which formed the boundary between Ardura and Loch Buie. Rising from a chain of lochs the river, a typical western Highlands spate river, was only about seven miles long. It rose and fell at an alarming rate as the Highland rain came and went, but given enough water a salmon could easily run up to their spawning grounds above the lochs within a day. There was only one place for them to rest, and that was the 'Falls', a series of four pools in a deep gorge, which the salmon could leap and swim when enough water was coming down the river. They were bound to rest there on their journey upstream, so if David heard heavy rainfall on the roof at night he would be up first thing and on his way to the Falls to intercept one or two salmon in the boiling white water. It could only be fished with a worm but could produce fish of anything up to 20lb in weight – exceedingly popular when brought back for the larder. But more exciting fishing were the sea trout which came and went with the tide up and down Loch Don, an estuary of more than two miles long. The technique was to start in low water and fish the pools upstream as the sea trout came in on the incoming tide to meet the fresh water coming down from the hills. If the tide was to flow in in the evening the additional excitement – particularly in the autumn – of the widgeon, teal and mallard that had been out in the sea loch coming over the brae to the top waters of the estuary was a bonus when busy engaged with the sea trout. Their cries, mingled with the roaring of rutting stags in October, created a symphony. Flighting duck flew invitingly low when he was engaged in fishing, but a specific visit to bring home some duck from an evening flight remarkably caused most of them to vary their route to pass out of gunshot. The fresh run sea trout, if there was not enough fresh water coming down to take them up to the hill lochs, fell back to the sea. They were tremendous fighting fish but with somewhat soft mouths so it was never easy to bring as many home as came to the hook. The success of this fishing depended so much on the state of the tide and its variants between springs and neaps. David's familiarity was to be a good grounding for his future nautical career.

By the mid-thirties they were being seriously menaced by poachers who used to come over from Oban by sea and net the mouth of the rivers, seriously damaging the fishing, which in consequence became harder to let. Poaching provided an important income for those taking part and Archie McColl, the stalker who doubled as fishing bailiff for the rest of the year, was put to it throughout the summer to keep them off the estate. This involved several fights – in the end running into all-out war – and David and his mother got involved in quite a few of these incidents. On one occasion poachers at work up at Loch Don were seen by the family out on a routine patrol, having left the car at Grass Point. David was sent to bring the car back on side lights so as not to alert the poachers and his mother taking a shotgun, set up a raiding party of Bertie and Violet de Klee from Auchnacraig and one or two of her houseguests, while Archie and his companion were left on guard. The poachers were found hauling up their motor boat on a making tide, clearly pleased with their catch, when they were subjected to a barrage of stones, rocks and seaweed and the noise of Bridget firing a shotgun into the air – at which they rowed away fast into the dark, leaving their motor boat. The Torosay party were delighted to find their shore-going clothes stored in lockers and scattered them about the beach, while Archie disabled the boat with a sledgehammer. The poachers had the nerve to summon the police the next day and pressed charges which were denied. John Bill, the butler, told the police that he brought the nightcap tray of drinks to everyone playing liars dice in the library at 11 p.m., the relevant time, so that there was no way the charge could stick. The following day when Olive went to Oban there were no smiling faces and no one smarmingly tried to sell her own fish back to her. This little action proved far more effective than the ten shilling fine which is all that the bench used to inflict on poachers, and until the outbreak of war poaching ceased.

Towards the end of David's schooldays the interest that grew most rapidly, sparked and shared by his mother, was sailing. A fourteen-foot dinghy was built in Oban in 1934 with a single lug sail; in this dinghy the pair of them used to sail endlessly round Craignure Bay. Following a modicum of success at the Tobermory Regatta, the ambition was to enter the Tobermory/Oban race, open for boats of all sizes up to 20-ton yachts. The champion and their mentor was a retired farmer, Hugh Carmichael from Lismore, who lived in Craignure and had an uncanny knowledge of the Sound. He used to win by pinching the tide close to the shore while everyone else sat out off the windless headlands in the middle of the Sound. He was also able to pick up the sea-breezes which came down from the Mull corries and managed to get a fine lead on everyone else. By this time the tide would be beginning to slacken so he beat all of the most powerful yachts.

After a couple of seasons they upgraded the dinghy by stepping the mast further aft and covering the foredeck for somewhere dry to put coats etc. They had her fitted with a bow-sprit and even installed heads which enabled them to go on wider sallies than before. Finally, in 1937, when David had left school they did enter the famous Tobermory race. They had very light winds for the first half in the Sound but it suddenly piped up to such an extent that a 200-ton schooner beating down the Sound caused no end of trouble. In trying to extract themselves they were hit by a squall and David inexplicably got a jamming hitch on the halliard but managed to get most of the wind out of the sail. They made the shore without incurring any damage, other than severe fright and loss of dignity. Rather ignominiously they had to take the boat over to Oban on the estate lorry by ferry to enter the Regatta.

The holidays were marvellous for a boy of that age, with his two families providing the exquisite enjoyment of hunting, shooting, fishing, stalking and sailing during his formative years. This inculcated in him a deep appreciation and understanding of natural life and its surroundings – and management of the country and its denizens which field sportsmen are so lucky to acquire.

*　　*　　*

After leaving Summer Fields he went on to Eton, having been entered at birth by his father. When it came to choosing a Housemaster, sensibly, instead of going to the authorities, Archie went to Mr Welsh of Welsh and Jeffries, one of the four West End tailors with Eton branches, to seek his views about Eton Housemasters. From this source he received a thoroughly practical and disinterested view from someone with fourteen years knowledge of the school. He was advised to go for Eric Powell who had done war service in the Royal Flying Corps.

When he first got there David found the place huge after the confines of Summer Fields and never managed to arrive at the right place at the right time or with the right book. However, he got the system of pupillage into his mind in due course and the first term went peacefully enough having elected to become a wet bob, ie oarsman, rather than a dry bob, ie cricketer. New boys were given three weeks of grace to learn their way around, including the whereabouts and names of all the houses and the significance of the colours. They then started to fag for the prefects which they did until they left the lower school. He got on well with Eric Powell, his Housemaster – or in Eton terms his Tutor – but very sadly early on, David, while at Torosay, heard the news that four Eton masters had been killed climbing at St Moritz. In his heart of hearts he feared that one was Eric Powell and so it was confirmed.

David was lucky in his successor, Hubert Hartley, who had also been to Summer Fields and had stroked the Eton Eight in 1915. He had served in the Coldstream Guards in the war before returning to Cambridge, stroking the winning crew three times and the British entry in the Olympic Games. He and his wife, Grizel, not having children, were devoted to the boys and ran the house with a bubbling cheerfulness. She was particularly remembered for the day she was riding in Windsor Great Park and appeared at the boys' dinner in her jodhpurs, overcome with laughter, having seen nineteen riderless black horses galloping through the Great Park in the direction of the barracks. The Household Cavalry recruits had been taken for their first instructional ride out of the barracks; a car backfired and all but one of them were deposited on the ground. Hubert was Housemaster for fifteen years and he and his wife were splendidly unconventional; it is rumoured that they had met roof-climbing when they were at Cambridge. She used to enjoy giving dinner for the House Eight where no one was over 18. The menu invariably started with crab (caught by members of the Eight) and went on through ducks and drakes, to port. It was usually necessary to break open the cellar door – because the key was invariably mislaid – in order to meet the demand for a third bottle.

Hubert Hartley was obviously the right person to steer David into his adult life, which was destined not to be entirely conventional. He proved that by taking one's own line life need not be entirely at loggerheads with the establishment. David did not get on so well with his Classic tutor, the Reverend George Snow,* and took an instant dislike to him. It was awe-inspiring to see Snow – 6ft 7in under a top-hat, towering over David's father – a mere 5ft 5in in a trilby – fulminating on David's failings. Those moments of dread were relieved by less austere moments when Snow let them listen to his, for those days, brilliant reproduction equipment in the school hall, playing his large record collection; this helped to build up David's appreciation of music. On one occasion George Snow's Latin report on David read, 'feeble, feckless and inefficient'. His father had to look up 'feckless' in a dictionary and David hoped against hope that it might mean capable, industrious or even brilliant – although none of those epithets seemed to be in keeping with the tenor of the rest. He was not surprised to find it meant 'lacking purpose or resource, helpless, futile', which just about summed up his attitude at that time.

Schooldays again introduced an acquaintance with death when Michael

* Later, when David was MP for Kemptown and Snow was headmaster of nearby Ardingly College, they became good friends. The friendship continued when Snow retired to Dorset and David represented North Dorset in the Commons.

Cecil – whose older brother was to become Lord Salisbury – failed to get up at half time when they flopped down to get their breaths back. Apparently he had a congenital heart condition and was never likely to grow up, but his parents felt he should lead a normal life as long as possible. The effect on the boys was profound and for a short time near catastrophic for his House-master, Hubert Hartley. From this tragedy came David's appreciation that all life was a matter of taking calculated risks. Sooner or later the outcome was bound to be unfavourable in terms of this world but one had to get accus-tomed to the hazards of living.

At about that time he joined the OTC, which in theory was voluntary but in practice compulsory. He hated every moment but was glad he had joined when, on 20th January 1936, King George V died and the Eton OTC were privileged to line the funeral route inside Windsor Castle. He was not very impressed by the historic grandeur but may have recognised his uncle, Bertie de Klee, marching on foot, cloaked, in his role of commanding officer of the Blues. First came the band playing the haunting *Dead March*, then the gun carriage, drawn by ratings of the Royal Navy, bearing the coffin, fol-lowed by the young King looking desperately lonely. Behind were his three brothers in line abreast and behind them all the crowned heads of Europe with their suites. King Carol of Rumania, true to form, got to bed late from a night club and was far from sober even then; he was flanked by two men dressed as Admirals who were in fact his physicians disguised for the occa-sion. David was present because in 1882 an Eton boy chanced to be on the scene when a lunatic, Roderick MacLean, had tried to shoot Queen Victoria and had deflected his aim. For this reason the OTC had this privilege. Less welcome was the decree that, instead of wearing khaki like the rest of the army, their uniforms should be made of something in the colour of French mustard. They were terribly noticeable at the regular OTC camps and became a natural target for other schools, probably being supported only by the neighbouring Catholic Beaumont (now unfortunately defunct) who used to come to their aid, reminding them 'that Beaumont is what Eton was, a school for the sons of catholic gentlemen'.

In 1935 there had been a General Election at which David made his first election speech, in support of his father, to thank a visiting speaker. He con-sidered it went well, but noticed a certain sense of embarrassment on the platform – not to mention titters from the floor – when he gave a vote of thanks to Lord Cork and Orrery. On being reprimanded he felt it was unfair that there should be two double-barrelled Irish peers; he should have been thanking Lord Dufferin and Ava.

Soon after, at the beginning of the Christmas holidays, he and Bunny were unfortunate enough to be on the Marylebone – Bradford express in the last coach which was slipped in the usual practice of the day. This technique allowed the slip coach to override its coupling when the main train braked then accelerated, leaving the single coach to carry on into the station under its own momentum. This night the main train suffered a break seizure so that the slip car careered on its own into the back of the original train. The first David knew of it was when he came to, lying on a hard floor, covered in cushions and luggage, with his sister crying; the faithful Agg was trying to get them out before something hit the coach. They climbed out and sat there. David, clearing the blood from his eyes, could see he had been in a railway accident and the carriage had been substantially telescoped; but he had no recollection as to why he was on the train. On being got home somehow, five stitches were inserted over his eye and he had to stay in bed with concussion until his memory returned. Nine people were badly injured, including the guard. On the good side, his father claimed no less than £15 damages from the railway company and, although David was angry that it did not come to him, he consoled himself with the fact that his father had to pay the doctor's bill.

As soon as he had recovered they were taken to stay with the father of his godfather, Mark Pelham. The fourth Earl of Yarborough, born in 1859, had succeeded to the title and property at the age of 16 – before death duties had been thought of. He had just completed a reign of 61 years, during which time had virtually stood still. He was a neat, courteous and precise widower who overlooked his 30,000 acres of light Lincolnshire loam, where the farmers were the first to gallop across their own crops. The scores of plantations were all heavily stocked with pheasants and the kennels of the Brocklesby, one of the few privately owned packs of foxhounds, were on his land. Just before David's visit the footmen had stopped wearing powdered wigs but they still looked impressive enough to him in their knee breeches. The Victorian luxury lasted ten days with alternate hunting and shooting. But the luxury was far less convenient than with modern central heating. There were regular interruptions as rows of servants carried coals to the bedroom fire, and jugs of hot water were brought up from the nether regions. It was a taste of a bygone age.

These holidays, which began with the railway crash, were to end with a visit to a London specialist to have the banging and bumping in his heart checked. It was diagnosed to be 'athlete's heart' – a quite common condition for adolescents, but, sadly, it meant he was taken off rugger and rowing for six months.

Another, but not unexpected, blow struck in the Easter holidays of 1935 when their parents told David and Bunny that they had resolved to separate. When it came about, it hit David deeply and set his mind on a search for some sort of stability, clearly missing in his parent's marriage; without doubt it was a further step towards embracing the Catholic faith in years to come. His mother and father had started to drift apart in earnest soon after the move to Brackley and by 1934 when her brother-in-law, Bertie de Klee, got command of the Royal Horse Guards, Bridget made her home with them in Windsor. She shared her time between Torosay in the summer and skiing in the winter – conducted with the same dash, verve and aplomb as her hunting.

The *Herzogin Cecile*, returning from the Australian 'grain race' under sail, ran aground on the South Devon coast. This triggered the restless Bridget with her friend Dorothy Laird to take passage at 10s a day on one of these ships called the *Viking* from the port of discharge in England to her home port in the Baltic. Her enthusiasm following this trip was to brush off on David – with significant effects.

At this time of her life Bridget was far too preoccupied and excited with the thrills of living to pay a great deal of attention to her children. In particular Bunny had the rough end of the stick; from the age of 7, during most holidays she was parked with David's godfather, Mark Pelham, at his home near Rugby. Starting at the age of 8 she was sent off to a variety of schools, usually unseen by her parents. Among them were Portsdown Lodge at Uxbridge and a school in Switzerland where she was taught French by an English mistress! But what she most resented was being parted from her beloved Agg.

Divorce proceedings were somewhat more protracted in those days and Geoffrey Miller made himself scarce in the Sudan while Archie continued his career in the House of Commons. He became Parliamentary Private Secretary to R.A. Butler when he was Under-Secretary of State for India and then Secretary to the Ministry for Labour from 1935 to 1937.

Geoffrey stemmed from different beginnings. Born in Australia in 1905, he was a descendant of Captain Henry Miller who, having fought at Waterloo, went with the army to Australia where his duties took him to the convict settlements of Tasmania in the early 1820s. The family moved to Port Arthur, which had been founded in 1835, and were thus in at the beginning of the colony of Victoria in 1850. They shook off the army and became involved in banking and insurance in the new colony. Fortunately this coincided with the gold rush in the 1850s and they became prominently established in what was to become the State of Victoria, in due course to own a large property at Bacchus Marsh outside Melbourne.

❧ *Little did the Millers know or care when they were getting established in the new Colony of Victoria that Torosay Castle was being built on the other side of the world on the Isle of Mull.*

As with all colonials 'home' was considered to be England and when the First World War started Geoffrey's father Clive dropped everything, and with his wife and baby daughter set off on their way 'home' to join up. War or no war, Geoffrey was to be educated in England, so at the age of 11, in 1916 he and a governess set sail from Australia. But as was to become a habit he did it the hard way by getting himself torpedoed in the Mediterranean. Luckily he found a raft and made a landfall in Malta. He eventually got to England, to be educated for a year or two at a prep school before going on to Eton.

Geoffrey's character was such that throughout his life he always wanted to do the right thing, and usually did it, but got there by the longest and most awkward way possible. Eton was followed by Sandhurst and his ambition to join a cavalry regiment was achieved when he was commissioned into the 11th Hussars, still a horsed regiment in 1920. His aptitude for doing things the awkward way earned him the affectionate nickname of 'Poggles' in his regiment, but nevertheless he played cricket and rugger for the regimental teams. He made his mark, as all cavalrymen in between the wars, in the equestrian world – not only in the hunting field, which was considered part of military training, but also winning steeplechases with his point-to-pointers, *Hy Brazil* and *Beau Cladach*. His romance with Bridget started in the hunting field but his capacity for enjoyment made heavy demands on his funds. He tried to alleviate the position by taking an interpreter's course in German to qualify for extra pay. But this was not enough and a posting to the Sudan Defence Force was arranged – the traditional way for impecunious officers to rebuild their finances. Not only was the pay better, but there was effectively nothing to spend it on. It was also a tactical move as it eased the progress of Bridget and Archie's divorce. Geoffrey then rejoined the 11th Hussars in Cairo, sent for Bridget and they went off to Beirut to get married.

◉ *This had the effect of further tightening the ties between David and Torosay.*

During the following summer holidays, Bridget's tales to David of her experience in sail, coupled with his growing impatience with the routine of Eton, made their dinghy sailing, confined to the Sound of Mull, seem tame. They hatched a plot and decided that he should leave school early and sample this way of life before it departed forever. Copious reading took place on the catastrophic decline of the sailing ship, to find that by 1936 those which went to Australia from Europe amounted to a mere eighteen, compared with 304 in 1921. The routine was that the ships sailed out in ballast to Australia and returned home around Cape Horn with grain to unload in British ports. The reason they had the edge on steamers, particularly with the smaller ports in South Australia, was that without the overheads of a steamer these ships could lie at anchor in the roads while cargo came out in dribs and drabs. They also provided free warehousing for the three or four months home, during which there was always a chance the price of wheat might rise. Off-season there were occasional charters carrying timber from the Baltic to South Africa and guano runs from Madagascar to New Zealand. But the main thing was that the crews were cheap, with captains getting about £40 a month and the ratings getting £2 50s. They also used a pool of foreign apprentices – who actually paid for the privilege of working.

David found out that Eriksons were the last decent firm operating the ships and that Clarksons were their London agent. He could get a place on one of their ships under Finnish law, as an apprentice, having paid an indenture fee of £50 and getting 10s a month back as pocket money. Also required were a doctor's certificate and a clergyman's letter of moral character.

By then David was getting bored with life at school, finding it restrictive, and convinced his father that there was no benefit in staying to struggle for

Higher Certificate (A levels). He tried to persuade him, aided and abetted by his mother, to let him go to sea. During the Christmas holidays at Brackley, after being taken to the junior hunt ball he got back to find a note from Bridget to say that Archie had agreed; from then on he was no longer at Eton in spirit and only in body for a short time. For his final terms, not going for the Higher Certificate had its compensations. He could specialise in French and German, the two languages he most wanted to learn, and Hubert, his Housemaster sensibly allowed him to resign from the OTC – a thing unheard of – to concentrate on dinghy sailing. There were no naval or air sections and he was inevitably destined for the Navy in the event of trouble. It was an intelligent decision because war clouds were looming on the horizon.

In his last days at Eton he was much involved in the formation of the Caledonian Society, limited to twenty-four members of Scottish descent who danced reels and country dances every week, except during the summer half. Expert tuition was available and this led to a life-long interest in Highland dancing. After the war David became a competent tutor in this form of entertainment. The

David James *at Eton in 1937.*

main spin off from this in the days to come, whether in prisoner of war camp or on Antarctic expeditions, was an inbuilt advantage of being able to raise morale in an all male community. His final feat at Eton was to remain Head of the River on the newly introduced Novice Fours and get his 'Lower Boats'.

There was a change in plans when Archie persuaded David that he ought to go to Oxford, but his commitment to go to sea in *Viking* meant he would not be around to take the entrance examination. However, the Master of Balliol generously arranged for him to have a private examination, which happily he scraped through. And so schooldays came to an end, but not without the inevitable valedictory talk from the Headmaster, which equally inevitably touched on the subject of sex. He assured the assembled group that this was the one exception to the rule of try anything once – but that if they did they should not wear their old school braces. With these words of wisdom David donned his OE tie and set off happily for the future.

There is no better person than his Tutor to give an assessment of the young man who was setting out to face the world:

'David's reports are not a good set and he has not done much work for his division masters, but it must be remembered that the one and only thing which mattered this half was preparing the Latin and French literature required for the Balliol exam and in this he was successful, though it had to be done out of school.

David is a complex creature, so muddle-headed and untidy, so full of ideas that cannot be expressed, so eager and sometimes so idle. One feels there are great birth pains going on that in the end something tremendous may emerge.

He has again made enormous strides this half in assurance and poise and I am sure he has found himself. Had he stayed on for a last year here all the seething and boiling which is going on within him would by the end have died down and we might have been able to say that he was marked out for such and such a career. As things are, the voyage in the grain ship will turn him into a man and he may or may not be able to face Balliol and books again.

He would make a good journalist if only he could learn to write; for that he would need Balliol. He would also make a good MP with his quick, acute mind. He would also make an explorer with his love of adventure, courage and strength, but there is no future in exploring, save the name.

I am most grateful to him for what he did for the House this half. The Novice Four could not have remained Head of the River without his strength and determination. I wish you could have come down for the last night of the Bumping Race when the crew rowed with confidence for the first time. I have never seen a novice move so much water as David did that first minute.

He has been a glorious enthusiast, loyal and friendly and I am going to miss his eager conversation when I go round the House next half. But I envy him his adventure and will be with him in spirit.

And now I must bid him farewell and wish him all that is best in life, for he is the most interesting, in some ways the most promising boy, that I have had at the House. When he gets back from the voyage I hope he will come and see us often. There will always be a bed and meal ready for him and the warmest of welcomes.'

This seemed heady stuff to David. He felt that George Snow's 'feeble, feckless and inefficient' was nearer the mark.

5

BEFORE THE MAST

1937 *to* 1938

*I must go down to the sea again, for the call of the running tide
Is a wild call and a clear call that may not be denied.*

JOHN MASEFIELD, *Sea Fever*

THROUGHOUT THAT LONG HOT AUGUST, *Viking* was loading timber for East London, South Africa, in Kotka near the Russian border in Southern Finland. About the 20th a letter came from Clarksons, the owner's London agents, that she would soon be sailing for Copenhagen to take on stores and that David should be there by September 1st at the very latest, to be on the safe side.

Accordingly, two days later he and his mother, who had decided to see him off, caught the night sleeper up to London. After a thrilling morning at Gardiners in the Mile End road, kitting himself out, he felt a real old sea-dog. On the way to Liverpool Street station for the Harwich Ferry, suddenly ten months seemed an eternity and 30,000 miles a long way to go – and the old salt became a very apprehensive schoolboy.

They arrived in Copenhagen and pottered around the Lange Linje, the waterfront. There in the Sound was Erikson's four-masted barque *Passat*, waiting to sail for East London. Much of the Baltic trade was still in softwood and schooners or barquentines were there and a real old-timer was being towed out with sagging wooden yards, and tattered sails being set. The scene might have been 1880.

They spent the next week looking out of the hotel window, anxiously fearing that *Viking* must have been wrecked, but it was just a very fine spell and she had a slow passage. One night they went to bed with the Sound empty of vessels, but the next morning his mother tapped on the door to say *Viking* was there. By the time he came down for breakfast he found a note from her saying, very sensibly, that she had already caught the boat train home. So he was on his own. He went down to the agent's office to sign on with two Americans, 'Junie' Clark and 'Frenchie' Howard. The captain, Uno Mörn, duly arrived and they signed their indentures. They were then told to go off and have a meal as the agent's boat would take them and the final provisions out at 5 p.m. It transpired that his new shipmates were both graduates in their early 20s, while David was not yet 18. They were both staggered to learn that he had never had a drink nor a girl, but they seemed to hit it off well.

An oddly assorted crowd met on the quayside. There was Captain Mörn and his nice homely-looking wife, Helga, who was accompanying him on the round trip. Then there was a young Australian girl passenger, wearing skirts that were short even by today's mini-standards, and which were not to prove an adequate defence against a score of lusty young Swedish–Finns; but whether this was by inadvertance or design was never ascertained. Finally there was the Major, a well-known alcoholic whom David's parents had met in India and who had been sent by his family to be dried out; once he sobered up sufficiently he became one of the best liked men on board.

Joining a ship is like going to a new school and David's anxiety was not allayed by the bearded and piratical countenances that leaned over the rail to inspect them as they came alongside. But one of them, Joe Cooper, the only other Englishman on board, had a reassuring Lincolnshire ring to his voice. Soon, by means of smiles, signs and broken phrases, far from their presence being resented, they were welcomed by the crew.

The following day the wind was not fair and David had his initiation into an eight-hour working day – 'Rise opp, rise opp. Vi segla!' It was 4.30 and the wind had come fair. Already there was a hissing of steam and a slow clank-clank as one by one the links of the cable came in. They started to make sail, winding up the huge upper topsail and topgallant yard on the winches and hauling away like demons on an endless collection of ropes that for David held no meaning at all. At the end of three hours all sail was set and they had leisure to view their surroundings as they bowled merrily along at a good seven knots, with Hamlet's Elsinore a mile distant to the port beam and Sweden a similar distance to starboard. They went below for breakfast, thinking that the day's heavy work was already behind them, but during that half-hour they nearly lost the ship when the wind changed. In spite of the largely untrained crew being mustered with the cry 'all hands on deck' the captain could not prevent her sidling crab-like towards the shore. Keeping his head, he let both anchors go in 90 fathoms of water and brought her up with the breakers less than a cable away.

Viking made a magnificent sight as she came into the wind, her lower top-sails being rapidly clewed up and all other sails bellying back over the yards. But it was only for a moment that they could enjoy the scene, for at once there rang out the age-old order, 'Up aloft and furl them'. So up they went and David, for the first time looking down on the deck pitching wildly 140 feet below him, felt sick with fear. As they lay at anchor with a force 8 gale from ahead, the sail was threshing back over the yard, doing its utmost to dash them off. An unpleasant initiation, and all he could do was to hold on tight while the friendly Finns laughed encouragement and did the work.

For two days they lay there waiting for the gale to blow itself out, then, at dawn on 11th September, the wind came fair and light and they set all sail, weighing the two 4-ton bower anchors by hand round the forecastle-deck capstan; no skipper would waste £5 on coal to keep the donkey boiler going for 48 hours when he had muscles to rely on. The following evening they rounded the Skaw light and headed north-west for the Pentland Firth. Here, in a region dreaded second only to Cape Horn, their luck held. A north-east-erly gale sprang up, putting them well and safely into the North Atlantic and by their tenth day out from Copenhagen they were 300 miles west of Lewis and felt safe in getting the anchors lashed on deck. The voyage was well begun and the last land lost to sight.

The 3rd October, their twenty-fifth day at sea, was one of those unforget-table days that can make a whole year of toil seem worthwhile. It was on that day that they picked up the north-east trades – bright sun after North Atlantic gloom; blue sea flecked with white horses; flying fish; dolphins; the island of Las Palmas rising sheer out of the sea abeam – and a Sunday spent in the bowsprit net with a gramophone. The old ship stormed along at ten knots; four great towers of canvas with every stitch pulling to perfection, and the shadow of the sails showing clear-cut in the white broken water to leeward.

Viking **in heavy weather off the Horn**, *by Tom Wells – himself a Cape Horner.*

During the following two days they changed sail. This was done four times in the course of a round voyage; for in the tropics any old rag that will hold the wind will suffice, while in the westerlies, north and south, nothing but the very strongest canvas will do. It was hard 'all hands' work, but joyous in the good weather, and made interesting by the rivalry between watches. But that it was hard needs no gainsaying, since the three lowest sails (foresail, mainsail and cro'jack) weighed well over a ton each.

For a week they held the north-east trades, reeling off over 1200 miles, averaging 175 a day without touching a sheet. Then for two days they fell light, and finally, in latitude 10°N, lost them altogether. The doldrum belt is 500 miles wide and it took fifteen days to work across it, by way of comparison averaging barely 30 miles a day. Those doldrums were every bit as bad as people say they are. The ship lay sweltering in a flat, oily calm with black rain-squalls dotted all round the horizon. A puff of wind was followed by a drenching squall in which the watch laboriously braced the yards round. No sooner had the hands coiled down and gone thankfully below to change wet clothes than the yards were flat aback and needed bracing the other way. And so it went on, watch after watch and day after day, while tempers got steadily worse.

By now David had become thoroughly familiar with his shipmates and the ship's routine. Captain Uno Mörn was not only a very experienced seaman, on his way to sail around Cape Horn for the thirteenth time, the sixth time in command, but a humane man too. David was in the first mate's watch; he had a loud bark but not a serious bite. The only disciplinary action ever taken was to be put on overhauling buntlines. These ropes made of wire, with a block and tackle for ease of handling on deck, were the means whereby the bottom edge of the sail was hauled up to the yard. Because their weight chafed the canvas, someone had to go aloft and haul up some slack, securing them with yarn to the jackstay which ran along the top of the yard as a sort of handrail. The mate would say 'Yames, overhaul the fore royal buntline'. So up David went to the top. On getting down the mate would say with an ill-concealed twinkle, 'I'm afraid the main royal has gone too'. So up again, since a hearty tug from the deck would have 'broken it out' while David was up the 'fore. If sorely displeased, the mate could do the same to the mizzen upper topgallant and David would easily climb 400 ft up the rigging before morning coffee at 5.30 a.m.

Paths with the second mate seldom crossed, nor were they particularly congenial. But as David had to turn a blind-eye to the second mate's girlfriends coming on board when he was nightwatchman in port, a truce was tacitly respected. The third mate was an amiable bull of a man, but like all bulls in china shops, the damage he wrought to the crockery when he came back on board tight in port was spectacular. The steward, also catering officer, was uniformly kind to all.

Of the other 'idlers', as they were called, who worked all day and slept all night, there was a bosun/sailmaker, a donkeyman, who did all the welding and metal repairs when he had not got steam up in his donkey boiler in port; the cook; and the carpenter, who was a pure Finn, and spoke less Swedish ultimately than David.

The other eighteen members of the crew who shared the forecastle were all third voyagers – leading seamen, waiting to sit their master's ticket; second voyagers, planning to sit their mate's ticket and Jungmän, Swedish-Finns, and apprentices – foreigners, who shared an equal disesteem. To the last-named on a strict rota basis, without any national bias, came all the really dirty jobs like 'backsturn', cleaning the pigsties and the heads. 'Backsturn' was the daily mess caterer, who had to wash all the dishes and scrub the place out; scrupulous cleanliness was observed. Cleaning the pigs was, of course, easy money to any countryman; but the 'heads', so called because they were situated under the raised forecastle head were anything but so. Basically the arrangement consisted of a 'three holer', which led to a trough in which twenty-four people left their daily offerings. As outlet there was a two-inch pipe, so if the ship was pitching, it all came back and hit one with force on the backside. The unpleasant alternative was to have it swilled out with buckets of water, with the residue shoved down by a bit of bent wire.

There was no refrigeration so the food was primitive but ample, with fresh bread baked daily. On Mondays and Thursday they had thick pea soup and glutinous salt pork, followed by pancakes. On Tuesdays and Fridays, stock-fish (salted cod) which had to be beaten with a sledge-hammer on a bollard to make it edible, but what they had the rest of the week David could not recall, except that none of it was fat! Thus, to him, it was all delicious and had the effect of putting a stone on him during the voyage.

The Scandinavian watch system meant that a long night on with only four hours in one's bunk was preceeded and followed by a full afternoon and morning off; conversely a short night on was paid for by the afternoon and following forenoon at work.

At night there were just three people on duty, the helmsman, lookout and policeman, which jobs rotated through the whole watch. The rest were allowed to sleep fully dressed but on immediate call. Calls consisted of one whistle: policeman only, for some minor duty; two whistles: the whole duty watch; and three whistles: all hands. In practice three whistles, for taking in the heavier sails, were reserved, whenever possible, for the change of watch, when all hands were on deck anyway.

This system worked well with what was in effect a schoolboy crew of about twenty; in the balmy days of sail there would have been more than forty seasoned men. It enabled the multitude of maintenance jobs to be done and gave enough time for rest and recreation. Effectively, a small body of youths was engaged in transporting 4,000 tons of grain from Australia to England by muscle power alone, aided only by capstans, winches, blocks and tackles. It is hardly surprising that they were physically tough.

But it was by no means all slog. The two Americans had a double berth cabin to themselves and when not at the wheel or on look-out they, Joe Cooper and David, used to have some marvellous musical evenings with David's Mozart, Beethoven and Wagner records and their Bing Crosby and Louis Armstrong. In the other forecastle was the Aaland Islanders' gramophone, much used for Sibelius – who had cult status – Grieg and all the jolly Swedish seamen's waltzes. They naturally, swapped musical occasions, but tended to prefer their own. The haunting tone poem of *Finlandia*, however, brought a lump to David's throat to the end of his days.

On Saturday afternoons and Sundays no work was done other than steer and sail the ship. Then the gramophone would be taken to the bowsprit netting or one could read a book, propped up against an anchor fluke. With towers of sail pulling perfectly and no noise or vibration, it was the perfect life, other than in high latitudes, when any such social occasions were emphatically below decks.

But to sail the ship all had to go aloft, which was fine once one got used to it. *Viking* had 202 lines leading down to the deck and within days one had to be able to go unhesitatingly to the right line, even on the darkest of nights. Luckily, every belaying pin had its special place and some key ones were of a distinctive size also, so it could be done by 'feel'. The mind boggles now at how many blocks this involved, each of which had to be cleaned, greased and, in many cases, painted each voyage; they must have exceeded 500.

The angle of the lower shrouds with their steel-rung ratlines was very gentle. But then just above the courses they jutted sharply out for about three feet, so one was in effect climbing a ladder leaning outwards and it needed a good heave and a firm grip to get oneself over to the topsail shrouds. The object of this overhang was, of course, to allow the topsail shrouds, with wooden ratlines, also to slope inwards. There was a much less daunting futtock shroud to the topgallant shrouds, which had rope ratlines, and from there there was a 'Jacobs Ladder' up behind the mast to the royal.

This was really much more daunting in harbour, where one was somewhat overawed because of the little cars and people far below; but at sea, with no sense of scale, the ship also usually had a list. This could make the lower shrouds, with the wind in one's back, almost an easy stroll and even the futtock shrouds could well become vertical rather than a perilous overhang. In either event, coming down was no problem; all one did was to slide down a back-stay hand over hand.

The voyage continued with the doldrums behind them. Forty-six days out, on Sunday, 26th October and flat becalmed 3° North of the line: 'Will this never end? "On deck!" – "Satan" say the Swedes; "Perkeli", say the Finns; and "Hell", say the English as up on deck they go . . . But wait a minute! The compass tells us that the ship's head points SW – can it be the south-east trades? Even as the ropes are coiled down the puffs of wind gather in strength and the ship begins to heel. The list increases and a strange sound is heard – it is the man at the wheel singing . . .' A week later they were 20°S with a dying south-east breeze. Once that lonely spot in the Southern Ocean had marked one of the great trade routes of the world, but now with the passing of sail it was empty. Drake must have sailed nearby in the little *Golden Hind*, and so must the lumbering East Indiamen, the fleet tea-clippers, the wool ships racing home with the season's clip, and the emigrant ships going out to Australia in the eighties. Hundreds of great ships must have passed by in the early days of the present century – grain from San Francisco, nitrates from Chile, guano from the Seychelles, and coal from Newcastle – all the world's bulk cargoes, where scheduled sailings did not matter. Now there were only fifteen windjammers left, apart from the memories or ghosts of departed ships that seemed to slip by in the soft evening light.

And yet at dawn they were awakened by a cry of 'Sail-ho!' It seemed impossible, but sure enough there on the horizon she was, plain for all to see. The *Viking* was close-hauled at the time, so that throughout the day she gained on them. By evening she was abeam and exchanging signals. It was the *Abraham Rydberg*, the Swede that had sailed a week before them and was going to Australia for grain. Two large sailing ships in company, outward bound. It did not seem like 1937!

The next day they saw their first albatross, some 500 miles further north than expected. Frequently the only companions in the limitless Southern Ocean, with their 12ft wing-span, circling eternally and never a wing flap, they are a beautiful sight.

In the evenings after supper there was often boxing and wrestling. David, never a good gymnast, fortunately could box, and usually ended up against a crew member called Eklund since they were well matched for weight and reach. Here the similarity ended, since David only boxed to score points, seeing no merit in giving a bloody nose, when a tap would do. Eklund, however, had no aim other than to knock his opponent cold. Luckily, as he was totally untrained, his haymakers could be seen coming a mile away and were easily evaded. Undoubtedly David had the support of the crew here; but it evidenced a weakness that was to follow him into business and politics in that he was always to see too much of the other point of view to want to go for the kill.

Each day they got further south and altered course more to the eastward, curving in an arc round Tristan da Cunha for the Cape. The westerlies lived up to their name and the wind began to pipe up, with one good gale which brought the ship down to six topsails and foresail. This was notable for the fact that it blew up slowly in the early afternoon and David was able to get some extraordinary photographs such as one from the fore royal looking down on Joe Cooper subduing the fore topgallant with the forecastle head and bow-wave visible 140 ft below.

At noon on 24th November, the seventy-seventh day at sea, they had only 100 miles to go for East London, and thoughts ran high for letters, green trees, fresh food, and beer. But at midnight the wind blew up to gale force and it was all hands on deck until five in the morning, getting the sail off her and heaving-to. It was during this brief gale that David witnessed the most daunting seas he was to see. Off Cape Horn, where the waves roll on forever, there are two or three hundred yards between crests, but off the Cape of Good Hope, where the west-bound Agulhas current meets a westerly gale, the seas are much shorter and sharper, with little distance between crests. Often, indeed, a following sea looks more like a wall of water rather than a slope, and it is easy to imagine that in the trough there could be a hole, such as some people believe engulfed the *Waratah*, a liner that disappeared, on her maiden voyage, between Durban and East London, just before the First World War. However, at 8 p.m. the wind came fair and all sail was set again.

Soon after daybreak on the seventy-ninth day they were greeted by a landfall – a green and pleasant horizon with white sands rising out of the sea. Then to their amazement they saw *Passat* and *Killoran*, under sail. They had left Copenhagen just before them and had been held up by the same head-wind – three big barques making port under sail together. No wonder aeroplanes circled overhead, while practically the entire population of East London was down on the long quay; next morning the papers were full of their pictures. Then the stevedores arrived to discharge the cargoes and they ceased to be the two-day's wonder while life resumed its normal course. The following week Erikson's grand old four-master *Lawhill* – built in Dundee forty-five years before – arrived, having made a smarter passage than the others. For a few days East London was a forest of masts and spars.

Thus began David's first experience as a sailor in port, with the thrill of longed-for mail and peaches at 5d for 30. Unfortunately the mishandling of rusty wire a few days before gave rise to a fast swelling, throbbing finger. A fortunate introduction to a local MP from his father led to hospital and an operation for a whitlow, with the captain's agreement and at the owner's expense. The sights and sounds of a public ward, before the days of modern painkillers, introduced him to another side of life and the realisation how sheltered he had been for his first eighteen years. The other side of the coin of this hospital stay was that he emerged with his first girl-friend. She was a pretty little nurse called Jean who came to see him the night before he was discharged, expressing a passionate interest in sailing ships, so was promised to be shown round on her next evening off. With hindsight David was probably the object of interest rather than any 'silly old sailing ship', but, if so, it was good thinking on her part, as it was far the best way to his heart. They started going out twice a week to the cinema and eating ice-creams on the beach afterwards*. This meant he kept up because of their mutual interest in women with his American shipmates, one of whom found an attractive reporter on the *East*

* This, despite the fact, as he wrote to his mother, 'East London is a fine town with three really good cinemas, but far too expensive. It is practically impossible to go out at night without spending 15s'.

London Daily Despatch. Joe Cooper had drawn the short straw and been given a fortnight off to accompany the Major on a trip to see game reserves. As the latter wobbled up the gangway on his return, it was clear that Joe was better fitted to be a deepwater sailor than a nurse-companion! David was taken on a motor trip about 80 miles up country one Sunday by another MP for his first contact 'with Kaffir kraals where the natives are still entirely uncivilised' as he wrote to his father. In those days this was written in the spirit in which the *National Geographic* might have reported on an unknown tribe up the Amazon – just a simple matter of fact. He felt they were lucky that neither industry nor politicians had yet got to them, and parted after swapping cigarettes and fruit, feeling neither superior, nor inferior, but different.

The duties in harbour were easy with much spare time for swimming and golf. But the greatest joy of all was to be lying in harbour with so many full-masted ships which still remained David's passion – more so having survived the Atlantic with no touch of seasickness and clearly a good head for heights. He took every opportunity to visit and compare the other ships. *Viking* had been built in 1907 as a cargo-carrying cadetship. *Killoran* was a three-masted barque of the most traditional kind with a raised poop which housed the officers – as the after castle in Nelson's day – and a forecastle in which the crew would have lived, ie 'before the mast'. *Lawhill*, a four-masted barque, was the oldest having been built in Dundee in 1892 for the jute trade and bore the reputation of a charmed life; she had sailed through the German submarine blockade in 1917 to Brest where she was bought by Erikson. She remained profitably employed up to 1939 and after the war continued to serve in the Southern Ocean until 1949 when her 58 years service came to an end. As a postscript, though, David was to encounter her off Cape Horn seven years later. But *Passat*, built in 1911, was the finest of Erikson's fleet and one of the last three square riggers to be built solely for commercial purposes for the Chilean nitrate trade.

The likelihood of Christmas in port looked increasingly improbable as each sling of timber emerged from the hold. On the last evening Jean and David went down to the end of the jetty and found themselves getting considerably better acquainted. In the end she had to go – but not before she had told him that if they had another night she knew of a sandy beach where he could have his heart's desire ... He got back on board to a great anti-climax as a right old rumpus was going on. A seaman had come aboard tight and could not be prevented from going aft to tell the captain his fortune. He was the same seaman that David found painting the rigging in Mariehamn thirty years later!

David's hopes were not to be fulfilled because on December 22nd a tug came alongside and took them in tow. Jean was at the end of the jetty to wave goodbye and it was a love-sick young sailor who turned to his duties. Perhaps it is as well that nothing happened. David left with a first aid manual she had given him and which was treasured, at least as a memory, for years to come.

However, during this leg of the voyage, there was a South African girl on board, who had previously been at Bunny's school in Switzerland. This opened the conversation, but fast becoming worldly-wise, he realised that she had something else on her mind. Having left his heart in South Africa, he was in no mood for a consolation prize. But she was, and presented it in good measure in the sail-locker – which might have been purpose-built. Luckily she was so fair-minded in her distribution of favours that there was never any jealousy. This all became too much for the Skipper who ordered her to leave the ship as soon as they reached Australia.

From the moment they left the tug the wind began to blow and, with the ship in ballast, they were either taking in or else setting sail practically every day, for the captain was determined to drive her. On Christmas Eve they had a short sharp blow and had to furl the fore and mizzen upper topsails, the only time that these sails were fast, except when hove-to. This took some time, so David saw in his eighteenth birthday on the yardarm of the fore upper top-sail. On 29th December they had the longest run of the voyage, making 290 miles at more than 13 knots, with *Viking* steering like a dinghy and with every sheet bar taut and every shroud humming its tone and overtone.

On 7th January, they sighted *Killoran* at daybreak and promptly both ships set more sail. Throughout that day they 'ran their easting down' in company like clippers in days of old. They lost her that night, but for the next week they were treated to some grand sailing, having average runs of 255 miles. On 15th January, heading north up Spencer's Gulf, they fell in with *Killoran* again and sailed neck and neck for Port Lincoln. It was evening as they dropped anchor, having sailed 5,060 miles in exactly twenty-four days, at an average speed of 8.8 knots. This was probably the best passage of *Viking*'s career, and certainly the best of the year, *Passat* taking twenty-nine days and *Killoran* thirty-six.

Early the following week they sailed over to Port Victoria on the opposite side of the Gulf to load 52,000 sacks of grain, which was sailed out in small ketches. Being anchored nearly a mile off shore, with the temperature in the nineties, there was no point in going ashore other than at week-ends. But on the night of their arrival David and his American friends did slip ashore aboard a dinghy on a reconnaissance. They found a single main street with clusters of buildings with corrugated iron roofs and verandahs, housing about 250 inhabitants, a couple of shops, a village hall, a post office and a pub. They opted for the pub, just a single saloon bar decorated with tatty pictures of sailing ships and naked ladies. By this time David had started drinking beer and found the Australian version had a kick like a mule. They were informed of an 'Abo girl' whose beat was the beach nearby but, even though the going rate was only tuppence, there were never any takers – not because of the exchange rate but rather because the poor girl had syphilis – Europe's least welcome export to the Indian and Pacific oceans. Eventually the adventure palled and unsteady progress was made back down the 300-yard length of pier. Unsteadily resenting having to go to sea again, the obvious course seemed to be to throw some of the ready-stashed cargo into the 'drink'. For five minutes they worked with a will, until one of them threw himself in with his sack. He surfaced near his slouch hat and, thinking it was the dorsal fin of a shark, panicked and had to be pulled out double quick. At least one of them was sober as they eventually climbed back on board.

While this frivolity was going on, the donkey engines had steam up, both to load their cargo and to unload 250 tons of stone ballast. Ten Australian 'wharfies' came to live on board, and fine chaps they were, carrying one-and-three-quarter-hundredweight sacks (196 lb) for eight to ten hours a day in stifling heat, and stowing them neatly in rows so that the cargo would not shift – which was the sailing ship's nightmare. It was one of them that first called David a 'whingeing Pommie Bastard'. He soon learnt that the right response to this was 'well fuck you for a start' – after which ritual exchange of insults firm friendship ensued.

Archie had once again, unknown to David, intervened and the local Empire Parliamentary Association Secretary, Captain Parker, negotiated four days special leave for him in Adelaide. The generosity of the captain in granting this – which in the nature of things could not be given to anyone else – and the forebearance of his shipmates in not resenting it was most reassuring.

The 'put upon' Captain Parker drove the 120 miles and back on unmade roads through freshly harvested cornlands and miles of desert to reach the contrastingly green coastal-strip that contained the garden city of Adelaide. A whirlwind tour followed; a trip to the university where they met Sir Douglas Mawson, the polar explorer; then to a stockbroker's office where David was introduced to a slim, modest figure whose name, he was assured, was Don Bradman; finishing with a stay with a lawyer, Mr Homburg, and his charming wife and very attractive daughter. Here it became a case of 'all systems go' and in rapid succession he was taken to the finals of the S.A. tennis week, meeting Budge and the popular German, Von Cramm; to dirt-track racing, (which did not appeal); to a cocktail party for the maiden voyage of the P & O liner *Stratheden* and to call on a great old lady of Scots origin, Mrs Barr-Smith, who had a garden paradise 2,000 ft. up on Mount Lofty overlooking Adelaide. This fêting all too soon came to an end. It had happened because of the still close ties with the 'Old Country'. A visitor from 'home' was a comparative rarity and doubtless David had been lionised because of the unusual manner of his arrival.

Occasionally through his life events coincided to threaten mild lionisation but this first taste made him realise that, by temperament, he was not suited to being a lion. After a very few days he was happy to return to the obscurity of the Wauraltree Hotel, Port Victoria – as in future he was to be happier in the Cock Inn, Wivelsfield Green or the Union or Saxons Inns, Child Okeford or the Craignure Inn on Mull. He knew he was lucky to have been born into a world where he did not have to climb.

It was back to Port Victoria in the country bus, laden with fruit, eggs and other goodies, to find that things had moved. The ship was approaching her load-line and the full hatches were being reinforced with baulks of timber lashed down for greater security. Life-lines were being rigged to prevent any-one being washed overboard and the footropes tested under stress between two capstans, because on them lives depended. Everything added to an air of expectancy. It was the middle of February and they were deep laden, down to their marks. Already the two training ships the *Abraham Rydberg* and the German *Admiral Karpfanger* had slipped out of port and it was David, doing a job aloft, who saw the German ship, formerly *Erikson L'Avenir*, beating slowly down the Gulf, quite unaware that human eyes would never see her again. Practically all the Erikson fleet were busy loading: *Passat, Pommern, Archibald Russell, Lawhill, Moshulu,* and *Olivebank* of the four-masters; and *Killoran* and *Winterhude,* barques. Only *Pamir* and *Penang* had yet to arrive, for they had gone to Madagascar for guano. These, with the addition of the Germans *Priwall* and *Padua*, which were still engaged in the Chile nitrate trade, com-prised the entire surviving fleet of commercial deep-water square-rigged ships.

Viking, *hove-to in the abortive search for Joseph Cooper, painted by Tom Wells.*

Viking, the first of Erikson's fleet, sailed on 16th February 1938, bound for Falmouth. There is drama and romance about the departure of a sailing ship on a 15,000 mile voyage, and all of them would have been wondering what would occur before they saw land again. The optimists, remembering their fast passage outward bound, were betting on less than 100 days: the prophets of gloom, thinking of the weed they had accumulated in the river at East London, were talking of more than her 136 days in 1934. Yet Finns, Swedes, Americans and English were a happy crowd as they ghosted down Spencer's Gulf.

There were new passengers to join the steadfast (if hardly steady) Major. There was a Dutch woman with her daughter, who spent most of their time playing bridge with anyone they could find. There was an English boy who liked the life so well that he signed on the following voyage, and there was Miss Lucy D. Plummer, a most enterprising globe-trotting retired American schoolteacher who had been to the headwaters of the Amazon – and most other places.

The start justified the pessimist's forecast, for no sooner were they out of the Gulf than they ran into a series of easterly gales, which twice within a week hove them to. It did not take long to find out that *Viking* deep laden was a very different ship, since for most of this period she needed two men at the wheel, and often, working the foredeck, they were up to their waists in water, jumping for the shrouds whenever they saw a big sea coming.

On the twelfth day out the wind came fair, and during the next five days the skipper drove her for all she was worth, making 1,057 miles of easting. Then, south of New Zealand, they had two days of light perplexing airs and from there on to Cape Horn they had the most extraordinary weather. Day after day it was cold but sunny, with a high glass and only moderate winds. The log showed that they only had the royals fast three times between New Zealand and the Horn. Only five times did the run surpass the 200 mile mark, and that in the 'howling fifties', where by all the rules they should never have made less.

During this stage of the voyage there was minimal work on deck and each watch in turn was engaged in chipping rust in the forepeak. The luckless mate had to be on deck, so the watch did not exert itself unduly; experience showed that as long as four hammers out of nine were at work, the noise was sufficient to allay his suspicions. This background gave David little excuse thirty years later as an MP to complain about productivity in the car industry, but they were only teenagers without families to support. Then tragedy struck which was to marr an otherwise perfect voyage.

It was 7.30 a.m. and there was a fresh beam wind, with the ship doing 9 knots under all sail. Suddenly there was a shout for all hands, followed by a frantic scuffling of feet on the deck above. Diving into anything handy the free watch rushed up and at once saw what was wrong, for there on the boat skids was a group frantically cutting away lashings, whilst others were letting fly the halliards. 'All right, there; back the main yards!' Figures in oilskins and figures in pyjamas rushed to the brace winches to heave the ship to and save a life; for there must have been a man overboard. 'Who is it?' 'Cooper', came the answer. 'Has he a chance?' 'Not a hope in hell,' said one of the older hands. The big ship came broadside to the wind and, despite her reduced canvas, heeled right over. A moment later and the lifeboat set out in search.

The decks went quiet while all stood in anxious groups on the poop, normally so sacrosanct. All the watch had been working below decks, except for the mate, the man at the wheel, and Cooper, who assisted by Junie Clark from inboard, was reeving a new weather fore-sheet. This had to be passed through a sheave in the bulwark, and, since the ship was heeled over to leeward, he had gone over the weather side standing in a bowline. This was done without the mate's permission, which would never have been granted. By sheer bad luck the ship happened to meet a sea wrong at the crucial moment, and he was carried away from his hold. At the same moment the cook came on deck to empty a binful of ashes, and it was he who had given the alarm and then rushed aft to throw a lifebelt. It fell some distance from Cooper, and he was last seen trying to get rid of his heavy sweaters and seaboots.

Armed with binoculars David climbed the 100 feet to the mizzen crosstrees and was amazed to find that even from that height the lifeboat was often lost to view, though less than a mile away. Then it turned, and as he rejoined the others every available glass was focused on it. For some time they felt sure that he must be there: but as the boat came nearer it was clear he was not, and with a sickening shock, they realised that they had lost a shipmate. The waters in 53°S, on the edge of the Bellingshausen Sea, are cold, but the cold is merciful, and he could not have lived for long – even if he had managed to reach the lifebelt, which was unlikely once his boots were waterlogged.

Watching their moment with care, the men scrambled back on board, the last two hooking on the falls, a highly dangerous business in the heavy sea then running. Silently, and with none of the usual cheers, the boat was swung in, braced round the main-yards and the crew mast-headed the topgallants and royals. The whole thing had barely taken an hour. As the next watch was relieved the mate said simply, 'Let us bare our heads to the memory of our lost friend', and there in that heaving great Southern Ocean they kept a minute silence ... No more impressive tribute could ever have been paid. Then, 'All right the free watch', and life resumed its normal pattern.

Joseph Walter Cooper was barely seventeen, but he had spent two and a half years in British coasting schooners and eighteen months in *Viking*. He was anxious to make round voyages in *Killoran* and *Archibald Russell*; for they were hard, wet ships and he dreaded the thought of going into steam. He was born in the wrong century. Captain Mörn and his officers had shown fine seamanship in heaving-to a ship of *Viking*'s size and launching a boat in less than seven minutes; and there is no doubt that the chief mate and boat's crew risked their lives. That evening there was a fiery red sunset and the sea was stilled as though in benediction.

Cape Horn was rounded on 30th March, forty-two days out, in calm, clear weather. Next morning the temperature dropped and they ran into patches of thick fog. It was ice. They could 'smell' it, and hear the shrill cries of penguins, but all that could be done was to keep a sharp look-out, using the foghorn to port, starboard, and dead ahead as a sort of primitive radar. It was not till they reached England that they heard the German training ship *Admiral Karpfanger* was overdue and had not wirelessed a position since rounding the Horn. In September the Lutine Bell rang to proclaim another sailing ship lost.

A week later, on Good Friday, they were flat becalmed in brilliant sun. Such a difference do a few degrees of latitude make. All the ports and scuttles were once again open and for the first time in six weeks they were dry. A pig was killed for Easter and blood pancakes eaten for tea. When leaving Australia bound for England, all seemed too remote. Now, in the Atlantic and heading north, Falmouth could be seen at the top right-hand corner of the chart stuck up in the mess-room, confirming the eventuality of their home-coming.

To enhance their optimism there were landmarks other than lighthouses and these were the stars. David had been bitterly disappointed by the Southern Cross, but the common denominator to both hemispheres is Orion, the Hunter, since he is as familiar to Cape Horn as he is to the Hebrides, his belt lying on the Equator. Luckily his zenith was at night as they worked their way north and, even though they were given their position and day's run regularly, to see Orion getting higher day by day was as much a tonic as smelling land ahead.

After Easter there began the great spring-cleaning of the ship that was to go on the whole way to England. First, all the rust had to be chipped – from chain-plates, rails, deck fittings, brace-winches, masts, yards and winches. Next the affected places had to receive two coats of red lead paint, so that soon the ship was a merry blur of conflicting colours. And, finally, the whole had to receive three coatings of the proper colour. It was a task that kept them more than busy the whole way home.

They were much afflicted with headwinds in the South Atlantic and looked like having a slow passage to the line. Then, in that belt of calms south of the trade winds which often holds ships up as long as the doldrums, a grand sou'westerly gale carried them right into the tropics. The south-east trade was light but steady, and they crossed the line on Saturday, 8th May, eighty days out.

They had but two welcome days of doldrums, for they were running short of water. Whenever a squall bore down, the scuppers were plugged and every bucket pressed into service to take the water to the tanks. They carried the north-east trades for ten days and did not lose them until latitude 25°N, but as they died huge lumps of Sargasso weed appeared to remind them that some distance yet remained to Falmouth. On 22nd May a steamer, the *Regent*

Panther, was sighted and closed on them to their immense enthusiasm as it was their ninety-fifth day at sea and the first time that anything had crossed their horizon. Having seen nothing but sea from Christmas Day until Easter it is not surprising that they danced and slapped each other on the back for joy. She promised to report them at Lloyds, so their families would know that all was well. They crept slowly north on the final lap, as they grew intensely proud of their ship which daily grew smarter. But for David the prospect of homecoming was shadowed by the prospect of signing off.

On 2nd June, while 1,000 miles west of Biscay, they had their last and best gale. It was warm and the canvas was dry, and they raced up the rigging in shorts and sandals to make fast the royals at two in the morning. Throughout the early hours the sea grew, and by 11 a.m., when David came to the wheel, the helmsman was frequently up to his waist in water – even though he stood on a grating more than twelve feet above her load-line and theoretically in one of the driest parts of the ship. They had to take in more sail and at one moment, when the watch were standing on the pin-rail clewing up the main upper topgallant, she dipped her rail under so that only a group of faces could be seen in the smother of white water to leeward. But they were a trained and youthful crew, who had worked together long enough that these things were taken as a joke.

Next day all sail was set again and soon they were in the main North Atlantic shipping route. The *Europa* passed them, her rail black with spectators. A cruising liner went by with an appreciable list, as many rushed over to gaze at a sight whose like they might never see again; and every humble tramp altered course and dipped her ensign in salute.

On Saturday, 11th June 1938, the 115th day at sea, they descried the flash of the Bishop Light dead ahead and the following morning closed the Lizard Signal Station. One of the last of the Falmouth 'bumboats' that always used to come out to try and sell sailors fresh provisions, arrived and, since none had any money, David engaged the old skipper in conversation. 'How are things in Europe?' he asked. 'Fine', he replied, although the Anschluss had taken place and Europe was heading for war. 'How are the Australian Test side doing? Who has won at Lords?' He didn't know. 'How has Ascot gone?' It seemed he didn't follow racing. At length, in desperation, David said, 'Look, I haven't seen a newspaper for four months, surely something has happened.' – He thought deeply and then his face was lit by inspiration. 'Yes', he said, 'the Duchess of Norfolk had a baby yesterday.' David could only conclude that while he was going round the world, the world had continued to go around by itself as usual.

To their joy they were given orders for London, where to their infinite disgust, they could see their rival *Passat* already lying at anchor. Sailing ten days after *Viking*, she must have missed those easterly gales and somehow managed to slip past in the Atlantic.

For exactly four months their ship had been a sentient living creature, whose whims had to be understood to get the best out of her. Now she was being handed over to alien people, who neither understood nor cared for all the work they had done. But neither, in reality did David, overwhelmed by the joys of home-coming. They locked into Millwall Dock within sight of Tower Bridge. His mother, father and Aunt Violet were there to greet him; his father, sacrificing Gold Cup Day at Ascot, even admitted that *Viking* was a spectacular sight.

The captain agreed to sign off David, Junie and Frenchie at noon the next day, but gave him shore leave to have a family dinner – after the red lead had been removed from his hair and his filthy working singlet and jeans had been replaced at Great Aunt Isabel's, in spite of her fear of a resulting invasion of 'beetles'. Sadly he returned to the ship for a miserable last night with a raging toothache, having lost a filling over dinner.

So hour by hour in utter misery he paced the deck under *Viking*'s mast with a wind singing in the rigging.

Then it came to him that he loved *Viking* in exactly the same way as he loved Torosay and the beautiful and historic ships, like beautiful and historic houses had to be preserved at all costs for posterity.

Viking's cargo was unloaded quickly into Thames barges, thereby ensuring it got from the Australian outback to Ipswich entirely under sail.

But before leaving in the morning, David had done a deal with the donkeyman, who throughout the voyage had been engaged in making a very beautiful model of *Viking* – into which he had put 676 hours of work. David's only £13, in the Post Office Savings Bank, was offered and accepted, probably because it was going to someone who loved the ship. It is now the centrepiece of a Torosay display.

To repay the crew's marvellous hospitality one or two jaunts were laid on. One night the first and third mates were taken to the Victoria Palace to see *Me and My Girl*, with Lupino Lane. Another day a bus was chartered to take the entire foreguard to see Windsor Castle and Eton. Naturally Junie, Frenchie and David scampered around a bit, taking girls to nightclubs. Only the captain and his wife missed out because he was still too much like God Almighty, but ample opportunity arose in later days to make amends.

Then Junie returned to the United States having sworn to keep in touch. For nearly half a century this was achieved, with encounters both home and away. By a happy chance, the Major got away from a carousal at the Cavalry Club the same day, still wearing his Sherlock Holmes-type cape – and no soberer for his health cruise. He had richly earned the affection of all, not least because his parting libation for the crew was a case of whisky, rather than a barrel of beer. And when David left, to his amazement the whole ships' company lined the rail to cheer him off. No greater compliment could ever be given, for they were real men.

His Housemaster's first prediction was right. The voyage in the grain ship turned him into a man, but would he be able to face Balliol and books again?

6

OXFORD AND THE EARLY WAR YEARS

1938 to 1943

I think one of the most lovely sights I have ever seen is a gunboat unit
at speed in moonlight, with the white pluming wakes, the cascading
bow waves, the thin black outlines of the guns starkly silhouetted,
the figures of the gunmen motionless at their positions as though carved out
of black rock, all against the beautiful setting of the moon path on the water.

LT.-COM. ROBERT HICHENS DSO DSC, 1944

WITH SUCH A GREAT ADVENTURE behind him came the emptiness of an anti-climax, seemingly bigger because of his mere eighteen years and harder to bear because of the thought of three years of sedentary scholarship in front of him. David turned to the comfort of Torosay and of his grandmother, Gran'Ol, which did the trick. The smell of Torosay stones, the fish in Loch Don and the stags on Sgurr Dearg were the medicine he needed.

Apart from the certainty of Gran'Ol in Torosay his family were all over the place. His mother Bridget, now married to Geoffrey, lived in Cairo and only through the misfortune of a miscarriage was she able to meet David on his return from *Viking*. She was now happily married to somebody who would be beside her until the end and was to support her and her home to the limit. This meant that David saw his mother only in snatches as she was toing and froing, either because of her miscarriage or to give birth to her daughter, Leonie, in September 1939. Meanwhile Geoffrey was to be perfectly placed, as Squadron Leader of B Squadron, 11th Hussars, to fire the first shot of the Desert War against the Italians in 1940 – at least it would have been the first shot had it not been a misfire, which was in keeping with Poggles' reputation. Nevertheless, he commanded the Squadron with dash and élan and was awarded the DSO for actions in June 1940. The citation read:

'At Ghirba (in June) the information gained and action taken by Major Miller's Squadron enabled reserves to be brought up which led to the total destruction of the enemy; his Squadron alone capturing 100 prisoners and destroying 5 light tanks and 15 lorries. The G.O.C. wrote complimenting his Squadron for their work at Gabr Saleh over an extended period. In September he did excellent work co-operating with the Coldstream Guards during their retirement. To his splendid leadership in all respects I attribute the outstanding success of his Squadron.

Signed A.G. WAVELL, *General, Commander in Chief, Middle East*

He continued to be in the forefront of action until February 1941, during which time his Squadron led the advance of the 6th Australian Division along the coast road from Derna to Benghazi. He was then recalled to the United Kingdom on medical and compassionate grounds as his daughter, only a year old, was extremely ill. Geoffrey was to see out the rest of the war in England, commanding the 8th Sherwood Foresters as an armoured car regiment. He was heartbroken not to take them into action as they were drawn on as reinforcements for other armoured regiments in Europe after D-Day. His German interpreter's course came in handy at the end of the war when he commanded a unit in the south of England set up especially to interrogate German prisoners of war. He retired in 1946.

David saw little of his mother in the months before he went up to Oxford but his father kept in touch with him. By then Archie had given up his post as PPS to R.A. Butler and as an active and nosey back-bencher started making trips to Spain to see the Spanish Civil War first hand from each side.

He first went on an unofficial parliamentary delegation in December 1936 and reduced the House of Commons to silence with his speech on return. He swept away the belief that the war was an ideological struggle between Communism and Fascism. Spain's unhappy soil has bred strife through the centuries and foreign interests had seized upon the unhappy condition to further their own ends. He had no solution, but after addressing the Foreign Affairs Committee in confidence it is interesting to note today that the intimate details which he presented to the committee were leaked to the public.

Archie and his son had one thing in common that they both liked being in the thick of things; their judgement was not always particularly sound, but their views and comments were bound to be interesting and, in Archie's case in particular, likely to be opinionated. He felt that David was having a dull, anticlimactic time vegetating in Torosay and extracted him so that at least he could have the excitement of a trip to Spain before going up to Oxford. David got his first baptism of fire before he had been there twenty-four hours, being given a severe fright by a sniper from the one side and then being subjected to a bout of serious shelling from the other side; they were lucky to escape unharmed. This kept both of them remote from the Munich crisis which was hitting the news at the time. A year later, in 1939, Archie was to rejoin the RAF, and marry Eugenia Stirling in 1940. His Spanish experience led to the post of Honorary First Secretary to the Embassy in Madrid, where he was engaged in intelligence and organising for escapees from France to go back to England until 1941. He then served in the Commons again as R.A. Butler's PPS in 1942, at the Ministry of Education. He was awarded the KBE in 1945.

In the autumn of 1938, before going up to Oxford, David's sister Bunny was again moved to a new school, and as he so frequently did, he acted in *loco parentis* and delivered her to her new seat of learning, Mrs Fife's in

Cambridge. He then proceeded to Oxford to read Geography. Arriving at the Balliol porters' lodge the first three people he met – whose paths were to cross in years to come – were Roy Jenkins, Dennis Healey and Edward Heath. The result of his year at sea at a formative time of his life was that he arrived at Oxford, having lost touch with his contemporaries. In spite of coming from a big school he was lonely and particularly sought out Roy Jenkins on the ground that both their fathers were MPs, albeit of different persuasions. David had left Eton very young and, having roughed it at sea at an early age with completely different people, he was developing a growing impatience and an adolescent rebellion to upper class social attitudes. At the same time he was in no way attracted by socialism because he mistrusted the excessive concentration of power likely to emerge under the threatened nationalisation. Luckily Aunt Auds lived in Oxford and was delighted to provide her nephew with a family welcome and food on demand, which made his transition a great deal easier. As it was, the shadow of war and the under-lying uncertainty of the times did not lead to the normal undergraduates' intellectual musings and arguments but was replaced with a tendency more inclined to drink and be merry – particularly with sherry at 15s a bottle. The effect of Munich and Spain made the threat of war seem too close to concentrate on work. But the usual – probably under the circumstances rather exaggerated – pranks of undergraduates were well to the fore. Strip-poker in David's rooms became a regular event as they were the easiest to climb into. Among the players were George Howard, in years to come to be Chairman of the BBC, and Leonard Cheshire who was to be awarded the VC in the RAF.

Meanwhile, back in Torosay, Gran'Ol had been doing some serious thinking and made the main part of the estate over to Bridget and the self-contained peninsular of Auchnacraig over to her younger daughter, Violet. She retained for herself just the Castle and its eleven acres of garden.

Torosay, effectively, was to go into hibernation for the war. Little labour was left, the lawns were not mown, the hedges remained untrimmed and all the rooms except Olive's suite were never opened or even dusted; fungus started growing in the entrance hall. Rare wartime leaves by various family members could do nothing to stop the progress of dowdiness nor overcome deterioration of the structure. Nevertheless, as long as Olive was there, Torosay's heart did not fail.

David's long vacation in 1939 was filled by going to sea as a second mate in a chartered schooner on an eight-week cruise in the Aegean. As they got back to Antibes, Hitler marched into Poland. David rushed back to Oxford immediately to go before the University Joint Recruiting Board, which consisted of a senior officer from each service, presided over by the Master of Balliol. Recommended for training for a commission in the RNVR on the strength of his previous experience at sea, he was told he would hear about being called up within the next ten days. Predictably nothing happened, so he went up to Oxford again to await developments. The onset of the war put paid to any serious education in what became a rather amusing town in an adolescent and alcoholic sort of way. Every day saw someone go off to the Phoney War and each departure became an excuse for a wilder party than the one before.

*   *   *

David's turn came just before the Christmas vacation when a letter came from their Lordships of the Admiralty. They offered entry for selected undergraduates to go to sea as midshipmen, attached to commodores of convoys. David's speedy acceptance resulted in an appointment by return in no less than two sealed envelopes marked 'MOST SECRET' and on an open postcard from a friend in the Admiralty! Thus came a bewildering metamorphosis from an undergraduate to a naval officer and after doing a short course at the Admiralty, David found himself and nine other 'snotties'* two days later in Liverpool, each appointed as an assistant to a Commodore.

These Commodores were retired Royal Navy officers of distinction who had returned at the outbreak of war to take on a most hazardous job. They had all flown their own flags in their own commands but returned to sea with a total staff of two pensioner signalmen and a telegraphist and were put in charge of a convoy, making one of the merchantmen their flagship. They then had to shepherd large flocks of up to a hundred eight-knot ships carrying vital supplies, equipment and human beings for the next five years, in all sorts of weather. Probably in their previous Royal Naval life, years before, they were on the bridge of a battleship but they stuck to their duties throughout the war, taking convoys to Gibraltar or Freetown and, vitally, to Halifax where many were lost at sea.

One of David's first tasks at sea was to count the flock at first light. The Commodore would ask David and the yeoman, 'how many have we got left this morning?' – not because of enemy action but because in the early days merchantmen were quite unused to keeping station at night and their unwieldy ships without revolution telegraphs often lost company. A count between the Commodore and his assistants would vary by two or three but by lunchtime all had closed up and were going well again. Another hazard with these convoys was that merchant ships seemed to be incapable of answering signals. Whereas their crews were incomparable as seamen they did not have the signalling proficiency which came from the constant practice not called for in peacetime.

David did only one trip with the Commodore, taking a slow convoy out to Gibraltar, where they stayed for four days, and returning to Liverpool with a fast convoy. The highlight at Gibraltar was that Midshipman James was co-opted to make up a tennis double match with three admirals. As far as is known this did nothing to enhance his progress up the promotion ladder. The voyage home with the fast convoy was in the savage winter of 1939–40 and for five days they ploughed up the North Atlantic without ever sun or

* midshipmen

star appearing to give them a fix. At last, feeling their way into the Irish Channel, they picked up an outward bound convoy burning navigation lights and, hopeful of some positional help, flashed a signal to the escort destroyer, 'what is your position?' The only help they received as she disappeared into a thick hail squall was the reply 'on your starboard bow'. On return David's Commodore went sick and he was sent out with a variety of other ships to keep him busy.

His next assignment was to be lent to a mine-sweeping trawler taking some divers out to investigate a wreck, claimed to be that of a German submarine sunk near the Morecombe Bay light vessel. It turned out to be an old collier that had been there so long it had disappeared off all the charts. Then he was lent to a Grimsby-class sloop employed on escort duties. This was a happy time but as there was a lull in the submarine battle in the Atlantic they never saw anything.

However, a week after the invasion of the Low Countries, David was sent to the RNVR training establishment, HMS *King Alfred*, at Hove. This famous shore frigate, which was the converted municipal swimming baths, turned out more than twenty thousand temporary naval officers during the course of the war. There was no specified length of training in those days. Theoretically, everybody stayed there till such time as they were proficient, but in practice the Admiralty manning demands were often such as to make this impossible. It was after David left that it was found necessary to increase the accommodation by taking over the famous girls school, Roedean. To the joy of the new intake upon arrival, they found each bed with a prim little placard saying: 'Ring twice for Mistress'.

It was a month after David had been in *King Alfred* that the military situation deteriorated. The sounds of gun fire over the Channel grew louder and louder and one Thursday evening guest night the Commander entered, apologised, stopped the concert and asked all those with a sound knowledge of marine engines to report to his office. Thirty volunteers left and found themselves at Dunkirk. Most, but not all, were back a fortnight later after their baptism of fire, in their grey flannel trousers and gaiters, doing gun drill as though nothing had happened. Uniforms were still at a premium and they had to work in their civilian clothes; those who had turned up with spare pairs of trousers were the fortunate ones.

It was on Monday, 17th June, with ugly rumours of the imminent fate of France, that several of them went to a variety show in Brighton. Even though it was first-class performance by a London cast, no one really got into the swing of enjoying it; all felt that this was probably the last day before all hell was let loose over England. Walking back to his digs from the theatre David was overtaken by one of the staff driving a car. He pulled up and asked David if he would like to go to France. David's instant reply was 'Yes sir'.

'Well then, hop in'. Three more officers were picked up in the same way and taken straight to the station without even being allowed to pack. They were given warrants and told to report to the Commodore's office at Devonport. It says much for the national capacity to cope with emergencies that they found first-class sleepers duly booked for them at Waterloo.

Things returned to normal on arrival at Devonport. No one on HMS *Drake* had any idea what they had come for and they were told to wait. They spent the day wandering around reporting to a series of people, none of whom knew anything about them; but in the evening a signal came through and things started to buzz. They were even issued with those rare commodities, revolvers, as well as tin hats, and taken down to the destroyer HMS *Beagle* where thirty special ratings awaited their arrival. The *Beagle* lay amid a score of British warships among which were the French battleship, *Paris*, their submarine, *Surcouf* and, alongside the submarine, HMS *Thames*. David, risking the reputation of RNVR 'snotties' as being *persona non grata*, asked an Engineer Lieutenant-Commander whether he could have a look round and to his surprise was hospitably shown round the submarine as well as being taken aboard the *Surcouf*. He was not to know that the *Thames* with her whole ship's company would be lost on her next patrol and that the hospitable Lieutenant-Commander who had entertained him, would be murdered by the Captain's steward on taking over the *Surcouf*. On boarding HMS *Beagle* they found the ship's company was augmented by thirty spare naval ratings camping on deck with about thirty Royal Engineer sappers. The steward was arranging sleeping accommodation for three army officers and the midshipmen by laying down stretchers in the ward room. There was a Wing Commander to act as interpreter who had a hammock slung in the after flat and, much to his surprise, David found that they were accompanied by the Admiral in charge of the operation who was installed in the Captain's cabin. It transpired that they were demolition 'experts' and as soon as they were at sea they found that their destination was Bordeaux where they arrived thirty-six hours later without having seen a German aircraft. Slipping past the coastal batteries at the mouth of the Gironde with their hearts in their mouths they learnt that the Germans were not expected to arrive for another twenty-four hours. Some of them immediately went ashore for dinner. Throughout the three days of their stay the ship was at twenty minutes notice but they were allowed ashore as long as they remained in sight of the masthead where the recall signal was to be hoisted. The demolition target was an oil refinery up-river, on a spit where the Garonne joins the Gironde.

Bordeaux itself was in a strange state, being the seat of the French Government during those critical days. Life appeared to be normal, though there had been a small air raid the night before and German troops were expected any moment. Alongside the quay were ships unloading munitions and the trams were still running. As time went by it became apparent that chaos was growing hourly as the ships that had been unloading munitions began to load them again, and a steady stream of refugees came pouring from the north. A detachment from the *Beagle* was sent off to man the British Consulate as the Consul himself had left for Spain and there was a large crowd of the strangest 'British citizens', few of whom spoke a word of English, demanding exit visas to Spain and transport to the frontier. They had to refuse all requests for a passage home on the destroyer, but one train did get away before the Germans arrived. That evening they slipped down the river to do their demolition work on the Bec D'Ambes oil storage plant. They surprised the guards – who, thinking they were Germans shouted, '*Kamerad*' – and locked them in the guard-house. The charges were placed in position with the fuses laid and they were just contemplating on the wonderful blaze there would be, when the ship's surgeon arrived with a signal from the Admiralty to cancel the whole operation on political grounds. Apparently the French were still wavering and we did not want to antagonise them, so all the charges had to be removed. The guards were released, with the explanation that they had only been locked in because there was a rumour that they were to be attacked by German parachutists. This lame excuse seemed to satisfy them and with many expressions of goodwill they oiled the ship.

Sailing back to Bordeaux they came alongside again to find even greater chaos than when they had left. But as they had not had a proper wash for five days some of them took advantage of the public baths which were still operating. Returning from their ablutions it was most comforting to see, through the confusion, one of Her Majesty's ships lying quietly there with the crew cleaning guns and sunbathing as though at home, and with the White Ensign fluttering bravely in the breeze. The merchantmen had by then reloaded their cargoes and were sailing back to England. The *Beagle* signalled to Whitehall that the French government had signed an armistice with the Germans. Orders came to return home and they slipped silently down the Garonne on a beautiful summer's evening, leaving the French to enter their four years of bondage. The peasants waved Godspeed to them as they passed. Once again they held their breath as they sailed past the coastal batteries at the mouth of the river, but there were still no Germans. So it was *au revoir* to France and the last British man-of-war to leave the continent of Europe left the French coast, to arrive back in Devonport the next day. There had been prayers for them in the barrack chapel but in fact they had witnessed one of the historic scenes of the war, without seeing a single German or hearing a shot fired in anger.

David came back to his training and he had another fortnight in the coastal forces class where he was busily trained in skills which he was never to use during his service in MGBs[*]. There was an intensive study of celestial navigation but he never had occasion to take a sight. The course duly completed, they were sent on indefinite leave, which was rudely interrupted by a posting for three months to AMCs[†] for sea experience before taking up their

[*] motor gunboats
[†] armed merchant cruisers

A flotilla *of MGBs with a patrol trawler.*

coastal force appointments. This again was rather a strange idea as it is hard to see why an AMC of all ships was chosen for this task. Three months in a ship of 16,000 tonnes, with a speed of 15 knots, did little to prepare them for handling the 70-ft, 40-knot MGBs. The AMC that David served in was a most unhappy ship; the idiotic rivalry between the Royal Navy, Royal Naval Reserve and Royal Naval Volunteer Reserve, which took three years to resolve, was at its height. Of all HM ships, AMCs were easily the worst to serve in. They were passenger liners, selected for the length of time they could stay at sea rather than for any other qualities, and the only prospect they held out was months of boredom, with the almost certainty of being sunk at the end of it. Their large silhouettes presented a perfect target for submarine and surface raiders and, having no armour plating and very few watertight compartments, they were especially vulnerable to the torpedo. Despite filling their holds with several thousand empty sealed drums it rarely needed a second 'tin fish' to send many of them to the bottom.

The first patrol of eighteen days was up in the Denmark Strait where they steamed backwards and forwards between Iceland's North Cape and the edge of the pack-ice; during this period they stopped and boarded several trawlers. Thankfully they did not encounter any pocket battleship or other surface raider. They returned home to spend ten days cleaning boilers and then set sail again for the same place, but just as they were looking out their heavy clothes suitable for the Arctic Circle a signal was received diverting them to escort a convoy down to Freetown in tropical West Africa. On the way to join the convoy a Focke-Wolf Condor came lumbering up the stern, but the officer of the watch was not bright at aircraft recognition and thought it was one of our Sunderlands – until it dropped a stick of four bombs. The first near-missed and exploded astern, the second hit the boat deck and bounced overboard, the third came down the funnel through the plating and wedged on the deck without exploding, and the fourth near-missed and exploded ahead. The Commander, hearing the crash, rushed on deck and told the midshipman of the watch to investigate damage; he turned a minute or two later, quite unmoved, and reported that there was a bomb lying on the upper deck. The Commander, midshipman and two of the bridge look-outs then calmly went down and rolled it overboard.

As they got further south the more uncomfortable the journey became. The ship had been built for the North Atlantic, the ventilation was quite inadequate for the tropics and no one had been issued with tropical kit. They spent only four days in the heat of Freetown before getting orders to return home alone. Every evening they clustered round the wireless for news of the Battle of Britain which was then at its height, and in due course arrived safely at Belfast.

David was thankful to leave the ship in Belfast and go on to his final spell of training, an anti-submarine course at Weymouth. A few Motor Anti-Submarine Boat flotillas were being converted into Motor Gun Boats, for it was realised that, with the Germans in the channel ports, the U-boats were operating too far afield for smaller craft to deal with them, while the E-boats were becoming the growing menace of the in-shore waters.

The end of David's training coincided with the beginning of the hunting season and he managed to get a day cub-hunting with the South Dorset Hounds before he was sent to the British Power Boat Company to stand by

The seventy-foot MGBs *were capable of a speed of 40 knots.*

an MGB flotilla, just building. He was most impressed with the energy, efficiency and charm of the senior officer of the flotilla, Lt. Peter Howes who had also just arrived; his qualities were to stand Coastal Forces in good stead in the months to come.

Early in December David was fortunate to have two blitz-free nights, the first for many weeks, during a weekend's leave in London. But when he got to Southampton he found the centre of the city had largely vanished. Luckily the club which offered hospitality to naval officers – known as the 'Honky Tonk' – was undamaged and the night after the blitz David ran into the only other officer there, a sandy-haired fellow, going thin on top, and wearing the ribbon of a DSC. There was nothing then to indicate how much he would feature in David's future service life. As they gossiped of this and that David found out he was a solicitor from Falmouth, keen on motor racing and music, and that they had a mutual enthusiasm for sailing, although at a higher level. He had competed against Peter Scott for the Prince of Wales' Cup. This first tenuous link with Peter Scott was to develop after the war. He too was standing by on MGB building and had come to Southampton in case there was a further blitz and he could be of use. Within two years this quiet man became a legendary figure in the Coastal Forces and David's hero. His name was Robert Peverell Hichens.

The flotilla of MGBs was commissioned between December 1940 and February 1941. Lt. Peter Howes commissioned the first, MGB 61, early in December and took her down to Fowey to work up, followed by the next three boats: No. 62, Lt. Whitehead; No. 63, Lt. Shore, with David as First Lieutenant; and No. 64, Lt. R.P. Hichens. They set off with great enthusiasm. Though it was calm enough in the Solent, it was blowing force 6 outside and their boats, being flat bottomed, began to pound as though they would break, as they rounded the Needles at 30 knots. The jarring was such that it broke the coxswain's back in Hichen's No. 62 and he had to return, while the rest continued at the reduced speed of 12 knots. They eventually arrived at Fowey and lined up with the three other boats in service, only needing two other boats to complete the flotilla.

The next three weeks were spent at Fowey, working up and it soon became evident just how inadequate their boats were for the job. The 70ft-long British Power Boats seemed to be over-powered, with three Rolls Royce Merlin One engines giving them a speed of about 40 knots. The engines themselves were designed for aircraft, but the marine installation such as salt water pumps, gear boxes and propeller shaft couplings, were not up to the mark and soon gave serious trouble. At the end of the working-up period most felt that if their boats were not going to be out of action through one defect, they would be through another. Strange to say only one boat gave no trouble, Hichens' No. 64, but that was thought to be just good luck! While the engines inspired a certain amount of confidence, their guns certainly gave them none. Each boat, costing some £65,000, was armed with a

Lt.-Cdr. Robert Hichens, DSO and bar, DSC and two bars

Boulton Paul power turret aft, containing four 303 Vickers machine-guns, with two twin Lewis guns positioned amidships. The power turrets caused endless worry as they too had been admirably designed for aircraft, but driven by an electric system, in heavy weather at sea they were soon put out of commission by solid driving spray. It seemed that they were destined to fight in flat-bottomed speedsters, driven by aircraft engines and armed with little more than pea-shooters.

They arrived at their operational base, HMS *Beehive* at Felixstowe in March 1941. This was an old RAF station and not used by them other than to maintain the Harwich balloon barrage. It made a perfect Coastal Force base with a 50-tonne crane which could lift their boats bodily out of the water and large aircraft hangers in which repairs and maintenance could be carried out. They did not get a great welcome from the MTB flotilla already installed there. They seemed rather to resent their intrusion – as did the captain of the base who rejoiced in being rude to all his juniors, particularly if they were RNVR officers. The thought of Hichens being in command of an MGB nearly gave him apoplexy.

For three weeks they sat at Felixstowe doing absolutely nothing, even though one night E-boats came over and sank five ships from a convoy, just outside Harwich. The Admiralty had no confidence in the reliability of these boats to use them in an offensive manner, and so were sitting on the fence much to the MGB commanders', particularly Hichen's, frustration. Peter Howes and he had faith in the boats and the vision to see what they could achieve. As a result of Howes energy and pestering those above him, David's boat, No. 63, was sent down to Brightlingsea as a prototype for rearmament. Confidence and hope reigned when the Lewis gun positions were scrapped and replaced with twin-operated .5 calibre guns either side of the bridge and the Boulton Paul turret was removed and replaced with a single 20mm Oerlikon gun; the addition of self-sealing tanks was also a booster. This job scheduled to take four weeks, finally took ten.

But during this time Peter Howes succeeded in intercepting some E-boats returning from a raid on a convoy route, giving chase and inflicting a certain amount of damage. This was the first Coastal Force gun action of the war and, although the results were negligible, it did much to restore faith in the small MGBs as a potential weapon – and boost the morale.

While kicking his heels at Brightlingsea David fell in with a strange Australian, Lt. George Syme RANVR, who was about to set off up the Blackwater to make safe an acoustic mine. He offered to take David and the Brightlingsea torpedo officer along 'for the ride'. They had to hang about in the local pub with some trepidation until the tide left the mine exposed high and dry. Impelled by curiosity they tip-toed along behind Syme, and hardly daring to breath, settled down to watch him get to work. Out of his tool bag came a brass hammer, brass pliers and a brass screwdriver and lying beside the bomb on his stomach he, with infinite slowness, began to unscrew a plate; a quarter turn, stop, ear to bomb, listen; quarter turn, stop. It took some twenty minutes to get the plate off. Long fingers probed into the entrails to bring out the detonator and with infinite care snipped the leads. Then, with slightly less caution, he next unscrewed a thing like a clock, tied a length of twine to it, retired about a hundred yards behind the dyke and pulled. With a sigh of satisfaction Syme stood up and said that it was all over, and there was no tip-toeing back to the corpse. He called up the Sappers in a

15cwt truck and they hauled off the mine. He explained that, to start with, he was not sure whether this was a mine which would be triggered off by contact or magnetically or acoustically. Slowness in removing the plate was because, if the mine was acoustic, the range of frequency was so great that the ordinary rhythmic unscrewing would have been enough to detonate it. The bit he removed first was the bomb fuse which could have gone off without warning, and the next part was the 17-second fuse clock. This was the twenty-seventh mine he had disposed of and they all returned to the Yacht Club to celebrate with something stronger than lemonade. The next day while at work David heard two distant explosions further away; this was Lt. Syme exploding his twenty-eighth and twenty-ninth land mines. Shortly after he was awarded the George Medal and later a bar.

Rearmament was not completed until near the end of June and they got back to Felixstowe to find that, during the good weather, the boats had been operating much more frequently and the commanders and crews were beginning to form some better ideas of their potentialities. A programme was then worked out to modify all the other boats of the flotilla as David's had been and two boats a month were sent down; boats 62 and 64 starting the ball rolling.

The Admiralty were moving off their rigid rule that only RN officers should have command and started giving boats to RNVR officers and David's C.O., 'Arty' Shaw went to a destroyer during the re-fit. His place was taken by a delightful Scot, George Bailey. Peter Howes was due to relinquish command of the flotilla at the end of August and – but in the teeth of fierce opposition from the loathsome station commander – he succeeded in getting Hichens recommended as his successor.

July and August passed smoothly with plenty of patrol work, even though there was little activity from the E-boats of the other side. A party took place at Hichens' little house at Felixstowe to bid goodbye to Peter Howes who was sad to leave these boats; he was sure they were going to make history, and events proved him right. He had faith in the boats when others had none and he had the vision to select an RNVR country solicitor as his successor in the days when the average Royal Naval officer might just tolerate a yachtsman but would never consider him a professional equal. Another change for the good occurred at the same time in that the bloated Base commander departed for a more alcoholic sphere, to be succeeded by Commander Tom Kerr RN. He was from the Navy of a previous generation, a submarine commander in the First World War and a farmer in Kenya up to the beginning of the present one. His mind was more elastic than most of the regular officers twenty years his junior and his comprehension of the needs of a new and rapidly developing weapon was such that he put his weight behind every suggestion for improvement and championed every good idea. During his three years tenure of office he never failed to be on the jetty to see the patrols set out and no hour was too early for him to rise and welcome them back.

The stage was now set for Hichens' two years of leadership. In assessing his sea-going officers he had to say of David, 'that he was a young Etonian from the Isle of Mull who was a seaman by nature and had sailed before the mast in square-rig and found it impossible to feel the slightest qualm, however disturbing the motion. He was a devotee of the ballet with a surprisingly active mind – and was quite incapable of noticing if he had a large smudge of ink on his face or had a rent in the seat of his trousers.'

Of the practices Hichens brought to his command he encouraged the midday 'gin sessions' as a boost to morale and a help in cementing the team together. The nature of the work, patrolling at night, did not allow congregating socially in the evenings but boats took turns to host their colleagues and members of the base staff from time to time. On one such occasion the conversation turned to leave and a brother officer complained that he had not had Christmas leave for three years and it would probably not come about as doubtless David would have pre-empted him by booking seats for the ballet about then. 'Hitch' explained to a recently arrived officer 'You see David has an effective method of fixing his leave dates. He books seats at the ballet, and then if he's not allowed to go he sulks and gets inebriated.'

The second more serious practice was to instigate the weekly 'tactical talk'. At the first one, a couple of days after he took over, while being an atrocious public speaker, his logical marshalling of the facts and his evident sincerity got across to his audience that they possessed a weapon, which although they believed in it themselves, still had to be improved. There was no previous experience how to operate the boats to the best advantage and it was up to them on the spot to evolve their own tactics. Since sixteen heads had to be better than one, he proposed to meet weekly to hammer things out and he wanted all officers, however junior, to attend and to voice their opinions as they would all have commands of their own one day. Shades of Nelson's captains 'a happy band of brothers'.

The first technique he started to develop was to get away from the time-honoured method of 'patrolling' which in the routine naval mind meant going up and down a line wearing out engines and making a noise that could be heard ten miles off, when visibility was only 50 yards. Only a fluke would enable an E-boat to be intercepted that way. Hichens suggested changing the whole method to waiting and listening for E-boats at likely places on convoy routes and using hydrophones to pick up the noise of engines. They must then develop a skill in estimating their course and speed by doing a sharp dash on an intercepting course and stopping and listening for a second time to ascertain whether the course had changed. These were the days before radar, which did not supercede hydrophones until 1944. For two years these tactics remained the standard method of defending our convoys.

Another aspect that Hichens took very seriously was how to treat their engines. Being an ex-racing motorist he was the one man who knew how to handle them properly and during the training at *King Alfred* and elsewhere no one touched on even the basics of large super-charged engines. Every embryo Spitfire pilot in training would know the basics before he even left the ground. In the flotilla they were completely ignorant why the engines broke down so often for the first year, but it was very soon after Hichens took over that their boats began to run better and breakdowns were the exception and not the rule. Hichens' boat, No. 64, had never broken down.

They now considered themselves a worked-up team, but as in all spheres of warfare this did not mean continuous action in front of them day by day, rather the tedium of nightly patrols for weeks on end without a contact. The only enemy they had to contend with for the most part was the weather. The effects of the weather took on enormous dimensions in boats of this size, emphasised by the shallow waters and banks of the North Sea. The effect of driving on into gales of 30 to 50 m.p.h. from crest to crest for several hours at a time, so that the boat reared and dropped as if struck by severe hammer blows, was that it seemed that the bolts holding the engine or gun mountings must shar at every shock. It was easy to lose visual contact and in one such action, albeit not against the enemy, David proceeding at speed took a terrific smack from the sea and his port gun, mounted over the officers' lavatory – the 'heads' – broke through the deck. He sent a laconic signal by W/T: 'Damaged by weather. Port gun now in heads. Request permission to return to harbour'.

Hichens' theories still had to be vindicated. The night of 19th November 1941 was the night set by fate for this task. The call came in the middle of dinner: 'E-boats on the convoy route' and the duty unit of three MGBs set out at once. This consisted of Hichens' No. 64, 'Boffin' Campbell's No. 67 and George Bailey, with David still as his number one, in No. 63. In spite of all the attention to engine treatment and maintenance No. 63's engines began to splutter just after they got through the boom and there they stopped, spending the night tied to a light vessel, leaving the others to go on their way. By eight o'clock they managed to get an engine going and coughed their way back to harbour. There they were greeted by a large group of people on the dockside, congratulating them for an action of which they knew nothing. They were in the middle of lunch when Hichens and 'Boffin' Campbell were sighted; the news spread rapidly and in a few minutes everyone was on the dockside. As the boats came in a loud cheer went up. Under Hichens' ensign hung a tattered swastika, the crew on deck were all waving German guns like pirates and the motor mechanic had a large picture of Hitler standing on the edge of his hatch. Eyes were red from lack of sleep and lids encrusted with salt from the spray, but they looked happy as they stepped ashore and they had reason to, for they had engaged and sunk an E-boat. What is more they had done it by successfully intercepting a group on the noise of their engines and actually made contact with them while they were lying stopped and facing different directions. Surprise was complete and they ran down the line pouring a broadside into each E-boat in turn. Losing contact they turned and came across one abandoned and sinking. The seacocks were open and she was too far gone to get home but before she sank they succeeded in boarding her and salving much of her equipment. For this action 'Boffin' won a DSC and Hichens got a bar to the one he had been awarded at Dunkirk.

Another minor operation took place a fortnight later, but in the New Year there was an epidemic of going aground, with three of them managing to find sandbanks. During the long winter nights the E-boat activity was mostly up off Sheringham and Cromer, but as darkness grew shorter they moved down to Ostend and operated nearer David's flotilla. Unfortunately his boat broke some valve springs and he had to re-engine and was on leave when the next burst of activity occurred, Hichens fought an action in response to the Germans laying a minefield on the convoy route north of Harwich and sinking several ships. He and Ronnie Carr set a trap, using their hydrophone technique, and intercepted six E-boats, sending them running, thereby saving a large convoy and earning him his first DSO.

David's boat was now working well and in between patrols friends appeared from London on many weekends to get away from the blitz. He and his sister Bunny, stationed at Petersfield in the WRNS, got great comfort and fun from the visits she was able to make to Felixstowe. The eastern counties in the winter provided the great recreation that only wildfowling can give, when the duck were flighting with beautiful regularity on to the salt marshes of the nearby estuaries.

Another visitor was his father, Archie, who could not resist a bit of action and considered one of his duties as an MP was to take part in an MGB patrol – shades of Spain. He was taken on an all-night operation to sweep the enemy coast, a trip of several hundred miles, but on the way home encountered fresh winds, a running swell and deteriorating visibility. Hichens despaired at getting his visitor back to catch the 10 o'clock train to make an afternoon appointment in the House of Commons, but luckily he nearly rammed a light vessel five or six miles from home and that saved the day. Archie thought the encounter was by arrangement and never knew that it was by luck he kept his appointment.

On Saturday, 27th February 1943, having survived the ordeal of his boat being inspected by an Admiral in the morning and playing a game of rugger in the afternoon, he took a taxi to the station to meet his aunt. They had a quick cup of tea before he set out on a patrol that night to escort a group of motor launches to lay mines off the Dutch coast. They saw the motor launches lay their mines and their unit of four boats stayed on for a bit of action and ran into a small German convoy just off the Hook of Holland. In the action which ensued, David's wooden boat was badly crippled, set on fire and had to be abandoned as she was blazing from stem to stern. They swam as far as they could from the boat so that if anyone was coming to rescue them they would not be damaged if the depth charges exploded. Immediately Hichens, having seen the signals, returned with two other boats. While this brilliantly illuminated stage was surrounded by the enemy, he calmly stopped his engines and started to pick up survivors. It is probable that the Germans must have mistaken him for an E-boat because it was some minutes before they opened fire. David was treading water in the background, waiting his turn to be picked up – which not surprisingly seemed to be an extremely slow business – when suddenly realising what was happening the German trawlers opened up again. Hichens had to move off, having picked up six men under heavy fire and, as a forlorn hope, thrown a heaving-line to David. As the speed increased he was forced to let go and make for a Carley float with three men on it. Almost at once the MGB commanded by Lt. Matthias gallantly returned for another attempt, but the enemy trawlers opened up again and he had to forge ahead in a hurry. His bow hit David's shoulder and in the confused water the MGBs three large scews passed over him, miraculously leaving him largely unscathed but thoroughly waterlogged. In the turmoil David eventually came to on the surface and 30 yards away saw the float with the three members of his crew on it. Five minutes later a German trawler closed on them and strong arms hauled them aboard. David's legs failed to hold him up but they were taken

The adversary: *a German E-boat.*

to the boiler room. One of the Germans pointed at David and said 'He is the worst' and pulled his jerseys off. He felt pain for the first time and realised that his temple and one hand were filled with shell fragments. The doctor appeared and David was taken to his cabin, where he had his wounds cleaned and dressed but declined the offer of the doctor's bunk so that he could return to his men and remind them that they need not say anything as prisoners of war. They were left to themselves, drying their garments on the gratings in the boiler room, their fitful rest being constantly interrupted by the engine room telegraphs.

The postscript is that Robert Hichens, who had won the Distinguished Service Order and bar, the Distinguished Service Cross and two bars and mentioned in despatches three times, was killed by a last stray shell after a minor engagement with the enemy on 13th April 1943. On 28th April, just after David had been confirmed as a POW, his mother Bridget received a letter from Robert's widow to say:

> I was so terribly glad that Robert was able to try to save David even if he didn't succeed. I know what he went through the next day. His logical mind told him he was wrong to risk other men's lives but he really loved David so much that he had to try and I was thankful that he did and that Providence spared him and his ships, and also when his turn came it honoured him with such a merciful death.

7

CAPTURE AND ESCAPE

1943 *to* 1944

*'Listen to the groans of the prisoners and by your great power free those
who are condemned.'* — Prayer said at David's Requiem Mass

THE NEXT YEAR OF CONFINEMENT would encapsulate David's character. It gave time for him to firm up his deep religious convictions. It gave him the chance to indulge in adventure. It gave him the opportunity to enjoy the companionship of his fellow men. It brought out the lack of hate in his make-up. His assumption that most people were fundamentally good ensured he never made an enemy out of his captors; this eased the less comfortable moments of recapture and confinement. He was to display courage and fortitude in his escapades and his naturally relaxed approach overcame his appearance and mannerisms which were those of an upper class British officer.

The reality of capture resulted in immediate reactions – stemming from his training – such as making sure he was not recognised as an officer so that he could get back to his men and ensure that they did not reveal anything beyond giving their name, rank and number. Having read escape books from the First World War avidly during his schooldays, he looked to get away before reaching the camp. So, during the escorted period from Rotterdam to Wilhelmshaven, he feigned internal troubles and made frequent visits to the toilet. But every time he poked his head out of the window his guard's head appeared further along the carriage smiling at him and twiddling his revolver round his finger. David's return to his seat was always rewarded with a cigarette and a look, which said 'don't play tricks with me'. The layout of Wilhelmshaven Station was like Felixstowe and David realised that 48 hours before he had been with his aunt in Felixstowe; and the realisation that all ties were cut was the worst single moment of his capture.

By that time he had been recognised as an officer and was shut alone in a barrack room and subjected to a series of interviews over the next week. All these seemed good mannered and rather pointless and were, in fact, a welcome break to the solitary confinement which David soon found a most powerful weapon to be resisted. The interrogator was a fine old naval gentleman who had a naturalised English son and did not push the questioning too hard but there was a sinister 'half back' in leather riding breeches hovering about at every session. One of the tricks of interrogation that David did not fall for was being interviewed by a 'civilian' who appeared with a Red Cross form, with questions which went far beyond those expected to be in the proper interest of the Red Cross. There were naval details required quite outside the scope of a charitable organisation. However, the man displayed no resentment when he refused to fill in this document and David got the impression that he had failed with it only too often before.

His solitary confinement was in a twelve feet square room with a bed, a table and a stool. Apart from his clothes his only assets were a shilling he had found in the pocket of his trousers and a drawing pin he picked up off the floor. Fourteen days with nothing to do led to brooding and self-criticism and among other things he convinced himself that he had made a mess of the action that led to his capture. In the time-honoured fashion of prisoners of war, he managed to carve his initials on the wainscoting of his cell with the edge of the shilling and, on a visit to the loo, luckily found an unsolved English crossword torn from the paper put there for his use. He rescued this and managed to fill it in by scratching in the answers with the point of a treasured drawing pin. His chief pastime, which gave him exercise as well until the effect of the appalling food left him too weak, was dancing Scottish reels by himself. He extracted long straws from his palliasse to serve as swords for the sword dance but the foursome, eightsomes and sixteensomes needed a considerable stretch of the imagination to dance with non-existent people and a table in the middle of the small room. At home, ballet had been the only music to which he gave serious attention and he used to visit the ballet eight or nine times a week during his leaves. Left on his own he worked through the ballet scores in his head, whistling the music and becoming depressed to find how difficult it was to visualise the action. These activities caused some raised eyebrows among his captors and although they did help him pass the time, they were only efficacious because he knew he would not be there for more than a few weeks. A prolonged period of 'solitary' was, to him, unthinkable.

After about fourteen days this state of captivity came to an end and about twelve of them were taken by some dozey guards on a train journey which eventually arrived at the prisoner of war camp at Tarmstedt near Bremen. The final stretch was a two mile walk behind an elderly German naval officer on a bicycle. Several times during the journey David reckoned he could have slipped away, but discretion was the better part of valour. He had no maps or compass and would have been a conspicuous figure with unkempt hair and twelve-days growth of red beard, and with his head and hand still bandaged from the not too serious wounds he had incurred in his action. Surprisingly, spirits rose at the sight of the prison camp which looked exactly as they had imagined. Surrounded by barbed wire and with arc lights round the perimeter it looked very picturesque. It was comforting to find that in the large theatre hall in which they were to be inducted an orchestra was playing – it stopped as they walked in – and they were given their first English cigarette for days. The induction consisted of filling in some harmless form, followed by yet another search and being issued with 'tallies' – metal discs with the name of the camp and their prison numbers on them. David and the one other officer were taken into the officers' compound and welcomed by Lt.-Com. Jackson who was busy making a model barge. This was followed by an issue of Players cigarettes, supper and a spring bed in the sick bay. After fielding inumerable questions from other inmates, some of whom had been in there for some years, they ended the day in a fitful sleep.

Unlike the British prison camps, in Germany each service looked after its own prisoners and this camp, Marlag und Milag Nord, was in fact two camps under one single command. Milag was for the captured merchant seamen and Marlag for the Royal Navy or allied navy personnel. When David arrived there were about 150 officers and 650 ratings who lived in a different section of the camp and were kept apart, presumably to make them less effective in the event of a rebellion. The officers' camp, in accordance with all conceptions of prisoner-of-war camps, consisted mainly of double-lined wooden living huts – which were reasonably warm and waterproof – a theatre, dining room, sick bay and canteen. From the escaper's point of view the lavatory building was to prove of the greatest importance; it was divided by an inner brick wall into two, one half being for the prisoners and the other half for the German guards whose entrance was by a wired-in passage. It was therefore possible to gain easy entrance to the German compound from the roof of this building. There were four living huts which consisted of a passage with five rooms each side, each room holding eight men, with a single room at the end of each hut for the senior officers. The senior British officer was Captain D. Graham-Wilson DSO, who had come back to the Navy because of the war. He played this most difficult hand for four years with consummate skill, getting the maximum out of the Germans, consistent with the maintenance of the prisoners' dignity. He was aided by a senior naval officer; this, was when David arrived, was Lt.-Com. Jackson and when he left, Com. Geoff Lambert, who was known as the 'man of confidence'. Theirs was the worst job in the camp and meant being in close contact with the Germans in matters of common interest, such as drains, lighting, etc., but remaining completely neutral on any part in escapes. The camp routine revolved around three roll calls or *appells* a day, otherwise the Germans stood right back and left the internal organisation to the prisoners themselves. The rations were very poor but, unlike other camps, the officers at Marlag pooled their Red Cross parcels to supplement the meagre bread, potatoes, sauerkraut, beetroot, liverwurst and weekly slab of horse meat; as a result the catering officer was able to provide a reasonable routine of menus. Whereas the ratings were taken out to other camps for manual work, the officers were left to look after their own amusements. To fill their days most got involved in study, passing qualification exams, learning languages, or drama and music; those of a more practical nature would be employed making scenery or costumes for plays or playing in the orchestra.

Now David could take time to read and contemplate without interruption, he took the chance to get his mind straight on matters of faith. Catholicism had been attracting him for some time but he never seemed to have time to deal with it and neither had he been subject to any proselytising. No one, as it were, 'got at him' so he just took advantage of moments to reflect on the attraction of the faith. He was helped by two Canadian priests who had been torpedoed and captured on their way to missionary service and were able to give him the necessary instruction and guide him through doubts and beliefs that had been lurking in his mind since prep-school days. Thus, on 1st November 1943, he was received into the Catholic church while a prisoner of war. He kept his family at home aware of his decision and in spite of their appeals to think it over and wait until he got back, he was sure he would be wrong to procrastinate any further.

The months went reasonably quickly as religious instruction made a counterpoint to his other main interest which was 'escaping'. The initial stages of theorising led him to the belief that the human mind seems inherently lacking in suspicion, and the best way to plan an escape was to base it on assuming an everyday character. To make it work, success would depend on mixing with the crowd with sufficient audacity and without hesitation. Escaping for David became a problem which was split into four sections: (1) Getting out of camp, either by using guile and concentrating on the lack of observance by the guards, or physical methods such as cutting the wire or tunnelling. (2) Getting out of the immediate area, relying on luck to meld into the crowd at Bremen; the escapee would then, in effect, be three-quarters of the way home. (3) Bremen to the point of departure depended on detailed homework covering good routing and good planning, preceeded by the acquisition of as much information as possible and memorising detail. (4) The final act of escaping was dependent on audacity, no hesitation – and luck. It was clear that an escape could not be achieved without a great deal of care and forethought, but fundamentally luck was essential.

There had been several attempts to escape before David got there and he soon became involved in an abortive sortie himself; his companion pulled back from cutting the wire owing to the lightness of the night but it whetted his appetite. The camp was surrounded by two ten-foot high barbed wire fences, six feet apart with concertina wire between. Each corner had a watch-tower with searchlights and *spandaus** to augment arc lights and sentries around the perimeter. As a result of the Germans thwarting a well thought out tunnel escape in 1942, there were microphones placed every 30ft around the perimeter to pick up any digging noises. The camp was situated on flat sandy country in the middle of a densely occupied military area – which did not make things easier.

After thoroughly chewing it over, David settled on basing his escape on train travel and his fluency in German. To keep his German up to scratch he took on the job of doing most of the camp black-market trading. The currency was a plentiful supply of cigarettes to barter with the guards, each

*German machine-guns

prisoner getting 50 a week from the Red Cross and being allowed an unlimited number in food parcels from home. As well as practising the language, David was able to assess the corruptness of the individual guards. They were all corrupt to some extent but kept to an established scale of exchange: at the top end was a bottle of champagne at 250 cigarettes or half a litre of schnaps for 200, at the bottom of the scale an egg warranted 8 cigarettes. The most corrupt German was the interpreter who had spent some time in America as a small time gangster and was tempted back to Germany by an offer of a cheap cruise in 1939 – to be slapped straight into uniform. Like all the other guards, to one degree or another, he bore a grudge against the regime. He was responsible for questioning and frisking recaptured prisoners but always pre-warned the inmates if a search was on the cards. He was a leading proponent in changing the camp marks, which were guaranteed by the British Government at a rate of fifteen to the pound, to German Reichmarks which were essential to carry out an effective escape. Like most of the elderly guards he had a vivid memory of the inflation after the First World War. All escape plans were co-ordinated by the escape committee which 'registered' anyone's patent and set the order for attempts, having approved the individuals concerned. The committee also organised a band of forgers, tailors, map-makers and linguists, as well as keeping an intelligence book on escape routes up to date with information that had been gleaned from returned prisoners or from other camps, added to information on train times and shipping movements from newspapers, or remarks that the guards might let slip.

David, having boshed his attempt to cut the wire, was one of forty volunteers for a new tunnel attempt. Nine weeks of tunnelling and disposing of the soil, ended with a draw for places as to who, and in what order, they would go out. David drew number twenty-three out of thirty-seven. With a week to go German suspicions were aroused and they arranged a complete swap between the Marlag inhabitants and the Milag inhabitants; ten days later the tunnel was discovered, filled in, and the prisoners were returned to their proper camps. Soon after David hit upon a fool-proof plan to get himself repatriated, by using one of the corruptible German guards to get hold of a standard form of document used by the German High Command for transferring prisoners from one camp to another and accompanying it with a forged letter:

> 'At the request of the Foreign Office (Western European Section) Lt. James is to be repatriated. He will be escorted forthwith to Hendaye and handed over to the requisite Spanish authorities for transmission to Gibraltar. Inform the Kriegsministerium in writing what action has been taken and the estimated time of arrival of the prisoner at Hendaye.'

He reckoned the journey would be through Paris, where he would get the opportunity to wire some Spanish friends, and in 48 hours be over the frontier – long before the fraud could be checked out. What really tickled him about the scheme was that he would be escorted to freedom by one of his captors. But the whole thing fell through. There was a change of staff in the office and the new ones not being so corruptible it became impossible to get hold of an original form on which to base a satisfactory forgery.

Soon after he was to make his first serious attempt. The escape would take place on a Thursday – which was the day that they were taken to the bath house outside the main camp – where, as nothing had ever happened, the Germans had become slack. They came into the bath-house with the prisoners, sitting about smoking and gossiping rather than patrolling the area outside. David discovered that a window at the end of the shower room would open; all that had to be done was to drop out and walk away, so long as all the guards were inside the building. He registered this plan and put his mind to work on a scheme to manipulate the numbers. It would mean overcoming three head-counts, one on the main gate on the way out, another at the bath-house before returning back to the camp and another back in the barracks. Not only would the numbers have to be manipulated but also time bought, as a half-hour grace would not be enough to get clear. Here David started to apply a psychological solution, the basis of which was that an escaper only got ten days for an escape attempt, but the guard held responsible got six weeks incarceration. David's assumption was that the bath guards, finding a prisoner missing would rush the party back into the camp and pass the buck on to the next watch. Secondly, the German Kommandant would be unlikely to tell the police that there was a prisoner on the loose until he was sure that there had been no miscount. This would mean calling an appell to check the tallies, at which David had noticed that the guards were keener to look at the bits of tin rather than the faces. It only needed the dentist to make a duplicate tally to leave behind and to find a similar sized friend to play the role if needs be. The two other appells during the day were to be dealt with by moving the sick around in the barrack rooms. They were counted separately and it would be quite easy to bogey the Germans into counting the same man twice. If all went to plan David would get a twenty-four hour start.

The route decided on, mainly from other escaper's experiences, was through the Baltic ports and the technique to get away from the immediate locality had been to walk to a station as far from the camp as possible before boarding a train. But David decided that, in order to get the most out of his twenty-four hour start, it would be to his best advantage to travel on the local shopping train from Tarmstedt, two miles away to Bremen.

Consultations with the imaginative Lt.-Com. Jackson decided the character. The obvious thing to be in a sea-port was a seaman of some description, so a Bulgarian naval officer was chosen and David's uniform was modified accordingly. A shoulder flash was sewn on the left shoulder with five gold letters on a blue ground, K.B.V. M.F. standing for; Kralov Bulgrski Voyenno-Mrskoi Flot, the Royal Bulgarian Navy. Bulgaria, being a monarchy, it

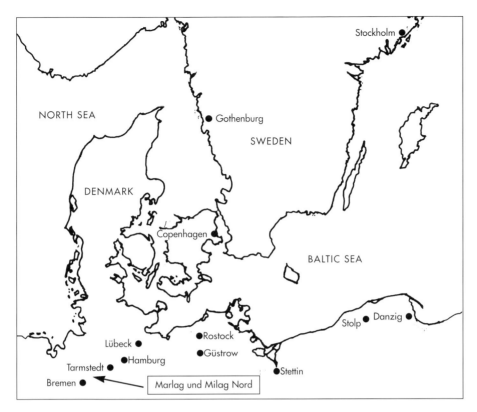

seemed that crowns on David's cap badge and buttons would pass and, any-how, Bulgaria had such a small Navy of some three ships that he would be unlikely to meet anyone who would recognise correct dress. A Bulgarian name had to be thought of which would come to his lips instantly at an interview or examination and it did not take long to choose Lt. Ivan Bagerov. A Bulgarian Naval identity card and a letter of introduction were forged with the expectation that they would be so rare as to be unfamiliar, but would appear authoritative enough to be acceptable. The letter was a masterpiece which said, 'Lt. Bagerov is engaged in liaison duties of a techni-cal nature which involve him in much travel. Since he speaks very little German, the usual benevolent assistance of all German officials is confi-dently solicited on his behalf'. The forgeries were endorsed by three German stamps, one counter-signed 'heartily approved' by a mythical German Foreign Office official, another by the Chief of Staff at Wilhelmshaven, 'Permission to enter dock installations numbers 9, 10, 11, 12 and 13 from 1st to 8th December'. The third was endorsed, 'Identity check by telephone from Berlin' and was signed by the Chief of Police at Cologne, whose name had been extracted from a recent daily paper. David then began three weeks of careful preparations. First it was necessary to get his Bulgarian accent right with his broken German and second to be able to sign his name in Cyrillic characters. There were two Greek officers in the camp who helped with this and with the marking of all the clothes in Bulgarian, having made sure all English labels were removed. For good measure in his pocket were enclosed a series of love-letters in 'off-Russian', accompanying a photo of Margot Fonteyn in a ball-room dress from the ballet *Apparitions* which had been sent out to him by a friend who knew of David's infatuation with ballet. This photo was inscribed as from his fiancée at the German Legation Ball in Sofia. The one time his case was searched this picture attracted more attention than all the rest of the contents put together.

All these preparations covered the main escape, having got to Bremen, but it was felt that the locals would be suspicious of any strange uniform so close to a POW camp. So for the first leg of the journey David decided to go out as a Danish electrician who was travelling for a medical survey, having had his nerves shattered in a recent raid. A temporary identity card was provided to cover for this and a 'quick change' was prepared so that David could go to the bath house in uniform with a pair of grey flannel trousers rolled up above the knee, cloth cap in his pocket, his buttons covered with silk and a civilian muffler hidden round his neck. Practice perfected a 30-second transformation and all was ready to change into his disguise in the shower room, jump out of the window, walk half a mile to a coppice to put on some bandages to change his appearance a bit and catch the 11.50 train to Bremen. Arriving there at 1.20, he would go into the station lavatory, emerge as Lt. Bagerov and set off for the Baltic ports.

*   *   *

Thursday, 8th December 1943 started off with Mass. The party got to the bath house to find the guards in rather a slacker mood than usual. Then came flutters of doubt. He was happy and busy in camp, the war was well on the way to being won. Why risk being shot for a hundred to one chance of escape? But all went well in spite of scarey moments. He was spotted by three Germans who knew him by sight, but there was no apparent recognition. Then he was stopped by a far too keen soldier on a bike and survived the grilling, before boarding the local train to Bremen where he successfully carried out his metamorphosis from a Dane to a Bulgarian. A mainline station meant that his papers were soon checked but passed the test. Between catching a train and leaving the platform at Hamburg he survived three more check points under arc lights. He fed off a coupon-free dish, available in restaurants for lunch and dinner, consisting mainly of vegetable soup known as a *stamm*. After one of these he caught the train to Lübeck, spending the night in a station waiting room wallowing in the thought that he was now fourteen hours and two hundred miles from his camp; and the next day he reached Stettin.

The search then started for a Swedish ship but not having a map of the docks, five hours of ineffectual tramping could not produce one so he returned to Lübeck by train. Here he left his bag in a hotel and finding the

Identität in Berlin
über Fernsprecher überprüft

Ulrich Wohltat

Der Polizeipräsident von Köln

Bulgarischer Marine Attache
Berlin
Krübekker Strasse 119

8. Dezember 1943

Leutnant Ivan Bagerov, Bulgarische Marine

Bescheinigung!

Leutnant Ivan Bagerov ist als technischer Verbindungs offizier
eingesetzt und muß viel auf Reisen sein.

Da er sehr wenig deutsch spricht, wird um die übliche wohlwollende
Unterstützung seitens aller deutschen Dienststellen gebeten.

Vladimir Solokov
Vladimir Solokov

Reichsaußenministerium

Genehmigung zum Betreten der Hafenanlagen
nr. 9, 10, 11, 12 & 13 vom 1.-8. Dezember 1943 erteilt.

Winfred Mössinger
Der Generalstab.

Lieutenant Ivan Bagerov's *forged lettter requesting assistance.*

dock layout much easier started his search for Swedish ships once more. This was interrupted by the heart pounding sight of a full rigged ship which he dared not try and get too close to it, being a German naval training ship; but memories of *Viking* came flooding back. Soon he did find two Swedish coasters lying alongside, bow to stern. Without further ado he returned to his hotel, collected his bag, got back to the quayside and, evading a sentry, boldly walked up the gangplank of the nearest ship. Going below he found a friendly steward who produced a cigar and a drink while listening to his story and David's spirits soared when he went to arrange a hiding place with the chief engineer. He returned with a glum face; they were low on coal and would be bunkering the next day, so the ship would be overrun with stevedores. It was a far better bet for him to try and get on board the ship lying ahead of them as it was known that the steward there had got some escaped Russians back to Sweden on the last trip. David was loathe to leave the safe haven but under pressure and with what turned out to be a short but critical delay while the captain came up the gangway, he shot down to the quay hoping to make the fifty yards to the next ship. Sadly, she had cast off and was pulling away and a pier-head jump would have been far too risky. He returned to the first ship and it was agreed the safest thing to do was to come back on Monday when they would take him to Gothenburg. It would be safer for him to spend the time on shore than it would on board, so he set off for the town once again, but unfortunately this time the sentry he had evaded on the way in, stopped him and demanded to see his pass. No pass meant a journey to the police station where an examination of his papers under a magnifying glass led to the direct question, 'Where did you escape from?' and all was up. While the following conversation made it clear that they had no information that he was at large, the important ingredient, luck, had fallen their way rather than his. After two extremely uncomfortable nights in Lübeck Military Jail, two guards from his camp came to collect him on Sunday, 11th December and they had a fraught journey back by train in the wake of several American daylight air-raids.

When he got back he survived several interrogations, in the process of which he managed to disclose neither the method of escape nor the use of the local train to Bremen which was vital for the future. He was sentenced to ten days solitary in the 'bunker' and told he would be court-marshalled in due course for uttering forged identity papers. Ten days, sadly, meant missing Christmas dinner with the rest of the camp but he was allowed out for midnight Mass where he first became conscious of hearing Holy Night; it remained his favourite carol from then on. He was back among his friends on Boxing Day and the New Year started afresh with preparations for the next escape.

David's assessement for the method of escape was quite correct in so much that, while the German officers had not discovered how he had left camp, all the other ranks knew. The bath party guards, after hasty consulta-

Paul Shädrich, *the German policeman who captured him at Lübeck, photographed with David when he returned.*

tion, had decided to push the party quickly through the main gate so that his absence should not be laid at their door. They had now started patrolling outside the bath house instead of coming in, so this method of escape was out for the time being. Escape attempts by other methods went on but by February the bath house guards began to get slack again so David made preparations to repeat his previous escape, this time going out as a different character. He chose a Swedish merchant service officer and took the identity of an old Swedish friend from his wind-jammer days who had written to him in prison, and told him he was now mate of the SS *Adolf Bratt*, Gothenburg. This could be checked on the Lloyds Register, but to avoid his friend being compromised he chose another name, Christof Lindholm. His story was that, while the ship was discharging cargo in Bremen, he had been caught in a daylight raid and had been badly burned; he was now being repatriated after two months in hospital. This was to ensure that he would not be recognised on the dicey first leg, the local train into Bremen, as he was able to assume a most effective disguise created by the camp doctor and the theatrical make-up expert, simulating burns. His hair was shaved back, half an eyebrow was burned off and the whole of the side of his face painted with acriflavine; scabs made out of cardboard were superimposed, dyed in Friars Balsam and stuck on with glue. The whole was covered in a concoction of violin beeswax and surgical spirit which, when dried, was a horrid, gooey mess – causing everyone to avert their gaze. There was a new forger from an Italian POW camp whose forgeries were responsible for getting five prisoners home during the war, but the old inventive Jackson produced the text of a forged letter from the Swedish Consul in Bremen before he himself departed from the camp. It read:

> Christof Lindholm, mate of SS *Adolf Bratt* was badly burned in the American terror raid on 24th December while his ship lay in Bremen. He is now on his way to rejoin her. Since this subject of a friendly power has suffered so much, both physically and mentally, during his stay in Germany it is trusted that the authorities will do everything in their power to make his journey home a pleasant one.

Lt.-Com. Sullivan, the new forger, produced the letter-heading and stamp on this document and turned out a beautiful temporary Swedish passport. The uniform was used again but with merchant service buttons and cap-badge. This time the window was not used as an exit but instead the inside lavatory, which was separated from the one outside by a wall which did not quite go up to the penthouse roof and had a big enough gap to allow a human being to wriggle from one to the other. David had done a lock-picking course in the camp – to cover the eventuality of the outside door being locked – and was relying on the guards once more not to report the escape. A day was chosen but on three consecutive Thursdays reports on the guards' behaviour were unfavourable and the attempt was put off. This was tiresome as it meant fresh application of the make-up and the re-forging of the papers to get the correct date.

Thursday, Feburary 10th was a propitious day. It was snowing hard and the first bath party reported that the guards were driven inside by the weather; his tracks would also soon be covered up. David did not leave the bath house until later than the previous time and having to lie up on a cold winter afternoon was a strain. He did not go for a train at Tarmstedt until after dark, to connect with the last train from Bremen at eight o'clock.

◉ *Walking through the snow in the half dark with his mind on avoiding patrols, his heart missed several beats when there was a crash beside him, but it turned out to be a good omen. A stag bounded swiftly across the road and it flashed through his mind that he really was on the first step of a journey to see the deer on the hills of his beloved Mull – and home to Torosay.*

Apart from some awkward moments and problems with not having any small change, he got to Bremen only to find that the last train to Hamburg had left. This meant sleeping in the waiting room until the 4.25 train left in the morning. It also meant surviving an inspection of papers by the local police. The trip to Hamburg was successful and the departure of a Lübeck–Güstrow–Stettin train, necessitated only a change from one platform to the other, with no barriers to pass. The train arrived at Lübeck in time for him to get a ticket on to Rostock. He got there and found himself going through the barrier behind an Underoffizier from his interrogation camp who luckily did not see him. He found only German coasters and a Danish tramp at Rostock so he had to set out on another rail journey to Stettin. The search of the docks there did not disclose any Swedish ships, but he thought he would celebrate being at large for a few minutes longer than the last time, and went into a pub for a beer; this nearly cost him his freedom. In removing his unwanted scabs earlier in the morning he had unfortunately removed a bit of real skin as well from his forehead. Exchanges in a lavatory, where David was trying to repair the damage, got him into a rather complicated conversation with a German who could talk fluent Swedish. It was quite clear, with suspicions aroused, that he must get out of town as soon as possible. On arriving at the station he luckily found a train leaving for Danzig in ten minutes time. Realising further suspicion would be aroused if he was to be seen as a lone figure walking round the docks on Sunday, when no work was being done, he took a train to the next big town, Stolp, where he had the comfort of being able to attend Mass. On returning to Danzig he took the precaution of looking up the Swedish Consul's name and address in the telephone directory and scribbling it on his passport so that when challenged he was able to say that he had just arrived off the midnight train, too late to go to the Consulate. So he stayed at the station till morning. He was feeling weaker, foot sore and harried – and his money was getting low. He had only about five marks left out of the fifty he had left camp with. In desperation he had contacted three separate groups of French prisoner-of-war workmen who were all sympathetic, but none had offered food or shelter so he finished his money in a restaurant on a last big feed. As well as beginning to feel physically exhausted, his nerves were feeling the strain, but he was determined to board a boat in the early part of the night. He found refuge in a cold dark alley and set about eating his forged papers, to lessen the offence in the event of being recaptured.

Whilst waiting he slipped into a reverie and, through the cold and dark, memories conjured up of the comforts of the mess at Felixstowe, and of his last hunt with the Grafton, just over a year ago, following Will Pope, the huntsman, fast across the Northamptonshire grass. Was it all going to end in the Marlag camp again?

Footsteps echoed over the docks and broke his reverie. By now it was ten to nine and time to take the last chance by boarding a Danish boat, the *Scandia*. Not the perfect choice but an even chance of finding friends. He eluded a sentry and within moments was on the deck – to find nobody about. So he made his way down the companionway through to the boiler room where he came upon an incredulous stoker, who agreed to hide and feed him, so long as the rest of the crew were not told. They were about to sail for north Denmark, a better bet than staying in north Germany. He spent the next five days half hidden in the boiler room, in complete darkness, with only the relief of the stoker arriving at eight o'clock every night with half a pint of water and three sandwiches. Eventually they arrived at Lübeck and he was told the sailing orders had been changed and if he stayed on board he would only go back to Bremen in discomfort, so he left the ship at 11 o'clock at night as he knew Lübeck well enough to find his way around in the dark to look for another ship. In even worse shape than ever he worked his way round the docks, finding three possible ships which he eschewed for one reason or another. He could not risk another day without any papers, and at 4.30 a.m. he took a chance and boarded a mystery ship with no markings on her at all. But she had steam up and time was drawing short, and there was no guard on the gangway. He found all the doors on the upperdeck locked, so he hauled down the ensign at the stern to try and ascertain her nationality, but it was still too dark to see. All the time he was being watched by a German sentry who had returned to his post by the gangplank and obviously assumed that David was a member of the crew. He eventually located the night watchman – who spoke no German but was persuaded that David was from the German Customs and produced the information that this was a Finnish ship, the *Canopus* about to sail for Stockholm in two hours time with the unlikely cargo of 2,000 tons of oranges. Leaving him to his devices, David made his way down to the engine room where he found a stoker to whom he broke the ice by telling him he had spent a year in the Finnish merchant service, before going on to tell him he was British and hoping to get to Stockholm. The stoker expressed difficulties, as their respective countries were at war, but David realised things were going the right way when he continued, 'I like England. I had one plenty good girl in Hull. Plenty risky to take you across.' This was the moment to offer a bribe and £200* did the trick. A very warm and uncomfortable two and a half days under the boilers followed – after surviving a very thorough German police search. But in two out of three watches he was able to at least have the manhole to the engine room open and was given vast plates of pea soup and porridge.

They docked in Stockholm about 1500 hours on Tuesday, 22nd February and he waited till dark when he went ashore and made contact with the British Consul. The official detailed to debrief him, by happy coincidence turned out to be his mother's old sailing companion, Dorothy Laird, who had voyaged with her in *Viking* before the war. The landing had to be carried out with the aid of the Finnish stoker friend who was bound to play his part

* David had to judge this carefully. On pay of £20 a month, it was all he could afford if the British authorities refused to honour the commitment.

if he was to see the £200 he had been promised. It transpired that he had been involved in a fairly extensive three-way smuggling ring between Germany, Sweden and Finland but this was the first livestock contraband he had ever freighted across. He was highly delighted to be received at the British Legation and collect such a large sum.

Twelve days after David got to Stockholm, two other RNVR lieutenants from Marlag arrived, having taken much the same route, and they were able to tell him how his cover had worked. As expected, to make sure they had not miscounted when they found they were one short on the bath party's return, the Germans had held a tally appell and Warrant Officer James of the RAF who was much the same build as David, as well as having the same name, succeeded in passing the guards twice; once with David's tally in a naval great coat and once with his own in an RAF coat. This cover had made sure that he got further than Tarmstedt station.

Three weeks after he arrived in Stockholm he landed at Leuchars in a Mosquito, after a very cold journey. He was given tickets on the *Flying Scotsman* from Edinburgh to London and, most unusually for wartime, the train arrived dead on time for David to find seven members of his family to welcome him home at the station barrier. In April it was noted on his records that he had 'rendered outstanding service whilst prisoner of war' and in July was awarded the MBE for 'gallant and distinguished service'.

The morning after his arrival he reported to the Admiralty for a hectic week of de-briefing, meeting among others, the First Lord of the Admiralty and the Head of the Naval Intelligence Department. He also had to report to the Foreign Office and was given lunch by R.A. Butler, at that time Secretary of State for Education, to whom his father was PPS. His contact with the guards in Germany and impressions he gleaned on his travels outside the camp, led him to express his conviction that a policy of unconditional surrender would only lengthen the war considerably. He had made this point to the Consulate in Stockholm, but it had already been settled by Churchill, Roosevelt and Stalin that unconditional surrender was the only way forward.

David, in his usual generous way, started his four-week period of leave by giving a series of cocktail parties – aided by his father and the Red Cross – in London and Glasgow, for the relations of those still prisoners in the camp. He also met a lot of people individually who could not get to either of the parties. One was a pathetic mother of a Merchant Service officer, the only person in the camp who had gone over to the Germans after being tempted by a luxury camp outside Berlin, from which he was sent off on recruitment missions round the various prisoner-of-war camps. After the war he was condemned to death for his treachery but the sentence was commuted to life imprisonment when it was shown that he had not given away the tunnel 'Mable' in the Marlag.

Before returning to his duties David spent a week in Mull at Torosay – much to the delight of Gran'Ol. The old place was looking a bit dowdier than when he had last seen it, the lawns were not mown and the hedges were untrimmed. Only Gran'Ol's suite and the library were ever opened or dusted and fungus was making good progress in the central hall. Meals were taken in the servant's hall for warmth and David was welcomed home with a 6 p.m. feast of stewed rabbit, strong tea and champagne – which left Gran'Ol, John Bill, the old butler, and David distinctly unsteady on their feet.

At the end of his leave David went on a brief course before being sent out as a Naval Intelligence Department staff lecturer; it was policy not to expose an escaped prisoner to the risk of re-capture. His role was to brief Naval invasion forces on German interrogation techniques and urge them, in the event of capture, to try and escape before getting behind barbed wire, which, of course, had been in his thoughts not so very many months before. This meant that the greater part of 1944 was spent on a lecture tour giving him a great insight into the various branches of the Royal Navy. Many tedious wartime train journeys followed until he was asked to visit a formidable list of Royal Naval air stations, amounting to two a day. Thankfully the method of transport changed from rail to air and his hosts conveyed him across Britain during a perfect summer and allowed him to fly the planes until it came to landing them – except for one easy-going Canadian who surrendered the controls in their entirety. He quickly grabbed them back when they hit terra firma, with the remark, 'you didn't land, you arrived'.

After briefing the Fleet Air Arm, he was told to make his own arrangements to cover the Fleet in Scapa Flow. He found himself in one of two Swordfishes, affectionately known as 'stringbags', about to land on a carrier in the Irish Sea. He was not unduly perturbed to follow the first plane in, but in his ignorance thought it would be removed and put in its 'garage' before they came down. Clutching everything, he awaited disaster, but the unknown miracle of the arresting wire halted them with only a jerk and a shudder; the ability to land on a flight deck whose rise and fall could be as much as thirty foot was to remain a matter of wonderment.

Having delivered his lecture, he was flown on to Scapa Flow to cover the ships at anchorage and was made welcome aboard HMS *Duke of York*.

This led to a memorable wartime experience. Arrangements were made for him to lecture the crew of the aircraft carrier HMS *Glorious*, while at sea on one of her strikes to the North Cape in the hunt to intercept the German battleship, *Tirpitz*. For ten days they sailed in company with a battleship, six carriers, two cruisers and some twenty destroyers. As they left Scapa Flow in line ahead, his pulse beat fast with pride and excitement. A naval force, redolent of Nelson and Jellicoe was recreated in his mind – and he was part of it.

They steamed north to the 75th parallel, then bore south to the North Cape, and marvelled on a perfect day at the jagged peaks and gleaming glaciers of the Norwegian coast. They stood muffled against the chill breeze on the bridge as the great carrier came round into the wind. There below them on the flight deck were grouped some 30 planes, Barracudas and Fireflys. The engines warmed up and then, every 30 seconds, one left the deck with streams of condensation flowing from her wing tips and tail. Suddenly it was silent and the planes had gone to find their targets in Alten Fjord. An hour and a half later they started coming back, fighters and bombers in ragged order. The first crippled plane, waggling its wings in distress, landed, the pilot was extracted and a crane picked it up and dropped it over the side. The deck was then clear for the rest and they all returned except for three fighters. The cloud cover had been too low for the bombers to be effective, but the fighters had been able to straff some ground installations, where they had lost their companions. David, for all his own experiences, saw first hand the different stresses and dangers that other branches of the service were required to meet. And so they came back from what was just another routine sortie carried out by one segment of Britain's terrific naval power.

There was just one more lecture tour to complete – to the 6th Airborne Division before they set out on their great engagement at Arnheim in September. In October the Admiralty, in their wisdom, suggested he could carry out a similar mission to the Far East. Fortunately the authorities were persuaded of the weakness of sending out someone who had never seen a jungle nor a Japanese. He was offered another – to David singularly attractive – opportunity, which he accepted with alacrity.

8

THE ANTARCTIC

1944 *to* 1948

*The risks one runs in exploring a coast in these unknown
and icy seas is so very great that I can be bold though
to say that no man will ever venture further than I
have done, and the lands which may lie to the south
will never be explored.* CAPTAIN JAMES COOK, 1775

HAVING DISSUADED THEIR LORDSHIPS from sending him on a jaunt to the Far
East, David put his thinking cap on to ensure that his next posting was to his
satisfaction. Since his prep-school days he had always had a hankering to go
to the south and it went through his head that now the war in Europe was
in sight of the end there might be a job for an RNVR officer trained in sail if
they were to commission the non-magnetic brigantine *Research*. He was
referred to the Hydrographer Royal of the Navy and found that *Research* was
not to be commissioned until after the war was over. But there was an expedition in which the Admiralty were very interested and David was put on to
Dr Macintosh of the Discovery Committee. To his surprise and joy he was
accepted by the leader, Lt.-Com. W. J. S. Marr*, in the role of an Assistant
Surveyor. The *raison d'être* of the expedition was kept vague and he was told
nothing more than it was hoped to establish a main base at Hope Bay in the
north of Graham Land.

So on 1st November, with three weeks to go, David started to settle his
affairs. His experiences of being cut off from the world – in *Viking* before the
war and as a prisoner of war – took him straight to Keith Prowse, where he
bought some eighty gramophone records and a good number of books.

🦉 *Of course there had to be a weekend with Gran'Ol at Torosay, the last time he was
to see this stalwart old lady. There was not time for long there but enough to get on
to the hill and peep over the rim, some two thousand feet up, into his favourite deer
corrie. Coming down he glanced back for a glimpse of the tops, to see them flecked
with snow. This memory was to stay with him and support him among colder times
and deeper snows in months to come.*

Returning south he found that his father had arranged for the Grafton hunt
to meet at his home. Will Pope, the famed huntsman, brought the pack to
the house to be greeted by a depleted wartime field of three farmers, two soldiers on leave, three children and David on his old hunter, Destiny, which he
had not ridden since 1938. But Destiny was as sure of foot as in the good old

* Lt-Com. W.J.S. Marr was one of the two Scouts taken south by Shackleton

days and kept David in the van. Rain eventually washed out the scent – not too soon for David as he was beginning to feel the effects of not having ridden for nearly two years. But it was enough to remind him of what the war was really about and provide inspiration for the next stage of his service life.

There followed a two-day visit to Cambridge, part of the unofficial briefing, where he met J.M. Wordie, a scientist with Shackleton in the *Endurance* some thirty years before, and Professor Debenham who was with Scott on his last expedition. Back to London, after a duty visit to the Colonial Office, he went to see Fonteyn and Helpman dancing *Giselle* at the Royal Opera House at Covent Garden. There were farewells on the steps of Boodles, his club, where he collected his fourteen pieces of luggage. At Euston he fell in with two other expedition members, Lt. G.T. Lockley, RNVR, going south as a biologist and Captain V.I. Russell, Royal Engineers, as surveyor. They arrived in Liverpool in the morning and by 10 a.m. were through emigration and safely on board R.M.S. *Deseado*.

On the after decks were Surgeon Commander E.W. Bingham, RN, and Captain N.M. (Freddie) Marshall, REME, standing by two pens containing 25 huskies from Labrador. Bingham had been in charge of the dogs on the 1934–37 British Graham Land expedition and had travelled over from Canada; after imparting his knowledge to Marshall he bade them good day and left. On Wednesday, 22nd November 1944, the *Deseado* sailed for the southern hemisphere and among those aboard was David, Russell, Marshall and Sub-Lt. G.T. Lockley RNVR, Tom Donnachie, a merchant navy radio operator from Glasgow; a zoologist and a meteorologist; also there were an old merchant navy engineer going out to become Chief on the Falkland Island steamer *Fitzroy*.

Before pursuing David's story it is necessary to explain why the Government were interested in establishing a base in the Antarctic under a cloak of secrecy. Before the outcome of the war was decided it was felt by the Cabinet in January 1943 that it was imperative that British sovereignty over what was known as the Falkland Island Dependencies and parts of the Antarctica should be secured by the occupation of strategic sites, even though they had been brought under British control between 1908 and 1917. Undoubtedly one of the main reasons behind this was the belief that the geological make-up of this Antarctic peninsula probably contained great deposits of minerals. It seemed essential that they were secured for the future.

So it was decided, following on from the work of British Graham Land Expedition of the thirties to establish Great Britain's first permanent bases in the Antarctic at Port Lockroy, Deception Island and Hope Bay by an expedition under the leadership of Lt.-Com. Marr, RNVR. This was given the code-name Operation Tabarin – a name chosen because much of the preparatory work was done rather late at night under seemingly chaotic conditions. This reminded the first organisers of their visits to a Paris nightclub of that name.

The first voyage in 1943 was not an unqualified success as the vessels chartered, SS *Fitzroy* and HMS *William Scoresby*, were not able to penetrate the ice of the Antarctic Sound. They managed to establish a base on Deception Island but failed in Hope Bay, leaving a party at Port Lockroy as a temporary base. The following season, in 1944, the Admiralty decided to send another expedition with the object of relieving the Deception Island party and transferring the Port Lockroy men to Hope Bay, which would become the main base for mapping the coast of Graham Land. The two vessels were augmented by chartering SS *Eagle*, the last of the old Newfoundland wooden sealing steamers, which could cope with the ice and act as a supply ship; all were under the command of Captain A. Taylor of the Royal Canadian Engineers. The expedition consisted of 21 men of whom 13 – including David – were to be at Hope Bay; four on Deception Island; and four at Port Lockroy.

And so they got under way with David finding himself teamed up with Freddie Marshall to look after the twenty five huskies, including a mother and her four puppies. He soon found that although their wolf strain gave them a ferocious appearance they were not as fierce as they looked; they were fundamentally bullies and it had to be made clear from the outset who was the boss. As with all dogs they soon made their individual characters very clear. The first day after sailing, having fed the dogs – and learning not to get nipped a second time – David and Freddie took till lunchtime scrubbing down the pens. Dog's names had to be learnt and David's admiration of a huntsman's job, with up to 50 couple of hounds to look after, rose considerably. He was particularly struck with the digestive system of the husky which enabled lumps of meat to disappear without any apparent chewing.

On 26th November they reached Lisbon and, gliding up the Tagus, memories were kindled by the sight of a four-masted barque which David recognised as the *Abraham Rydberg*, last seen by him sailing in company with *Viking* for twelve hours in the south-east trades in 1937. Of course as soon as he could get ashore he was on board and up aloft. After three days loading a cargo of wine and chestnuts for Rio – as unlikely a wartime cargo as oranges were on his escape from Danzig to Stockholm – they were at sea again.

For the next twelve days the dogs were their main preoccupation, for as well as feeding and cleaning them out, exercising and separating them from fights, they had to have codline collars fitted and pulling harnesses made. The whole harness was made from a single piece of lampwick about 80ft long and it took a few trials before a technique was developed to harness the individual dogs. On the whole they withstood the heat rather better than the humans but it was too much for one called Jumbo, who in spite of his name was rather a miserable specimen and became their first casualty.

They docked in Rio, where the news of David's award of the DSC 'for courage and skill during an action in light coastal craft' obviously enhanced their celebrations on Chilean Liebfraumilch at the lively floor show at the Lido.

December 22nd found them in Montevideo berthed next to *Fitzroy*. Sadly they were told they could not stay over Christmas but that they were sailing for the Falkland Islands the next day. The expedition members, dogs and all had moved across to the *Fitzroy* and were at sea on Christmas Eve; by Boxing Day it was noticeably cooler, the dogs noticeably happier and wandering albatross and cape pigeons were appearing in the sky around the boat – indisputable signs of their approach to the great south continent. On 28th December they sighted the Falklands, looking not unlike the Shetlands, and came alongside at Port Stanley in the evening to be welcomed by Lt.-Com. Marr and Lt.-Com. Marchesi the skipper of the *William Scoresby*. They had no idea what to expect from this funny little wooden, dolls-house town sitting in a bleak landscape and were quite disconcerted, having already had a meal aboard the *Fitzroy*, to receive a summons to dinner at Government House. This precipitated them into the first bath for five weeks and made them dig out their crumpled uniforms to sit down with the Governor, his Excellency Sir Allan Cardinall, and fourteen other guests, all in evening dress. Some of them had ridden for twelve hours from their farms to get into Port Stanley. It transpired during dinner that while most of the expedition was being housed in an army mess, David and Victor Russell were for some reason to be billetted in Government House.

And so began their last period of some four weeks in contact with civilisation. There was a lot to be done ashore, mainly checking all the stores, but from David's point of view the most important thing was the welfare of the dogs who went into a quarantine station after being cooped up for two months at sea. First they were dipped to get rid of any mange then fed to get them fit for work. As usual there were the accompanying temperamental occurrences which go with the huskies' nature.

The outline plans for the season were explained to the expedition members. After the arrival of *Eagle* from Newfoundland in about two weeks she was to be loaded with stores and the three ships, *Eagle*, *Fitzroy* and *William Scoresby* would sail in company to re-victualise and relieve the party on Deception Island. Then *Fitzroy* would proceed to Port Lockroy and take off the personnel who had been there for several months but leave behind John Lockely, a wireless operator and a handy-man, to continue weather observations for the coming year. The old crowd from Lockroy would be transferred to *Eagle* at Deception Island and then *Fitzroy* would leave on her own for Coronation Island in the South Orkneys to build a hut for future occupation. *Eagle* was to take the main party, assuming she could master the ice, land them at Hope Bay and establish the main base. There would be too much cargo to do this in one run and she would have to leave some of it on the beach at Deception Island and make a second run to complete the job.

The Colonial Office administered the Falkland Islands as a Crown Colony, along with its Dependencies, South Georgia, the South Orkneys, the South Shetlands and a segment of the Antarctic continent based on Graham Land. The economy relied on very few people over a large area, surviving off sheep and rendering a quantity of sea-elephant blubber for soap. The Colonial

Office had some vague idea that it was of strategic importance to the Empire, and that the naval power controlling the Falklands would hold the shipping routes to the River Plate and round Cape Horn. It can be no coincidence that in the early months of two world wars, the South Atlantic Squadron fought decisive battles there. The attitude of Whitehall to the colony was shown by a signal received by the Governor in 1940 just after the fall of Norway. It was a circular addressed to the Chief Constables of the Orkneys, Shetland Islands, Faroes and the Falkland Islands to warn them that German saboteurs might be expected to arrive from Scandinavia by canoe; therefore a sharp lookout should be kept at night!

On January 15th the four week holiday was over as the last of the wooden sealers, the *Eagle* arrived; the last but one was Scott's *Terra Nova* also of Antarctic fame. Designed for the rigours of sealing in the Arctic she had struggled through the tropics, with the bridge acting as a rain trap for the saloon below and quite unable to cope with the tropical storms. She was found to be weak amidships and looked like a caricature of an old fashioned steamer with her clipper bow and the 'crows nest' – a large barrel in her fore-top. Her skipper, Captain Shepherd was a veteran in the eyes of the expedition, being a young looking 50; he had given up his job as harbour-master at St John's in Newfoundland to commission this ship at a fortnight's notice. Two days were spent caulking the bridge seams and putting steel ties athwart the bunkers, then started the jigsaw puzzle of loading the cargo. The capacity of both *Fitzroy* and *Eagle* had to be used to ensure the right supplies were accessible in the right order for unloading at the right base.

By January 23rd all the loading was finished and the final job was to fetch the dogs from their quarantine and get them on board. In the evening twilight *William Scoresby* left, followed by *Fitzroy* – towing a 500 tonne oil barge to moor at Deception Island, to save *Scoresby* returning to Port Stanley for fuel.

With a lump in his throat David watched as the expedition set sail for the Antarctic. He and Marr followed in the *Eagle* twenty-four hours later in a flat calm and with a glorious sunset and a high bank of clouds hanging out of a pale green sky, like a fiery tapestry over the Falkland Islands.

The passage proceeded smoothly until the adrenalin started coursing through David's veins again at the sight of a four-masted barque – a tower of square-rig canvas out of the morning mist on the horizon. It was the South African Goverment's *Lawhill*, steering a course south of South Georgia under full sail. It had the legs on them but to mark the encounter they gave her three blasts on their sirens to speed her on her way. The last of the 'wooden walls' of Newfoundland saluted a 53-year old barque in full sail. Coincidentally when Marr was setting out with Shackleton in the *Nimrod* in 1922 they had encountered the great five-masted barque *France*. The sight of *Lawhill* must have made David's heart miss a beat as they were crossing the course he had taken in *Viking* only eight years before. What a lot had happened and how much he had experienced since then.

During the voyage David began to find out more about the *Eagle*'s crew. The bo'sun 'Old Skipper' Tom Carrel was 81, with a powerful frame and the ability to race anyone up to the crows nest. He had served with the same sealing company for over 60 years and was in the ship's company that dropped Peary on his succesful attempt on the North Pole in 1909. The Chief Engineer was also an octagenerian who kept up a good humoured state of war with his captain, while nursing his engines in their groaning hull but making every mile he could. The wireless operator 'Sparks' lived in an elevated hut abaft the funnel with his dilapidated mongrel called Tiger. Unfortunately the captain slipped off a companion ladder during the journey and broke a couple of ribs; Marr strapped him up and provided some relief.

On January 28th, after a misty morning start, David was in the crows nest when it cleared to a sunny day and revealed the Antarctic in all its glory, quite unlike anything he had imagined. He was not looking at snow country, as he had experienced in the Alps, but an ice country. The smooth, rolling white expanses were vast sheets of ice, which on close inspection were rent with fissures and crevasses. The cliffs which, from afar, appeared like the soft chalk white cliffs of Dover, as they got closer turned out to be cold and ice-blue. The silence was broken by crashes and distant rumbles as they gave birth to icebergs. As they turned in that night they were overwhelmed by the awesome beauty of the Antarctic.

The next morning they made a landfall on the slightly active volcanic Deception Island. This circular island, about nine miles in diameter with a crater lagoon in the middle, is connected to the sea by a narrow entrance, Neptune's Bellows; it had provided a safe harbour over the years to the early sealers and whalers. They dropped anchor to be welcomed by the resident party waiting to be relieved and went over to *Fitzroy* to get their orders, which were to 'moor and secure the oil barge'. This left them the afternoon free to look round the old whaling station, built in 1929 and subsequently blown up by an armed merchant cruiser – such as David had served in a few years before – to remove the temptation from any German raider to use it as a base. The next few days, until 3rd February, were busy unloading and stacking stores including 8 tons of coal. Meanwhile *Scoresby* was sent off to Port Lockroy to fetch a doctor to examine the unfortunate *Eagle*'s skipper whose ribs were not improving; he was ordered complete rest! There was considerable to-ing and fro-ing between Deception Island, Port Lockroy and South Orkney to juggle with coal and stores and erecting huts as well as relieving the stations. Between these destinations they took on tasks such as anchoring for an hour to maintain the Melchior Light which gave them their first experience of pack-ice. It was a fascinating experience standing up in the bows watching the sea being cleaved and hearing the reverberating crunch as they hit a floe. The scores of crab-eater seals looked disturbed and baleful as their ice pans were rocked before they slid gently off into the sea. This early part of the expedition was so relaxed that they even stopped the ship to allow the steward to collect a bucketful of ice to put in their midday cocktails – upsetting David's preconceived notions about exploring.

It was on one of these excursions that David and Marr were put ashore on the rock beach in the Neumayer Channel for a geologising trip, their first real work in the Antarctic. The Channel, about one mile wide was flanked by two hundred foot high, sheer, ice cliffs which were the foot of the 9,400 ft Mount Français and other dramatic peaks of Anvers Island, which in the dawn were tinted red, orange, gold and dazzling white. The beach they landed on was at the foot of Copper Peak, glistening mildew green with copper where they struggled on the slippery rocks and ice to collect samples of what seemed to be 100 per cent copper ore. Rocks of all hues and sizes were gathered but the most brilliant green one to the uninitiated eyes was cast aside contemptuously by the experts as being an 'erratic block'. After an hour they returned to their boat and were back on board without incident – other than David disappearing through a snow crust and landing up to his waist in icy water.

Marr's back began to play up badly while all this was going on and he was taken off in the *Scoresby* and returned to Port Stanley. David was sorry to lose him as they had become quite close in the six weeks they had been together. They would also miss the experience of someone who had led the expedition during the 1943–4 season and had also been involved in the earlier *Discovery* investigations. Fortunately the doctor gave a clean bill of health, or nearly so, to Captain Shepherd of the *Eagle* who was now able to proceed to Hope Bay. Marr's place was taken by Captain Andrew Taylor, with whom David was not so close. Later Taylor was to write 'James and I had occasional differences, for confrontations are indigenous to politicians and Scotsmen, when exposed to each other.' In days to come they had all melted away.

On February 11th they set out on the last leg of their outward journey and, with the right stores on the right ships, they started for Hope Bay. They set off looking like a Christmas tree. On the forecastle head were the dogs; the well deck for'ard was flush with lumber, anthracite, beds, benches, ladders and more dogs; coal was piled round the bridge; athwart the after-hatch was the scow with lumber piled round it and dogs inside. So they sailed on in warm sun and calm waters with the mountains of Graham Land fifty miles away, accompanied by a school of whales a cable length away. They slept where they could on the saloon table, on bunks, on benches and curled up in the wireless cabin with the anxiety that when they woke in the morning they would find the ice which had kept the *Fitzroy* out of the Bay the year before, and the Swedish expedition forty years before that. But at 6 a.m. their fears were dispelled and they entered a deep bay free of ice, headed by a glacier with either side the sheet cliffs of a mountain mass rising some 3,000ft to a flat table top covered with a thick ice sheet. There were several acres of pleasant hilly ground below this which were entirely devoid of ice or snow and it was somewhere on this ground that they hoped to erect a base.

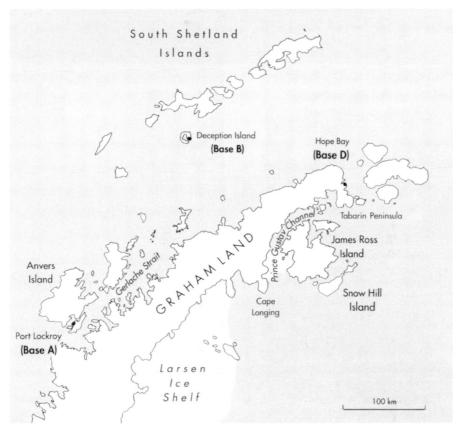

Antarctica: *location of Operation Tabarin bases.*

A conference was called by Taylor who divided them into pairs, each pair being given an area to scout for a site which should meet these criteria:

(1) Level and large enough to accommodate all the buildings.
(2) Accessible to a decent landing place.
(3) The maximum distance from the stench and noise of a penguin rookery.
(4) Minimum distance from a water supply.

David and 'Old Skipper' Tom went off in a dorey and sounded the *Fitzroy* into an anchorage protected by a projecting rocky foreshore, Seal Point. After lunch they set off in six parties of two, having had a good look over the 40-year-old Swedish stone hut. David's area had been taken over by several thousand angry Adelie penguins, so they made straight back to the rendezvous and basked in the sun. The others duly returned and compared notes, a site was selected and they returned to the ship well pleased with the day's work.

On getting back to the ship they found that the crew had shot a seal and

'Old Skipper' flensed it on deck, watched by an intrigued audience of men and an extremely enthusiastic audience of dogs. He took only ten minutes to do what two unskilled men were later to take two hours over.

With little to say to each other, but their minds inquisitively ranging through the months ahead, they sank into contentment having arrived at Hope Bay on a still evening, the sea calm and transparent, the hills aloof, with only the penguins making a racket returning from their day's fishing. They could see great parties a mile out at sea porpoising and plop plopping to the ice foot and then, in tens or twelves, jumping straight out of the sea to land on the ice edge and gossip there before waddling on to find their chicks in the rookery and surrender their undigested food to their clamouring offspring.

While wallowing in this unexpected and animated scene in an undemanding dusk, their intuition told them that it would not remain a land of milk and honey much longer. Serious work soon began and it was to take them over a month before the main buildings of the base were complete. David's first tasks was to row out in the dory to take soundings in the approaches to the chosen site and having given the tide two hours to make, the first load was landed from the scow. It was not long before a pre-fab hut had been erected to serve as a galley while the rest of the work was going on. This started an endless backwards and forwards of unloading which went on for the next few days. *Eagle* had anchored in a nearby cove and her crew had landed non-essential feed-stuffs to be sledged over to the main base later.

On the main site the foundations for the living hut and the Nissen hut storeroom were laid. Cement was mixed and poured for the piers and all was going according to plan when the wind started its temperamental activities, the gusts getting stronger completely destroyed the half finished Nissen hut; this put everything back by two days.

There was no let up the next day. The gale blew up and found *Eagle* steaming into her cables to lessen the strain when a large 70ft-high iceberg bore down on her. There was no time to steer clear, nor weigh anchor and all looked lost as the titanic mass loomed over her puny bow. Then some underwater spur of the berg must have grounded and it pivoted off to starboard. Captain Shepherd spun the wheel hard a'port and the iceberg swept by within feet of her side.

By February 24th the main frame was assembled and the Nissen hut finished with the stores stowed away; then came the first snowfall. David took charge of the dogs from Freddy Marshall, releasing him for more time for his marine biological work, and his life took on a new and embracing aspect. The dogs had been landed from *Fitzroy* in quite good health and were tethered in two long lines along the nearby shore. The first job was to feed them, which in principle was simple enough as they only needed a penguin a day each. In practice David found this task a long and wearysome business. On his first outing, armed with a heavy iron cudgel, David was chasing a penguin and slipped on some rocks, cutting his eye and knocking himself out.

The doctor soon fixed it up with no lasting damage but he never came to enjoy the nasty business. Penguins were as tough as old boots and a heavy iron cudgel had to hit them with accuracy to have any effect. The Adelie penguins were the easiest to deal with as they stupidly stood their ground, but the wiser Gentoos left the rocks for the soft snow and tobogganed away faster than David could run, hence his downfall. With winter approaching the penguins were starting to leave for warmer climes and another source of food was going to have to be found.

By the end of February *Eagle* had landed all her stores and returned to Deception Island for the final lift. Racing against the snow flurries penetrating the half-finished constructions, lining the walls and roof went on as the conditions got more and more uncomfortable. David had been taken on as number two on the wireless set, albeit his morse was slow and shaky, but he was able to report that *Eagle* had reached Deception Island on March 4th and all was going well. On March 11th David was able to leave the tin shack galley which he had made his home in order to be near enough to hear the dogs at night, and move into the main hut which was named Eagle House, and indulge in a bath. The baths were hip baths, and the water was produced from frozen snow, which had to be carried in. The expedition members were now installed in the winter quarters which were to remain their home until the following January.

The new quarry, in lieu of penguins, for dog food had to be the only alternative – seals. David's first hunt was far easier than the exhausting first penguin attempt, and he went out and shot and gutted four seals on the point,

The Eagle *at Deception Island.*

towing all four back to the landing beach behind the dinghy. The day they moved into the hut, a rumpus disclosed the dogs surrounding a young Weddell seal. This windfall was despatched and buried with the others, so the larder was beginning to take shape. The dogs were temporarily being fed on mutton which had become unfit for human consumption but, while David was cutting it up he was harried by 'Paddies' (*Chionis alba*), voracious white pigeon-sized birds – as bold as they were hungry – which continually interrupted the procedure, in spite of being bombarded with stones.

Eagle came back and, having landed coal and anthracite, landed the vital timber necessary for building the annexe. As the work continued ashore David, still hunting for dog food, had added a further four seals to the larder, making eight which would last them till May.

March 17th dawned with a high, but unsteady, glass, a gale force wind and driving snow reducing visibility to twenty yards; it turned out to be a disaster day. They struggled through their normal chores until it was time for their morning cup of tea, when David switched on the radio for the morning's scheduled contact with *Eagle* and was surprised to hear they were at sea. Their faint signals reported that in the night the weather was such that they had carried away an anchor and had been forced to put out to sea but were now not sure of their position. Twice they had hit ice in the low visibility and had suffered damage for'rard but luckily were not making much water. To make matters worse they had had to cast adrift the scow and the dinghy. David went off with three others to Eagle Cove on the off chance that the scow had come ashore but there was no sight of any wreckage. The weather had improved enough for them to see *Eagle* forging back into the bay, her bowsprit hanging from the shrouds and her clipper beak bent up. She came up on the air to enquire about an anchorage and David, having taken the soundings, was able to give them a spot. The snow was driving too thick to see her come in but the next signal was a shock, 'we have carried away our other cable, given up hope of saving the ship. Skipper thinking of beaching rather than risk taking her out to sea. Go to handy cove and stand by with ropes.'

A party set out at once to the rocky beach, where in the gale it would be a forlorn hope to get anyone ashore and she would in all probability rip out her bottom. Just as the first sledge started off *Eagle* came on the air again to report that the Captain had decided to run for it; with indescribable relief the sledge was recalled.

The story from the ship was that, with the water gaining control, they were searching for the best place to beach among the mass of grinding growlers and bergs. When the old Chief said the pumps had regained control Captain Shepherd called his crew and gave them a choice of beaching, with a likelihood of only half of them surviving, or a fifty/fifty chance of running for Port Stanley. The reply was 'Skipper, if you're in command this old ship is certain to reach port' – and the die was cast. Fortune favoured the brave and the next morning they ran into peaceful sunshine for twenty-four hours which gave them a chance to make good some of the damage, trim the coalbunkers, jettison useless cargo and stuff blankets in the gaping forepeak. Soon the gales came back and they spent a day and night hove-to stern first to save the weakened bow. They then made a slow passage back to Port Stanley and tied up alongside a coal-lighter. She was preparing to continue her journey on to Montevideo when the weather made yet another attempt to finish her off. A cyclone, with gusts of 100 m.p.h., blew the captain off the forecastle into the well of the ship and all the mooring lines parted – except one, which miraculously held. But she made Montevideo where her wounds were healed in dry dock and after three months she set out on her final 600-mile trip back home to Newfoundland. The sequel was that fifteen months later when Captain Shepherd was back in Montevideo in his little motor ship *Trespassey* on his way to relieve Hope Bay, he was summoned to the British Consulate and told that His Majesty had awarded him the MBE. *Eagle* continued working with the sealing fleet out of St John's, Newfoundland and eventually, at the end of her useful life, was sunk off the coast of Newfoundland.

Back at Hope Bay all was proceeding according to plan except a supply of seals which they had relied on being shot by *Eagle* had not, of course, materialised and, with the dinghy lost, a proper hunt could not start. This meant that David and Vic Russell daily patrolled the foreshore and by dint of hard work added another eight to those already buried – the bare minimum to get the dogs through the winter.

On the building side the finishing touches were coming on. The Esse cooker was installed and seemed to work well in spite of a printed notice on its side, 'For pressure mains only'. The interior fittings were worked on as the weather closed and by April 1st the Bay had frozen over for the first time. There had been hopes that there would be one more visit with mail from *Scoresby* and these hopes were raised as a heatwave set in, bringing the temperature from 9°F up to 45°F by Friday, 13th April, when they woke to see that they were entirely free of ice again. There was still a lot of work to be done on the interior fittings, bunks, etc., but they declared the Friday and Saturday as days of rest so that they could get down to their mail which *Scoresby* should be delivering to them by lunchtime. All of them sat down to write their last letters home and were scribbling away on the Saturday when a signal arrived in the evening to say that *Scoresby* had run into heavy pack-ice in Bransfield Strait and had been forced to turn back and make for Port Stanley. So near and yet so far. Vic Russell and David, returning from an excursion to try and assess the conditions, got a seal before lunch which was a bonus for the dogs. A very slight recompense, but after dinner they drowned their sorrows in a rum-punch and song. The next morning they woke up to a declining Indian summer with the temperature starting at 28°F. and by the time they went to bed dropping to 9°. Then they knew that their next mail would not now be with them until December or January.

A two-day blizzard descended on them as a harbinger of winter and for the last time cleared Hope Bay of ice before it reformed and thickened enough to bear a sledge. Taylor for some reason gave them a holiday on the last warm day, April 30th. So a party, including David and Vic Russell, climbed the 900ft Pyramid to get a glimpse of the land to the south of which they had been reading and thinking for so many months and which was to be the destination for the sledge trips to come. They were back by 4.30 to find the temperature had risen to 39°F. the last 'heatwave' before five months of absolute quiet descended, broken neither by the dash of waves on the shingle beach nor the squawk of penguins in the rookery. Graham Land became as austere in death as the mountains of the moon.

*   *   *

They settled down to their winter routine knowing that there were three possibilities of weather type to expect ahead of them:

(1) Blizzards and winds from the south-west between 30 and 50 m.p.h., with the temperature at zero in whirling, thick, drifting snow with zero visibility. No one would venture out in these conditions except for the one who had to go and feed the dogs, and another, the 'Met' man, who had to go out to the Stevenson Screen to record the routine synoptic readings. In bad weather there would be a rope between the hut and the screen.

(2) They could expect days on end with calm, cheerless, gray, overcast skies and occasional snow. They would find jobs outside – if only for exercise – when conditions were like this.

(3) Such spells would be relieved by a day without a cloud in the sky and the sun hanging like a giant red ball just over the horizon but without any warmth in it. The sight of it would cheer them nevertheless and they would rush for their anoraks, seal skin boots, skis and dog traces and think of tasks to do out of doors.

A typical day through the winter would start at about 7.30 in the morning. The duty 'bogeyman' who was responsible for the messing and domestic arrangements for that day, would light the Tilley lamps because with the snow piling up to the windows, most light was excluded. Tea would be followed by the first of 42 weekly meterological readings being taken. At 8 o'clock the first radio transmission would be made, reporting the weather to Port Stanley. The 'bogeyman' would sweep the mess room and produce hot water for somewhat unwilling washing and at 8.30 breakfast, usually a spam omelette followed by tea would be served. After breakfast tasks would be undertaken and, typically, Taylor would work on his journal; Chippie would have some fitting to make in his workshop; Taffy and Jock would be helped to bring in the weekly coal ration; scientists would work on their tasks in the laboratory and David would feed his dogs. They would stop at 11 o'clock for a cup of cocoa and then carry on until lunch at 1 o'clock when

The five-man party *about to depart to climb the Pyramid. From left to right: Russell, Donnachie, Matheson, Back and David James.*

they would call up the BBC World Service – if only to indulge in the nostalgia of hearing a female voice. Outdoor work would continue till 3 o'clock, when it got dark and indoor chores would continue until dinner-time at 6 o'clock. In the evening the workaholics would continue their experiments and those enjoying recreation would indulge in chess or a session with the gramophone. On Fridays everyone was glued to the BBC's Overseas Service of *London Bridge* which was a special request hour for Falkland Islanders. By eleven o'clock, by mutual agreement, lights would be out and silence would reign, except perhaps for the quiet hiss of the Tilley lamp of one lone, obsessive reader. Day by day they would mark off the winter as being another day towards the oncome of spring and the sledging expeditions.

Each member had his own sphere of responsibility and David's was the dogs. On April 18th he became an amateur vet when Beauty produced two good dog pups and he had to ensure she was mothering them well and having enough food away from the main pack. Early in May they started learning to drive the huskies by moving the twenty-five tons of non-essentials, dumped by *Eagle*, back to the main base. This became a perfect training course with the round trip, depending on the weather conditions, averaging about an hour and a half. They experimented on different conditions such as soft snow and hard pack-snow and found the amount the dogs could shift on the sledges varied between 40lb to 120lb per dog, according to the conditions.

The tedium of this winter routine was interrupted when they heard with joy over the wireless of the German surrender to Montgomery in Europe. But it all seemed far away and somewhat unreal – although five months before most of them had been vitally concerned one way or another in the course of the war. Now their preparations for coping with the oncoming winter seemed much more important. Nevertheless they did celebrate victory day in Europe by making it a holiday and listened to the speeches by Churchill, the Prime Minister, and the King before they sent a message to the Governor of the Falkland Islands reading: 'In these lonely outposts, His Majesty's loyal subjects from England, Scotland, Wales, Ireland, the Falkland Islands, New Zealand and Canada, join with the Empire to celebrate this historic day.' That evening they drank the loyal toast after dinner. It seemed rather trite to David that on this, one of the most important days during his life, he should spend most of it cutting up seal meat for dog food.

The main occupation – when the conditions were right – was to continue ferrying supplies from Eagle Cove. This had now become easier because the ice in the Bay had frozen to a thickness of eighteen inches and they were able to speed things up by sledging the stores home 'by sea'. Practice was making perfect and seven dogs were managing 800lb, so with two teams doing a double trip they were bringing in a ton and a half daily. It was getting too dark to do a third trip in the afternoon.

On May 28th Pretty produced a litter of four bitches and a dog and David's veterinary practice was extending as he worked hard to save two of the bitches which the young mother had laid on – all to no avail. The other two bitches were to earn their living; by 1947 they had spent 235 days sledging as well as producing a litter each – after spending the first year growing from pups weighing but a few ounces to 75lb huskies. On the other side of the coin, things were not proceeding so smoothly. The day the pups were born four of the dogs went hunting on the sea-ice when the temperature rose by 30°, cutting the edge of the Bay ice back by 300 yards, with the sad but inevitable result and reducing the three dog teams down to two. David took it very badly, blaming himself. But he had a tricky balance to weigh up between risking losing dogs by letting them wander into trouble, or keeping them permanently tethered on a line when it was probably only a matter of time before one or two might throttle themselves on their chains, however carefully they were managed. Realistically the only solution was to have enough dogs and enough pups coming on in various stages of development over the life of an expedition. By now he had become really taken with the dogs and to him they presented the chief charm of his polar life. He learnt how to live with their social life and their hierarchy based on age, experience and gangland connections. He was

OPPOSITE: **David James with Pretty** *and her litter.*

able to assess which dogs made what part of the camp their territory and how stoutly they would rule over it. He learnt to live with their trials of strength, the sad sight of an old ruling dog in decline and dogs getting lost in fights – but the balance being restored by more pups arriving. With it all continued the incessant job of cutting up frozen seal meat.

June came, cold and windy, with Force 12 gales and temperatures of 7°F. They were only able to move outside on all-fours; even then in the driving snow it was easy to get lost trying to find the puppies tent, which was only fifty yards away, to take them their food. This simple task of feeding dogs and pups, while being nothing in warmer conditions, became extremely time-consuming. In the middle of the month the weather let up and one day David, supported by a dog-team, was able to get out and shoot two Weddell seals which they took back, one at a time, travelling into the most wonderful sunset. The north face slopes glowed a golden red under a pale green sky, turning to black to the south, with a back-cloth of wisps of clouds of all colours of the spectrum. The silence was broken only by the swish of the sledge runners over powdered snow and running behind the team of dogs, with their plumed tails arched proudly over their backs, produced an evening of awe and contentment. After the second seal was got home in the pitch dark and gutted by candle-light, to recover the liver for the pot, they retired to a gramophone concert of Beethoven's *Emperor Concerto* – which seemed entirely in keeping with their mood.

David had been accepted as the provider of culture, having brought a selection of classical records and also a library. Several expedition members found in later years that *Eine Kleine Nachtmusik* or Gibbon would evocatively recall Hope Bay.

And so came June 21st, mid-winter day, and the thirteen isolated men, having completed the last ferrying of the *Eagle* stores, could now look forward to preparing for their spring journeys as the days got longer. The day was marked by David's first editorial effort, the production of the first number of the *Hope Bay Howler* – a humble rival to Scott's *South Polar Times* – which consisted mostly of 'in' jokes and articles only truly fathomed by the band of thirteen themselves.

An activity which contributed to passing the time, and to the larder, was fishing through holes in the ice, using either mangey bacon or red flannel for bait. The quarry was a small tasty, half-pound fish, *Notothenia*, and their record was to bring to the larder some 600 fish in a month. The skill involved the ability to sit still, well wrapped up on a sunny day, contemplating one's good fortune, while occasionally pulling in the line and relieving the hook of its fish – until the whistle blew at lunchtime to signal the gastronomic delights of a dish of spam.

July started with six days of blizzard. The weather gods distributed their favours evenly so that the second week of July was one of uninterrupted sunshine and good weather which brought about a sudden and unexpected winter thaw. This exposed faults in the roof and leaks in the window – to everyone's discomfort. Not unexpectedly a period of bad weather was to follow; sudden rises and drops in temperature was one of the features of the Antarctic and, in August, it varied from +49°F at the highest to -43°F at the lowest.

In the middle of the month David received a wireless message telling him of Gran'Ol's death and that he had been left the castle and the gardens of Torosay but, as on previous occasions, no cash came with the legacy. Her death in between VE and VJ day was well timed in that it was easy to persuade the authorities that David could never live at Torosay on a Naval Lieutenant's pay, so the castle and contents were accepted for probate at £1,000. Gran'Ol had predictably directed that her ashes should be interred beside her husband, Murray and that the faithful butler, John Bill should carry the urn to the cross by the slipway. What she had not foreseen was that after a good wake it was going to take two men to carry John Bill, let alone the urn – but this would have appealed to her Irish upbringing. So Torosay had to wait until David returned the next year before finding out what was in store for it ...

A sense of purpose was engendered when Taylor called a conference to plan the sledge journeys for the months ahead. The main trip was to start as soon as possible, with two teams, the first consisting of David and Russell and the second, Taylor and Mackenzie Lamb, the botanist. Their trip down the Crown Prince Gustav Channel on the east side of Trinity Peninsula to Cape Longing, across to Snow Hill Island and back up to the base, was planned to cover over 270 miles and take some 35 days to complete. Spirits were high and the conference ended by being well lubricated with a bottle of port, which David had bought in Lisbon, and music supplied by the Hope Bay Band, which consisted of an accordian, comb and paper and percussion effects on pots and pans. Their preparations then involved careful calculations of sledge loads of rations based on 27.5oz of food each per day, for thirty days. They were ready by the end of July but on August 1st the glass rose steeply with a windforce of 8. It dropped suddenly and on August 8th they were able to set off.

From the hut, they first had to climb some 1,000 feet to the summit of an isthmus, and then down the other side and on to the sea ice of Duse Bay – called the Bay of a Thousand Icebergs. This would lead them into Crown Prince Gustav Channel. Their journey was to be almost entirely on sea ice from then on.

David, while not being of an athletic build, had just the right stocky physique for the sort of adventure ahead of him. He was fit and hard as his adventures as a prisoner of war had shown and with his upbringing on the Scottish hills, his stamina was not in doubt. In racing parlance he was a stayer rather than a sprinter which was just what was wanted in a member of a sledging team about to set out on the unknown. David and Vic Russell were first away, with the 'Big Boys' team harnessed to the sledge pulling 900lb of stores, while Taylor and Lamb followed with their team the 'Odds and Ends' harnessed to the twelve-foot sledge carrying 800lb. With the aid of the rest of the expedition, and some relaying, they got themselves up to the summit and made camp. The next day was a blizzard, with thick drifting snow and nil visibility, and they had to lie up. But the following day they reached Duse Bay – new territory and all very exciting. By August 12th they were getting the measure of the teams' capabilities and they changed sledges and adjusted loads making great improvements so both teams could now cope with their burdens. At lunchtime they relayed their loads to the top of a 200ft snow-covered isthmus and had a magnificent view, with Vega Island about twelve miles away and thereon the frozen surface of the Crown Prince Gustav Channel. David naively thought that all their troubles were now over, with the bad going and difficult country behind them, and nothing would stop them making decent progress over the channel ahead. But soon a tell-tale streamer of snow blowing off the cliffs held a few 'whirlies' which began to scud past them and within half an hour they were in drift snow with a visibility of about 100 yards and with the snow getting thicker and thicker. They were forced to camp early and had to erect the tents in appalling conditions which made it difficult to get their drying fug up. Both Vic and David were having their first warning blisters of frost-bite.

The unpredictable Antarctic weather on August 13th produced a glorious day with the glass as steady as a rock and not a cloud in the sky. Their convoy discipline was not well developed yet and as they did not both start together the leading sledge was unaware that the nine-foot sledge, which had a tendency to tip over, had got itself bogged. From then on they made a rule that they must give each other mutual support and one sledge must never start until the other was ready. They made good progress and, confirming that Cape Corry was an isthmus, they swung west into the Crown Prince Gustav Channel, heading for two islands shown on their chart, on one of which they intended to leave a small depot. Just short of the island they passed a grounded iceberg beside which lay a seal and David took the rifle to shoot it while the rest went on. After firing several shots with no more than a click, he realized that the temperature of -20°F had frozen the grease and he was impotent with a frozen firing-pin as the seal made its way slowly to the tide-crack.

The next day a fast rising glass brought some 'whirlies' and caught them at their morning activities, literally with their pants down, which was exceedingly uncomfortable. The weather became such that they could not travel so they constructed the depot they had planned 50ft above sea-level. This consisted of two and a half days food for four people, seven primus fills of paraffin, three and a half days of dog pemmican and other odds and ends which experience was suggesting they would not need, but which turned out on the return journey to be their life-saver. The 15th August was a good day for travelling and they stopped for surveys, having made over eleven miles because the dogs benefited from the 100lb per sledge left behind at the depot. They were disturbed to find out, however, that they were getting through their paraffin far too fast and had already used 40 per cent of it.

They continued making their way over the frozen channel, passing some seals which thankfully the dogs did not get wind of, collecting lichens and taking measurements as the opportunities arose. To their right lay the mass of Graham Land in full glacial thrall with nothing to break the monotony of the backbone of the unbroken forty-mile-long wall, crowned with a dome of ice rising to some 4,500 feet. It was a relief to look to the left-hand side, to the mass of Ross Island which seemed to be returning to life, being ice free in parts. The travelling was good and they made eleven miles in one day again.

But on August 18th progress slowed, with poor going, a falling glass and a deteriorating surface and they did not get to where they expected to have lunch until early afternoon, so Lamb went off collecting while David had a look around a rather promising looking berg and found a couple of Weddell seals. They made their camp and left Taylor mending his tent, while David went off to shoot the seals. After removing the liver and a bit of rump steak for human consumption the dogs had a field day both teams being allowed to gorge themselves on one of the seals, but discretion made them cache the other against the possibility that they might get held up with bad weather in that area for some time. As it was, the next run made only about seven miles, but they went on and did about ten miles the next day on an improving surface and found themselves by Sjögren Fjord. They encountered a serious rift about 200ft across, which drove them off course out on to the sea-ice, but the dogs were running well and anti-cyclonic conditions were continuing – as was the cold at -15°F. At camp, Lamb capably put a new stopping in a wisdom tooth of David's. They also managed to take a couple of rounds of star observations by shouting to Vic, ensconced in one of the tents so that his hands were warm enough to record the data. The next morning David woke to find that everything round his back was thick with rime and there was a difference of opinion among his party as to whether it was better to sleep with head in or outside the sleeping bag to prevent condensation turning to rime inside. David's technique was to sleep with his head inside, with a small airhole, and he was as dry and as comfortable as a chrysalis.

When they set off they found the boulder moraines at the base of the glacier coming down from Sjögren Fjord made the going extremely difficult and it was hard to make any distance. However, on 20th August, they camped down at 4.30 and treated themselves to a good fry-up of seal's liver – for the first time for a fortnight eating cooked fresh food. They decided that they would try to make contact on the radio, could not raise base but managed to get the BBC and received a wonderful surprise to hear that the Japanese war was nearing its end. Preoccupied in their own distant world they had not given a thought to the passage of the war but the news ranked an extra bar of chocolate and a cigar before they went to sleep that night. They pressed on the next day and came upon a large bridged rift across a glacier and had to rope themselves up for the first time, but they got themselves, dogs and sledges over satisfactorily to continue their journey.

By now the routine of making and breaking camp was getting pretty successful. The technique was that the 'outside man' tethered and fed the dogs while the 'inside man' erected the pyramid shaped tent. The poles had to be set as wide apart as possible to maximise the floor space and the ground sheet laid on the floor completely clear of snow. The outside man having dealt with the dogs was free to pass inside the various items in the right order that would be needed to keep things comfortable. The first were the sheepskins, and after food, cooking material, etc., had been passed in, the outside man then shovelled the snow on the tent skirting to tamp it down securely for the night. The inside man got the primus going and started cooking the meal while they thawed out and dried their boots. After the meal David and Vic often moved over to the other tent to do the work required, such as diary writing and mending, and thus save paraffin, before returning to their own tent for a cup of cocoa and eight hours sleep. At six o'clock in the morning the whole operation went into reverse, so as to have breakfast, strike camp and be ready to move in about one and a half hours. There was a certain amount of mental pleasure in thinking and working out the quickest and most efficient way of dealing with the tasks during the mechanical slog of sledging.

They continued over going that was not too bad but the gales brought the march to an early halt on some days. One night when they had to camp early and lay over they settled down for a good rest after the gastronomic delight of enjoying a haggis made from seals liver and oats, accompanied by pea-soup which got somewhat muddled with the coffee but turned out to be quite nourishing. About this time they had the misfortune to burst the minimum thermometer, trying to warm it up to expel some bubbles. This was a pity because it was an historic thermometer; on its box was written in pencil; 'Originally made for Captain Scott, 1900–1902 or 1910–1912' and under this was written:

> British Arctic Air Route Expedition 30-31 Greenland,
> Watkins Greenland Expedition 32-33 Greenland,
> British Graham Land Expedtion 34-37 Antarctic,
> Winter Warfare School 41-42 Iceland.

Against one of these expeditions a note had been made: 'minimum liquid displaced very obstinate 1933' so David was glad to know that he was not the only person to have had trouble with this piece of equipment.

By August 23rd they had reached their southern-most point at Cape Longing where exploratory trips confirmed the sedimentary nature of the island unlike the rest of the mainland which appeared to be volcanic. They then set off in perfect weather for a quick passage in an easterly direction across the frozen sea towards Snow Hill and made a record of over eighteen miles in an eight-hour march to the camp off Cape Foster on James Ross Island. It was on such marches that David found that when the only interest was eating up the mileage over bare and featurless ice, trudging along beside the sledge the mind becomes detached from the body. However, two topics did frequently impinge on his mind – food and dogs. The character of the dogs became very plain on a trip like this and the steady pullers, never causing trouble on the march, carrying their tails lying flat along their backs were soon noticed from the bad-tempered, sulky brigade who complained when their harness was put on and taken off and pulled with their backs arched and tails above the horizontal. They were the ones forever looking around and growling at the dogs behind or to one side. It was important to choose a good leader who always pulled his heart out, although these were the ones apt to act first and think after. Riding the sledge, contemplating the dogs and their characters with their smart bushy tails waving rythmically to and fro, a state of near hypnotism set in.

The journey became difficult, with weakly bridge fissures and softer conditions but later on the going improved and they made another good run of seventeen miles up through Admiralty Sound. By 26th August a blizzard caused them to lay up again for a day. They had to sort out the dogs – who had caused some entertainment by pulling the ice-axe at the end of the span out of the ground getting the wire and their chain in a most fearful mess – difficult to resolve in extreme cold and minimum visibility. Otherwise the day was spent inside where they just had enough light to read. In Davids' case he got stuck into *Anna Karenina* and played peggity for light relief between chapters. On August 27th Taylor and Lamb pushed on for the end of Snow Hill Island, Vic Russell visited the cape on Ross Island to look at a small Swedish depot while David spent three hours trying to make radio contact. David and Vic then ran on for another hour and a half before camping. Their dinner was augmented by aged ingredients of apple rings and sugar, the food from a small packet that Vic brought back from the 5olb tin that had been cached some 43 years before. The following day they moved on to catch up the other members of the party at Snow Hill where they intended to explore the rest of the island to try and find Dr Nordenskojlld's hut in which he and his team had spent two fearful winters between 1901 and 1903 after being left by their Swedish expedition. The only visitor since had been the American, Lincoln Ellsworth, in 1935, so there were hopes that they might find some Swedish and American goodies to help the menu. But Taylor and Lamb had been to the house and reported that it was an empty wreck and they found it just like the *Marie Celéste* – abandoned as it had been 43 years before, with the corpse of a mummified dog on the porch. They took sights and readings and then the party ran on to Seymour Island where they made camp and started to explore round the coast and across the middle of the Island to Penguin Bay, where the *Uruguay* had made a depot on the voyage to relieve the Swedes. They spent the next day taking scientific readings, collecting fossils, lichens, etc., as well as mending and maintaining sledges before setting off in different parties to meet up on Penguin Bay. They returned back to the camp by noon so that they could make a good start on the leg home, but Taylor was missing. David and Vic harnessed up the 'Big Boys' and made their way over to Penguin Bay where they found a wooden cross set in frozen penguin guano to mark the site of the depot. They found some useful primus parts and one or two tools including a coal chisel and a knife, and a certain amount of still edible food in tins that had not blown. There was even a case of drink – including incongruously, orange bitters. They started back without finding Taylor but were relieved to find that he had returned to the camp just after they had left.

On August 31st they set off homeward bound on a northerly course to make the last run of any distance for some days. They had to use the compass in appalling visibility to get to Cockburn Island, where luckily gusts of warm air to the north of the island raised the temperature to 18° Fahrenheit and dispersed the fog. Scree slopes, topped by a basalt plateau, were revealed to David – reminding him immediately of the west coast of Mull. Cold blasts of air put paid to the daydreams, the fog returned and with deteriorating visibility the necessity for keeping the sledge in front in view took precedence over other esoteric thoughts.

With a worsening surface they managed eleven and quarter miles before camping, where taking stock of the supplies they found that, while being well off for food they were into the last tin of paraffin and had only one and a half days of dog pemmican left. They laid up on September 1st. Preserving fuel became the priority and they tried cooking some 42-year-old corned beef on solid fuel and seal's blubber and found it worked. They set off the next day with the expectation that they would have a pretty clear run over the sea to base, but the next four days they barely made four miles per day running over exceptionally deep, soft snow which was also drifting badly. Whereas Taylor and Lamb could manage to keep the twelve-foot sledge going, the none-foot sledge developed a temperament of its own. First one runner and then the next sought out and sunk in every pot hole. The more it got bogged down the more the dogs lost interest and the more the dogs lost interest, the more it got bogged down. The only solution to keep things moving was to start a relay system with the risk of the weather setting in and so leaving a load of food or chattels at the far end of a lift in closing weather. However both sledges made camp at 3.30 in the afternoon but the shortage of paraffin meant no evening cocoa. Morale was briefly lifted at the sight of some snow petrels – the first birds they had seen since they had set out. The next day, while the twelve-foot sledge made progress, they had to continue relaying with the nine-foot, struggling into camp through waist deep snow in the surprisingly colder dark. David's feet were getting that burning feeling which presages frostbite, and he also felt very bad at being able to give the dogs only half a ration of pemmican, all that was left – and there was still over 65 miles to go They agreed that they should leave a depot so as to lighten the load when they moved on. Eventually, when David got into the cheerless tent and got his boot off there was a hard, white left big toe devoid

Vic Russell *with the 'Big Boys' team.*

of any feeling; nor did prolonged thawing efforts produce any sign of life. All
he could do was smear it with resinal and hope that eventually feeling
would return. It did, with a constant burning sensation which ensured that
he had a sleepless night.

September 4th was a day of decision and they spent it sorting out among
the tool-kit, extra clothes, books, cigarettes and even the wireless and batteries what to leave behind to save a further 60lb. They then adjusted the
sledge loads so that David and the 'Big Boys' strong team on the nine-foot
sledge was down to 400lb and the 'Odds and Ends' were at 350lb. The order
of march was led by Taylor with the only snow shoes on a man-hauling
trace; Victor Russell and David alternated on the remaining skis in front of
their sledge, also man-hauling. Lamb just wallowed in the soft snow behind,
not able to add to the march but fully engaged in getting himself through
the heavy snow. They were able to make about one mile an hour and they
rued the moment on the way out when they had decided to leave 'junk, like
skis' in a depot. They were struggling and floundering for the first time and
realised they would have to call on deep reserves.

They made 23 miles in the next three days and were left with something
over 40 miles to go with completely unknown going ahead, little dog food left
and precious little fuel. Doubts – and determination – took over from the easy
coasting of the past four weeks. At the rate of progress they were making, it
looked like a further nine days before they would get back to the supply depot
that they had cached on the way out. They had rations left for three days in
addition to a little sugar, rice and corned beef, which should be able to sustain

them for a week. But there was only enough food for the dogs to last for two days, which meant that they would have to start killing dogs in two days time. The fuel situation was more dangerous because without fuel in the Antarctic was like being without water in a lifeboat. Not only was it essential, to melt the snow and produce drink, but it would cut out any precautions that they might need to make to prevent frostbite when they settled down to camp in the evening. They therefore set off, restricting themselves to one hot meal a day and hoping that the last solid fuel and a few candles would hold out. But they would have to risk not unfreezing their boots and accept the frostbite danger. If the weather got no worse it might be possible to make the same progress but if gales intervened and slowed things up, all that could be said about being forced to lie up would be that they were using less energy. With these thoughts they treated themselves to a warm meal of half a pemmican ration, topped up with corned beef and a cup of lukewarm cocoa before getting into their frozen sleeping bags to generate what warmth they could. David puffed his last cigar through an enlarged airhole in his sleeping bag, possibly increasing the warmth minutely – a strange mixture of opulence and poverty.

On September 5th they set forth at 9.15 and floundered about, making 100 yards in the first quarter of an hour, by proceeding in five to ten yard jumps out of the waist deep snow. By one o'clock, nearly exhausted, they thought they would have to make camp, but imperceptibly the drifts became less deep and the spurts forward extended into fifty yards and they realised that the sledges were actually kept moving. Hard patches of snow became the rule rather than the exception and they thankfully finished the day camping on a little island off Vega Island – with the sun blazing across a featureless landscape, like a frozen desert – having made nearly five miles. The euphoria they felt made it seem more like twenty. The fuel situation now was that they only had the candles to cook with and it took two hours to melt enough snow to produce some near hot cocoa.

The next day they made good progress in the face of a blizzard and the going was so good after what they had been through that the dogs, who usually curl up and give up under such circumstances, were pulling with a will. But they were brought up short after nine miles by a force 8 gale in which they were just about able to pitch their tents. They reckoned that they were, under reasonable circumstances, near enough to get to the depot the next day and, on balance felt, that they should build up as much energy as possible and risk using up the last of the pemmican ration with the last bit of fuel before they went to sleep. They could do nothing about the dogs who curled up and went to sleep without any food.

September 7th started looking good with the glass high but a temperature of -22° Fahrenheit and the going unpredictable; they were looking at a new countryside, shaped by the newly fallen snow. This was too much for the dogs who having been listless for the last day or two were not fit to withstand a hard day. Mutt, Geoff and Sydney of the 'Odds and Ends' team and

Jimmy of the 'Big Boys' could not keep their traces taut in the soft going and only two dogs out of each team were really pulling which meant that the sledges were being moved by man-power with marginal help from the dogs. Jimmy worsened rapidly and by lunch time was a passenger on his sledge and was soon joined by Mutt on the other one. By 4.45 they realised that they were not going to reach the depot and that they would have to shoot one of the dogs for food and take a break in order to stop the fall in canine morale. Just off Cape Scott Keltie they camped in the last of daylight and made the unwelcome decision between Mutt and Jimmy. Mutt, being the most stroppy member of his team, was chosen; it would be easy to incorporate two of the up and coming pups in his team while when Jimmy recovered he would remain a valued leader. In temperatures of -27°F, the revolver was warmed up so that the hammer would work and the deed was done; at least Mutt gave 2 lb of feed each to the other dogs. When they took stock they realised that they had run nine miles during the day.

The next day started off fine, with temperatures rising from -13°F to +15°F and they got off at nine o'clock with hearts beating with expectation as they drew near the island on which the depot had been cached. The teams split to circumnavigate the island to double the chance of seeing a seal and were excited when they met the other side to find their month-old footprints still *in situ* – but there were no seals. David dug out the depot, to find everything in perfect order, so they repacked the sledges and went on further to camp at 5.15, after making another thirteen miles. It is impossible to convey the pleasure David got from feeding the dogs a double whack of pemmican that night – particularly from watching his favourite, Little Dainty, standing between two lumps unable to make up her mind which to eat first. The only recollection he had of that evening was WARMTH.

On September 9th no one felt in a hurry to move off – even though the weather looked like turning tricky – and having got going, they soon started feeling lacklustre. They camped in sight of the depot glacier and the Pyramid, the other side of the Bay of A Thousand Icebergs. They were secretly worried that the fact that they were not feeling well could be put down to the Marmite or paté that they had found on Ross Island – and which had been there some forty-two years – might have given them ptomaine poisoning, even though it tasted so good. But when they came to put their tent up they realised it must have been carbon monoxide poisoning as they found the air vent at the back of the tent had got stuck closed. Having set up the camp, Vic Russell and David set out with their ice-axe and revolver and filled the larder with three seals. Taking out the steak, the liver and blubber for their own use, David drove the two teams in their traces to the sight of this plenty and watched each team have its fill on a carcass. They then tended to their own gastronomic needs, and without much delicacy filled a frying pan with butter, seal meat, onion rings, oats, a dash of pea-flour and anything else that came to hand.

A last look out of the tent before they dropped off to sleep in a force 8 gale disclosed a colour scheme of ragged low clouds chasing each other across a background of iridescent cirrus framed by flaming reds, golds and silvers to the west and delicate light blue, shading to deep purple in the east. They needed no alcohol to go to sleep, intoxicated by this wild scene.

On the following day the dogs saw that they made a good run of fifteen miles, while the humans were lethargic, as a reaction to success and from accumulated fatigue. The teams were completely restored and, pulling much lightened sledges, made easy work over what had seemed an impenetrable zone of bergs and pressures on the way out.

The next day they really were getting near home, with less than ten miles to go but they had the presence of mind to stop for photographs in case they forgot on arrival. They first had to negotiate the tide-crack but then, with very light sledges, the dogs made easy work of climbing up the glacier. By this time there was a force 7 gale and the light sledges on bare ice were being blown sideways. Soon the dogs saw the hut and were off down the final slope at a gallop, to warm greetings from the others at base camp who had seen the sledgers approach.

David's first act, having tethered the dogs, was to go and see the puppies who he found had grown enormously. Then reaction set in and only very vague recollections of the rest of the day remained – other than one coherent conversation on weather which it turned out had been some 10–20° colder with them than it had been at Hope Bay. Then followed a long, hot bath and a gala dinner. They dropped off before the party was over – being more celebrated against than celebrating themselves – and the night ran into one of fitful sleep.

Contemplating their journey, there was satisfaction with the work done, readings taken and samples collected, but probably more on the testing of the mind, body and soul under hardship. The experiences of human relationships reacting under stress were forgotten on return or faded. Trivial incidents or decisions on the march which produced temporary outbursts of anger, lack of judgement or even animosity, had been blown up out of all proportion. Marked irritation among expedition members is commonplace but as in this instance faded away to nothing when the goal was achieved.

They soon settled back to the routine and made plans for the future which were now limited by having only two dog teams available. This meant that the southern push could not take them further than they had already been. It was proposed instead that a six-man team occupy the archipelago at the south end of Duse Bay for a month of intensive work during October. David, unfortunately, was excluded from any further sledging work as the damage to his toe was much deeper than it first seemed and he was left to a slow and painful healing process.

October produced the foulest weather of the year with continual fog, snow and wind, but the penguins, sensing the days lengthening, started popping up on the ice-foot and tobogganing to their nests in the rookery. Everyone was more or less confined indoors except for essential work. As well as the now commonplace Weddell seals, some crab-eater seals turned up which were much better eating. Even more exciting was a visit from a leopard seal – a streamlined, graceful, killing machine compared with the other two species. November was heralded by six days of force 9 to 10 gales. However, getting out on the 4th they were overjoyed to find their first Adelie penguin egg, the harbinger of a very welcome addition to the diet. A 5 a.m. start was made over to the Bay of A Thousand Icebergs with stores for the forthcoming trip and conditions were so good that the party was back for supper; this allowed the sledging party to set forth on the 8th. David was thoroughly envious of the team. He would love to have seen one five-month-old and two seven-month-old puppies in action and making the sledge teams up to full strength. When they had departed he set off discontentedly to the penguin rookery to collect the eggs. He was partially appeased when he started his journey back with some 400 eggs – but less pleased when he slipped up on some ice and all his efforts would have seem to have come to nought. Fortunately, when it came to the count only eighteen had been broken. He kept his mind from the departing explorers by teaming up with someone else for another afternoon's collecting, coming back with 1300 eggs – all unbroken this time. This haul would have lasted twenty six families back home for a year but nine hungry Graham Landers took only three weeks to consume them.

The sledging party was having success in the south. David's foot was back in full use by December and he got to work among the dogs. All the mature animals were of course out, but some bitches were left behind to pup and Beauty, seven months after giving birth to Hobbs and Hinks, produced a small litter of two more bitches. Pretty came next with a better litter of seven pups, only one of which was a dog. Dainty, who the sledgers had wanted to take with them because she was a super lead dog, came up trumps and supported David's insistence on their leaving her behind when she spent a day producing nine whelps. As she had only seven teats, David moved two on to Beauty which she took to even though her two were ready for weaning. David looked upon all this as a great feat. He had now reared eighteen pups and the expedition would go into the next season with four or five teams available and not be crippled for transport as they had been this year.

David's other ploy was to carry out a plane table survey of the neighbourhood, which fitted in with plotting the nests of the local breeding birds. These were the Adelie penguin, the Gentoo penguin, the Sheath bill or Paddy (the only land bird), the Dominican gull (cousin of the Great Black Backed gull), Swallow-tailed Tern (akin to the Arctic Tern and reminiscent of Scotland in May), the Wilsons Petrol and Brown Skua (the arch harasser and egg-snatcher of penguin rookeries). He then set about a census of the Adelie penguin rookery which took four days to complete, ending up with a grand estimated total of 54,000 Adelie penguin nests and 162 Gentoo penguin nests.

With December came the anticipatory waiting period for news of the summer shipping movements in the Antarctic. Although they knew they were going to be picked up it was very difficult to settle to anything. The day after David's twenty-sixth birthday, Christmas Day, the wireless picked up a signal from the *Scorseby*, returning from a refit in Montevideo, with the names of some of the reliefs she was bringing out on the way to Hope Bay. On 29th December a signal was seen from the Pyramid summit that the sledging party were in the area – returning after 51 days and 500 miles sledging, rich in achievement and with a mass of geological and metallurgical samples. New Year started with a heatwave of 49°F. and with it the craving for spring which seems to excite the physical forces in man, particularly after their senses have been subjected to long periods of cold and desperation.

January 6th 1946, was the day that the great news came that they were to be evacuated in ten days. The *Scorseby* was to sail from Port Stanley on January 9th to relieve Hope Bay but they remained on tenterhooks when she was diverted by Deception Island because of heavy ice. But she did arrive on 14th January and David, who was remaining behind, went down to the beach, casually waving the rest goodbye at 3 o'clock in the morning. He was to stay until the new meteorologist had come in and he was determined not to break the continuity of readings that had so faithfully been taken over the last year or more. On returning to the base, five hours later, all had gone except Vic Russell who was also to stay for another season. Thirty-six hours later his old friend, Captain Shepherd, with his new little ship the *Trespassy*, arrived with a fresh cargo of supplies for the base including ten new dogs. After two days she sailed off taking David and leaving Victor Russell and eight men behind. As she sailed away David went on deck and stood gazing with a lump in his throat at the tawny, black, white and multi-coloured dogs spaced out on the rocks, getting smaller and smaller. In their endearing way they had indulged in midnight fights, escaped, failed to pull or had run off with the sledge at full tilt. Generally they had tried to show who was boss. David realised he had not really won, but at least an honourable truce had been declared and the dog teams had flourished. The huskies had certainly won his heart.

He was busy again for another month, building and stocking bases from Deception Island until he was transferred to *Scorseby* on the 16th February and arrived at Port Stanley. One of *Scorseby's* officers five days later had returned to Great Britain on compassionate leave so David took over from him with the approval of the Governor. He did a final mail delivery run in the *Scorseby*, had another last look at his friends at Hope Bay and Deception and paid 'adieu' to the Antarctic. He returned to Port Stanley to take up the post of acting ADC to the Governor before they both set sail in late May for Devonport in *Scorseby*. They arrived on July 8th and so the nineteen-month Antarctic adventure was over – but was it? Two years to the day after his first arrival at Hope Bay he was to be found again sitting in his old seat in the Survey office with Vic Russell at his desk beside him.

9

PROGRESSING INTO PEACETIME

1946 to 1949

Sir Michael Balcon's production of Scott of the Antarctic
*is a tale worth telling as some record of a great
adventure that has occupied two years of the lives of
a strangely diverse group of people and has raised
problems of film production never before encountered.*

DAVID JAMES, 1948

ON THE 10TH JULY 1946, David was 'dispersed', in naval terms, as a prelude to his formal release from the RNVR on 7th December. This meant that he was now a free agent and would have to decide what to do with his life, his sole asset being a crumbling castle in Scotland. The previous nineteen months had fulfilled yet another of his tutor's predictions that, 'he would also make an explorer with his love for adventure, courage and strength, but there is no future in exploring, save the name'. Luckily his father produced a tenuous *pied-à-terre* for him in London by letting him use his house, No. 3 Cheyne Row, in reality his step-mother's. London was the perfect place to keep in touch with his service colleagues as well as renewing his social life. Scottish dancing came high in his priorities along with visits to his beloved ballet. But his first objective was to get back to Torosay to reunite with his family and take stock of his inheritance.

So it was back to Mull where he found his mother Bridget and Geoffrey, recently retired from the Army on the grounds of ill-health, settled in Java Lodge, the dower house in Craignure that had come into her possession when she was left the estate. Java Lodge sat prettily among the trees on the north promontory of the little bay at Craignure and was a perfect place to take stock of the castle and the estate after the years of wartime dereliction. Straight away money had to be spent to clear the main drain out of the well in the castle roof through which the water had seeped into the main hall to create the invasion of fungus, which also had to be removed. The delapidations in the garden were also considerable and at the enormous expense of £4 a week a gardener was engaged to start on the formidable task of bringing order among the chaos. The estate was riddled with debt and so the first positive action was taken in David's absence to let the house as a hotel.

A very engaging couple, the McCrimmons, who had been running a boarding house on the Isle of Skye, answered an advertisement, and early in 1946 Torosay Castle was translated into a residential hotel under the name, 'The Tangle of The Isles'. The operation got under way with the minimum of management skills but with the maximum amount of hope and enthusiasm. Somehow they attracted a select and distinguished clientele – which included Sir John Reith, the first chairman of the BBC – possibly because of petrol rationing and the limited travel allowance, 'The Tangle of the Isles' was the nearest thing to an overseas holiday. There was a singular lack of servants, running water and bathrooms to match the large bedrooms in which the guests found themselves, but the enthusiasm of the host and hostess was enough to outweigh these deficiencies. A most optimistic brochure was issued which omitted to mention anything so tasteless as a tariff. The available activities and services were presented under the following headings:

> MOTORING. We hope the guests bring their own car. It is a very pretty island. *(This in spite of the fact that strict petrol rationing existed and the ferry could only handle four cars at a time, once a day).*
>
> ADEQUATE TAXIS AVAILABLE. *(This in spite of the fact that the only known taxi was at Salen, some eleven miles distant.)*
>
> WALKING. Maps readily available.
>
> SWIMMING. Too cold for some.
>
> EATING. Through the home farm there are unlimited supplies of food off the ration. *(This was an inaccurate but tempting sounding statement.)*
>
> DRINKING. The hotel is licensed.
>
> GOLF. A nine hole park course, not up to St Andrews. *(This course was built on the promontory north of Craignure in 1903 for the family's entertainment and had had no attention for the previous six or seven years.)*
>
> MOTOR BOAT TRIPS AND PICNICS. These can be arranged and bicycles are available for hire.
>
> SEA FISHING. Mackerel and saithe are invariably plentiful and the hotel has three boats.
>
> STALKING. Can be arranged.
>
> IF POSSIBLE COME IN MAY, JUNE OR JULY as the hotel will be emptier and sleeping berths from London are easier to obtain.

The McCrimmons' public relations were adventurous. A press-cutting exists from the *Oban Times* reporting a party that took place during 1946 to mark the coming of age – belatedly – of David and his sister, Bunny, who were away during the war. It was said to have been a Highland Ball attended by 300 guests but Bunny has no recollection of such an occasion, nor could it have been possible to squeeze more than a hundred people into Torosay for such an event. The furniture must have lent a degree of elegance because most of it had come from Stratford House in London when the house was sold at the beginning of the century. The setting alone – for any guest arriving through the wooded drives – was immediately breathtaking.

David arrived in Mull on 8th August, a month after he had shaken off the shackles of service life. He found his mother trying to make something of the main estate through the tenant farms and hill-grazing, while letting Geoffrey the tenancy of the home farm. She was also trying to induce some income from David's inheritance of the Castle and gardens through the hotel venture.

David stayed at Java Lodge and quickly renewed his acquaintance with the locals. The obvious venue for this was the Craignure Inn which belonged to his mother, who had sensibly taken out a licence while putting in a manager to run the pub. The first reunion would have been with Archie McColl, who had taught David so much about stalking before the war; he could not wait to tackle the hill again with him. He wasted no time in renewing his acquaintance with the sea-trout at Loch Don Bridge, when the tide was right, and in the Lily Loch, nestling at the foot of the hill behind the Loch Don crofters' grazing – arguably the most romantic place to find a sea trout in the west of Scotland. It is no more than a peat tarn some two or three hundred yards across, set in an amphitheatre of sparse oak trees, behind which rises Johnson's Glen, each side of which are the great peaks of Sgurr Dearg and Mainnir nam Fiadh, making the most perfect backdrop. In the opposite direction, down which the burn flows out of the loch, are glimpses of Loch Don leading over the sea to Oban and the mainland. Lying in this loch, while waiting for the autumn rains to take them further up the hill to spawn, are sea trout of up to 4lb which need to be attracted out of the lily-edged bays, in to which the boat is allowed to drift, by a well placed fly. If taken the ghillie must row swiftly for the middle to put the fish out of range of the sanctuary of the lilies. At the first sign of a spate David would make for the Lussa – probably to try the Sea Pool on his way to the Falls – to put a salmon in the larder.

By September he was up on the hills with Archie to get his first post-war stag, when getting a stag off the hill still depended on pony power or dragging. But both the ponies and the locals who acted as pony-boys to bring stags off the hill were no more. All that remained was Bunny's pony, *Comrie*, who was small enough to be pressed into service to carry a stag on a deer saddle, or bigger ponies that were owned by the farmer at Scallastle, which could be borrowed to drag a stag down when necessary. This was probably how his first stag was got down from Creagach Bheag – a nine-pointer of nearly fifteen stone.

The one he really relished was on the day he set out with Archie McColl up a burn that runs into the Lussa off the steepest face, known as 'Archie's Burn' which was deep enough to give cover for an approach well up to the sheer face of the hill, after leaving the oak woods and the riverside road behind. The good stags at that time of the year would have been at the top of the hill, away from the flies and in the moving air, probably still getting rid of the remnants of their velvet. After steadily climbing up the first thousand feet they would have taken a rest below the steep rock face on which the golden eagle's eyrie of their pre-war adventures still remained, half way up Ben Bhearnach. Below them they would have looked down at the Cruach on Ardura, that part of the estate that had gone to Murray Guthrie's sister in the last century and which was no longer owned by the family. Beyond this they would see the low hills of the rolling peninsular of Auchnacraig, which had been left to David's aunt, Violet and was to remain the treasured home of the De Klee family. Further over, looking towards Loch Don and Duart Point, the black woods of the Forestry Commission below the Lily Loch would have reminded him of sales his grandmother had been forced to make during the thirties to keep the estate going. The stalkers would then have continued their ever-steepening ascent over the rock steps leading to the flat moraine-like top of Ben Bhearnach and, spying carefully, would have looked eastwards down the great Corrie Bhearnach to see parties of hinds scattered well below them among the sparse trees and the flats running downwards towards the Lily Loch. On the high ridge of Ben Bheac opposite and below the steep cliffs falling from the summit of Sgurr Dearg they would have seen parties of stags of all ages grazing in the sunlight. To the west, looking down into Corrie Nan Each, in the centre of which lay the great black Castle Rock, there would have been other parties of stags grazing peacefully. As they moved forward cautiously to get a better view of these beasts they disturbed a covey of the tamest of all gamebirds found in the wildest of all places, the ptarmigan. In its grey speckled summer plummage, walking about with a bright red eye comb and smart plus-fours, a step too close made them explode like a firework and disappear curving round the contours of the hill.

They chose to go for a beast among those grazing in Corrie Nan Each as it would be an easy pull down to the road and the wind was in their favour. Working their way along the inside lip of the Corrie among the steps of rock, they were pleased to see one good shootable stag among the party of beasts which grazed across the ridge in front of them on the sheer face above the river. The stalkers turned and went back to look over the face, down to the River Lussa and the woods some 1800ft below, and spied the beasts settled some 300 yards away among rocks in front and a bit below them. Using the rock shelves, they made their way down on top of the beasts, who seldom seem to expect trouble from above, and got to within 150 yards when David took the shot that felled a good-bodied stag with a poor eight- point head. On their way up a raven had croaked in the sky, signifying to them in stalker's lore that the 'croak of the raven means blood on the stalkers knife'. They gralloched the beast on the spot, leaving the entrails for the eagles and ravens, and washed their hands in the beginnings of a burn emerging from the sphagnum moss. They enjoyed their 'piece' and a dram and while Archie's probably consisted no more than a sufficient cut of bread and cheese, David's doubtless included sausages and marmalade as well as a bot- tle of beer. He smoked one of his inevitable cigarettes and then they dragged the beast some 1500ft down the sheerest hill to the road below on the Torosay estate. They were grateful not to have to pull the beast over the 'flats', carpeted with tussocks and hummocks – near impossible to walk through and which caught the antlers of deer being pulled behind. Back in the larder the deer was found to weigh 15st 12lb, a respectable stag by any account; it was prepared and labelled to be taken out to the boat when it called in Craignure Bay on its way to Oban the following day. And so David contributed a few pounds into the nearly naked estate coffers.

That month, before he left Mull, David shot six stags, all of very respectable weights when compared with mainland beasts, the heaviest of which was 16st 4lb. None of them carried a very good head which confirmed that Archie was the most competent and selective stalker, leaving the best to breed. He was also the firmest of friends and companion to David on the hill.

David returned to London and through his Antarctic contacts managed an introduction to Michael Balcon* who appointed him polar adviser to the film *Scott of the Antarctic* which he was about to make. As well as promising him at least a year's employment it gave him the chance to go back to his stamping grounds in the south, the yearning for which he was finding so difficult to shake off. He approached the Colonial Office on behalf of the film for permission to go back to the Falkland Island Dependencies Survey at Hope Bay with a camera team and use the facilities there; it was granted so long as any spare time would be used for the filming of a documentary. David secured a passage for, Bob Moss, the camera operator, on a Falkland Islands Company vessel, to take all the cameras and equipment out to Port Stanley. David, accompanied by Osmond Borrodaile, a foremost lighting cameraman who had specialised in outdoor locations, set out together to take a stock of background shots of the Antarctic to use in the film. They flew to Montevideo and then joined David's old friend, the *Trespassey* from Newfoundland, now under the command of Captain Burden. They went to Port Stanley where they joined his other old friend, the Falkland Island Company ship *Fitzroy* and retraced their seaward steps back to Hope Bay in the New Year. And so David found himself employed in an area and on an activity that he loved.

After an Antarctic winter the ships were sailing from Port Stanley to refurbish the bases that David knew so well. It would have been much more apt for David and his colleagues to go to Ross Island, where the Scott story actually took place, for their background, but there had been few visits since Scott's time and there was nothing due to go to McMurdo Sound during the season that they had to do the work. There was, however, his contact in Graham Land. Even though it was 4,000 miles from Scott's old base, at the opposite end of this vast continent, it would produce an identical background populated with wildlife such as penguins, seals, killer whales and skuas and a state of extremely heavy glaciation off the east coast, so similar in make-up to the Ross Barrier where so much of the real tragic story took place.

On January 21st, making good progress on one of Heaven's own days, the mist rolled off the hill to reveal the northern-most tip of the Antarctic continent and they started encountering pack-ice. From then until they arrived at Hope Bay that evening, bashing through it gave 'Bordie', as the cameraman was known, a marvellous opportunity for shots in colour and in black

* Sir Michael Balcon, a renowned film producer at his peak in the 1940s and 50s. His films included *Whisky Galore*, *The Blue Lamp*, *The Lavender Hill Mob* and *The Cruel Sea*.

and white. The 'extras' included numerous crab-eater seals, Weddell seals, penguins, and birds that live and feed in such surroundings. David was overjoyed to get back among the members of the FIDS and to find that there were spare berths in the hut which Surgeon Commander Bingham RN, who was leading the expedition, let them use. They landed their heavy equipment and gear, and the *Fitzroy* went about her business while David hitched a lift in *Trespassey* on a four-day survey trip with his old friend, Victor Russell, the base leader at Hope Bay, whom he had left behind but a year before. The trip into territory unknown to David, provided some very good shots for Bordie. A stock of good shots of 60ft-high bergs were invaluable for use as shots of the Ross Ice Barrier.

They then settled down on-shore for three days of continuous blizzard, which gave them a chance to map out the sequences they were going to shoot, and prepare the various properties they might need. Straight away David was back doing familiar work, making three extra man-hauling harnesses, altering an expedition pyramid tent to make it resemble Amundsen's and sewing up a small Norwegian flag. During the following three days they were able to take extensive shots of the enormous Adelie penguin rookery – which they had to do before the young started to shed their down and started on their great migration north. They then set about the long distance shots needed in the film and the first thing was to create an artificial South Pole, with the tent and Norwegian flag which Amundsen had left behind just before Scott reached it. This was done on an 800ft-high rolling, desolate plain of windswept snow and ice which resembled the summit plateau on which stands the real South Pole. Against a strong wind David had to work quickly to see that the sledge was loaded right and the 'pole party' was dressed according to plan, muffled up in their sledging anoraks, hoods, gloves and goggles. While they were concentrating on shooting, the huskies amazingly managed to chew up the leather ends of the camera tripods and tore up David's reference copy of Scott's diary. Three weeks of blizzard followed, in which they were able to snatch odd moments to take the documentary shots that they had promised the Colonial Office. But it was not until March that perfect visibility of about eighty miles returned. This they used to good effect, going out every day for background material or action shots with members of the expedition acting as doubles. It was as strenuous as the sledging of the year before as the camera equipment weighed nearly 800lb and it was a hard tussle to get it up to the glacier each morning, calling for a team of eleven dogs as well as their own concerted efforts to pull the load to the top. The magnificent country in which they worked was well worth the effort, as for David was the run home, riding the sledge with the dogs proudly trotting along with their pink tongues hanging out and their tails curled over their backs. It brought back a feeling of nostalgia for the happier side of an explorer's life.

Then the Arctic weather did its unpredictable best by producing a force 8 wind and blowing in excess of 100m.p.h., making expeditions to get anthracite from the stack risky. David was frightened lest he and Russell were blown into the seething, smoking sea, less than 50 yards away. They could only move about by crouching behind boulders and crawling on all fours over snow, making sure they lay flat during gusts of wind. Meteorlogical instruments were blown away and the kennels for the young pups were covered by snow drifts which the heat of the pups reduced to slush but subsequently froze them to the ground. They all recovered, thanks to the application of hot water. Two days later the *Fitzroy* and *Trespassey* arrived, delivered the always welcome mail and were delayed by a fire in *Trespassey*'s engine room which *Fitzroy* managed to put out with hoses. They just got away before the ice closed up the base and by May 2nd they were back in Montevideo where their ways parted. Bordie flew to Hollywood to supervise the processing of the film stock and David returned home after three months on location – at a far better rate of pay than he had received from the Colonial Office a year before.

By the time he had got back to England the cast had been chosen and a suitable location found in Switzerland, the Jungfraujoch glacier. Travelling by train and changing on to a cog railway through the longest and highest tunnel in the world for the last 4,500ft, the party emerged at 11,342ft at a hotel looking northwards to the deep, lush valleys of summer Switzerland and southwards to a totally Antarctic scene – the proud remains of Europe's former ice-age. This great glacier was to represent the Beardmore Glacier. The group included a technical team of some note, including Charles Frend, the director; Osmond Borrodaile, who had accompanied David to the Antarctic and Quintin Riley; he was one of the five men to have been awarded the Polar Medal with both Arctic and Antarctic clasps, with an impeccable pre-war history of exploration and had been on the British Graham Land expedition of 1934–7. Only two of the lead actors went to the Swiss location: John Mills* was playing Scott and James Robertson Justice was playing Petty Officer Evans in his first big film role, having previously been a taxi-driver, an engineer, a policeman, an ornithologist and an officer in the Navy. He was a large Falstaffian figure, with a never-ending repertoire of stories. There was also an essential party of fifteen magnificent Swiss guides to act as doubles, help to haul the gear about and to rescue people who fell down the crevasses.

The main shots were on scenes of the Beardmore 'pressure point' which called for some nerve-wracking camera positions. In getting equipment and sledges into position great care had to be taken not to go over the route that in the film would have been virgin territory. This incurred a lot of extra heaving and lowering of sledges which was achieved only with the complete assurance and help from the guides. They not only managed to get the equipment about but gave full support to a team, inexperienced and not acclimatised to the altitude. Another hazard was the visitors staying in the hotel, who had a knack of being in the wrong place at the wrong time. Summer also brought butterflies and alpine choughs which, intruding in the shot, immediately ruled it out of

* Later Sir John Mills CBE

court. A further hazard was the snow melting the ice during the main part of the day turning it from pristine white to a slushy yellow. This meant that the only dog team in Switzerland which commuted daily to work on the Jungfraujoch by train had to follow up with Quintin Riley later in the day – by which time it had invariably became a morass. Only by starting early could they man-haul the heavy sledges up before starting a day's work. The compensation came at the end of the day when they had five miles of perfect skiing back to the starting point. Far too quickly the work on this location was over and they were back in England to prepare for the next spell.

The people making up the location teams had to be chosen carefully and kept to the minimum because there was the problem of getting Treasury permission for foreign exchange for anyone leaving and working outside England. Only twenty-four went to the Swiss location, including the two main actors.

On his return from the Antarctic, David had been sent to Norway in early June to check out a further location for the film. He flew to Oslo and took a train to the chosen location which was in the centre of Norway near Finse. Their destination was at 4,000ft, just above the tree line, where only two miles on the far side of a small lake there lay a dome-shaped ice field, the Hardanger Jøkel, about eight miles in diameter and rising to 6,000ft. There was a hotel at which coincidentally, early in the century that Captain Scott stayed while trying out his experimental motor sledges. Captain Amundsen had also practised driving his dogs on the very glacier they were intending to use. David made accommodation arrangements and did a reconnaisance of the ground to check its suitability for the film; it was deemed just acceptable.

David returned early in September with Leonard Douglas, the assistant director, to make the final arrangements. The visit was not encouraging as it had been the hottest summer on record and the top of the Jøkel was just bare and dirty ice without any snow covering whatsoever. This put doubt over the location but they appointed a contact man in Oslo to make arrangements and undertake negotiations; his diverse brief included the following items:

(1) Obtain a motorboat in which the unit might cross the lake.
(2) Hire ten ponies – to play the part of Scott's Siberian ponies and carry the camera equipment over the rocky foothills.
(3) Hire three army 'Weasles' with drivers to take the party up the glacier.
(4) Secure the service of a dozen guides and porters who could also act as doubles in the film.
(5) Borrow fifteen huskies from the Norsk Trekkhund Klubb, a charitable organisation that kept dog sledges available around Oslo, to bring in injured skiers.
(6) Mend the bridge over the river at the bottom of the Finse Lake and prospect the best route for men, 'Weasels' and ponies over the foothills up the glacier, marking any likely crevasses before the snow bridges froze hard.

The Swiss guides *manhandling a sledge.*

David returned to England to report that these projects were underway and two days before the unit was due to sail from Newcastle, he flew back to make certain that all was in order. He found everything he had requested assembling at Finse. Even better news was that snow had already fallen on the summit. He met the boat at Bergen on October 3rd and welcomed the unit of thirty-seven men, including three more artists to play the principal parts: Harold Warrender (Dr E.A. Wilson); Derek Bond (Captain Oates); and Reginald Beckwith ('Birdie' Bowers). The casting was brilliant; all these men had a remarkable resemblance to the originals, not only physically but they also seemed to have developed the same mannerisms and voices. They travelled by train from Bergen to Finse, to find a hard thaw had set in and the next two days were completely shrouded in cloud. But they had work to do unpacking equipment, becoming familiar with the motor sledges, jerrycans, skis, cases of clothing and everything that goes to make such a project work.

Shooting was scheduled to start on Monday, 6th October, but typically for Arctic conditions was postponed by a blizzard; they secured only three shots in the next two days. The complication of directing pony men who spoke no English and were hard to recognise from the English team, muffled up as they were in windproofs, made them realise that there were some formidable obstacles lying ahead. Both David and Quintin found that the work was far more strenuous than any they had been used to as explorers, as they were not on the move. On sledging exploration there is a very bad half hour in the morning while tents are being struck and sledges lashed, or a cold hour or so round a theodolite of a survey station, but even this work cannot be done in a blizzard. David soon found you can shoot polar films in bad weather, which made filming a perpetuation of the explorers' worst possible moments. He took his hat off to the camera crew and continuity girl for the way they stuck at it.

Coming into the back end of the year they knew that daily the light would get less and they were racing against time, as well as the vagaries of blizzards and weather. This led them to reduce the number of essential set-ups from about 150 to just over 100 and the shop stewards agreed to put breakfast forward to 6.30 a.m. and suspend the luncheon interval to take advantage of every minute of the waning light. They made slow progress during the week with the continuing thaw and the snow pouring off the glacier, making travelling extremely difficult and the ice too dirty to shoot. They managed two days when the sun came out and were able to complete the sequence at the foot of the Beardmore Glacier with the ponies. But it was 14th October before they got a really fine day and were able to do some work on the glacier top and get some good long shots of the ten ponies winding their way across the Barrier and being passed by one of the dog teams. Progress remained slow until 20th October when, with half their time expired and only twenty shots taken, the whole location looked like being a failure and there was ugly talk of going home. On October 21st, however, they could see the top clearly at breakfast time and the glass had put in a sensational rise during the night. This thankfully proved the prelude to eleven days of unbroken fine weather.

They rose at 6 a.m., had breakfast at 6.30 and by 7 o'clock were on the trail which meant a tiresome hour's walk over the foothills, limited by the speed of the ponies carrying the cameras or other properties making slow work over rough going. They were able to secure scenes at an average of about seven a day and thankfully the weather was so settled that they were able to save considerable time by leaving the properties on site at the head of the glacier. David's skill with the huskies was put to the test and they became a great trial; the only thing they could be relied upon to do was to fight at every opportunity. This was because, not only were they mixing the teams of dogs belonging to the hotel with the dogs borrowed from the Norsk Trekkhund Klubb, but more importantly were having to run them in a different hitch from any that they were used to. The Norwegians drive their dogs in tandem with small teams in line ahead, kept in position by twin bamboo shafts run from the front of the sledge. Scott's teams, however, were of eleven dogs running in pairs herring-bone fashion off a single centre trace. This, of course, gave unrivalled scope for biting the chap in front or to one side, or even the one from behind, an opportunity they never missed until they got used to each other. The first time David took a team up the glacier there were nine major scraps in the first half mile – which slowed down his rate of ascent considerably. His rapport with the husky was undoubtedly of immeasurable benefit to the making of the film.

The most striking thing was to see portions of bulwarks, deck and rigging – made in the studio – being carried to create an exact replica of *Terra Nova* on a wheel track at the edge of the smooth ice which covered the boulder clay at the foot of the glacier. Therefore, in the heart of Norway and more than 4,000 ft up, they were able to shoot as though from the deck of a ship, coming alongside and landing the ponies and the motor sledges and the steady flow of stores over the ice to the hut. Then they were able to photograph the expedition members on the ice edge, waving goodbye as she left. The only alternative to this sort of cheating would have been to build a real ship and sail her to the Antarctic – without improving the result at the end of it.

After ten days of intense work the eleventh day broke fine but things went completely wrong from the beginning as everybody by then was on edge for fear of opportunities being missed. In addition to ten or eleven hours hard physical work in the cold air, most of the members of the unit had a lot to do in the evenings, such as typing out continuity notes, arranging the following days call sheet, cleaning cameras and loading film magazines; it was usually midnight before most got to bed. Therefore, when the weather broke the next day, thankfully it was called a day of rest. But even so, with only seven shooting days left and twenty-eight vital set-ups to be secured, they spent most of the time in conference, fixing schemes of work to suit the various days that might occur: grey days, blizzard days and foggy days. In fact in six days they had all sorts of weather they required and were able to round off the work to a fine crescendo. When the location came to an end, a great *esprit de corps* had been built up and the locals threw the Norwegian equivalent of a Scottish ceilidh in their honour in the village school, with a fiddle and accordian band. To complete the illusion James Robertson Justice appeared in his kilt, playing his bagpipes which made David feel quite homesick. The next day the advance guard was on the way to Oslo to catch a plane to England, while the remainder returned from Bergen by sea. All felt they had done a good job of work and left with a tinge of sadness.

There had been a most fortunate coincidental interruption for David on 17th October when he returned on studio business to London and was present at the wedding of his sister, Bunny, to Bruce Cheape. Bruce came from the Isle of Mull where his father had retired to his family home Tiroran, having served as a Brigadier General in the Kings Dragoon Guards. His grandfather, Bruce Ismay, had been Chairman of the White Star Line and on board when the *Titanic* made her unfortunate maiden, and only, voyage. Although they lived on opposite sides of the island, Bruce and Bunny first met in 1945 at Gran'Ol Guthrie's funeral when her remains were being conveyed to the cross by the Torosay boat house. Bunny had come up to Torosay from serving with the WRNS at the Royal Naval Air Service station at Ayr and Bruce had just returned to England after being liberated by the United States Army from a prisonor-of-war camp. He had been with the 8th Battalion, Argyll and Sutherland Highlanders when the 51st Highland

Division were trapped in France in June 1940. After a long incarceration, made endurable only by his bagpipes, it was wonderful to return home and discover that he had such an attractive neighbour on the island. Soon after their marriage they set themselves up at Fossoway on the mainland. There they farmed until they retired to South Lodge, Torosay, which had been given to Bunny by her mother in 1962.

David spent November and December in London working at Ealing Studios, recreating the scenes of snow with plaster, epsom salts or urea formaldehyde and artificial glass icicles filled with distilled water, to match up to the Antarctic, Swiss or Norwegian long shots. Shooting was to start as soon after Christmas as possible but David was called to Mull for Christmas to deal with the news that the hotel the 'Tangle' had lived up to its name and gone broke. The McCrimmons had sadly failed to make a go of it. Being young and eager, and taking advantage of the fact that it was off-season David appointed himself managing director and returned to London to complete his commitment to *Scott of the Antarctic*.

The shooting 'on the floor' started on December 30th and when they started shooting the ship close-ups it most fortunately coincided with the Antarctic Club dinner and the members were invited to see the cast at work on the set. Thirty of them turned out, including Admiral Skelton of Scott's first expedition, and five survivors of the *Terra Nova* who found themselves in the unusual situation of being introduced to themselves. David found the reality of the ship entirely convincing, so much so that he was sad to see the ship, having taken six days to build, being dismantled after only ten days of life. The blizzard scenes were seemingly more unpleasant than the real thing, with the huskies from Whipsnade and three pure-bred Norwegian cream duns to match those which were used in Norway, adding a final touch of reality. They reached the Pole after twelve week's shooting, leading up to Easter; after the Easter break a fortnight finished it off. The status of the film is such that it is still shown as an instructional film to new recruits at the British Antarctic Survey headquarters at Cambridge.

David all through had been most impressed by the actors. Many routine operations such as sledging, man-hauling and tent pitching – which came naturally to David and Quintin Riley – would have been done most unnaturally by the unpractised actors. But the Polar advisors only had to do it once and demonstrate the emphasis that was needed and to rest assured that the scene would come out looking authentic. During this episode in his life David made many lifelong friends, including Michael Balcon, the producer, Quintin Riley, the fellow Polar advisor and last, but not least, John Mills, whom he found to be most genuine, most conscientous and far from conceited.

Being based in London for the first part of the year, with the new responsibilities of a managing director of an hotel, he made enquiries among his ex-RNVR contacts, in particular, Billy Astor* who recommended a young lady

* Later 3rd Viscount Astor.

A blizzard *on the set.*

who had been in service with him and who was, without much further thought, appointed as manageress of the Torosay Hotel. David then giving more serious thought to his new venture realised that the lack of sufficient ablution facilities was serious and had running water and basins installed in every bedroom – as well as investing in a large sized Aga in the kitchen. Such lavish expenditure, coupled with the new manageress and his occasional appearances, in his view was the recipe for establishing a successful hostelry – but sadly the clientele, such as it was, started drifting away.

Another great first in David's life happened when *Prisoner's Progress* was published by Evans Brothers Limited and was on the market by the beginning of the year. It was well received as a brave escape story of the war and was to run into a second edition, published by Hollis and Carter in 1954. It was published by W.W. Norton & Co. Inc. in the USA under the title *Escaper's Progress*, with yet a fourth edition in 1958, a Corgi edition twenty years later, and reprinted privately in 1986. All this after it had been published in *Blackwoods Magazine* in serial form. It confirmed another of his tutor Hubert Hartley's predictions that, 'he would make a good journalist if only he could learn to write'. This was further confirmed by the publication in 1949 by the Falkland Press of *That Frozen Land* which he finished in August 1947; this was an account of his time in the Antarctic. In 1948 *Scott of the Antarctic, The Film and its Production* was published by Convoy Publications Limited; it ran into a second edition in 1949. All these books had been written 'in between whiles' during his time in the Antarctic or during the making of *Scott of the Antarctic*.

When the film was finished in July he got word that *Viking* was only 250 miles west of Scilly so he gathered together a few enthusiasts and went to Falmouth to await her arrival and see her slide out of the mist in the middle of a heatwave. The captain, with orders to sail for London agreed to take them aboard and so ten years and one world war after David last stepped off her decks he went out by motorboat, with those familiar spars towering above him. They sailed at once, so still clad in his London suit he swarmed aloft, awakening familiar emotions. But getting back on deck he felt things were not the same. Ten years before everyone knew exactly which rope led where but now there was a good deal of confusion, even after a passage of 140 days. The watch did not start deck work until 8 o'clock and the loss of a daily two hours maintenance was very apparent. The mate did not call the duty-watch to square all the yards – which admittedly made very little difference as there was so little wind. But with a channel full of shipping, in the old days it would be regarded as a matter of pride to have everything perfectly set, even though the steamers had no thought of dipping their ensigns in salute to a bygone age. The post-war generation, young as it was, had already forgotten about such things and scurried on their way with indifference. It was also evident that the ship's company were much less contented than in his days – which was confirmed to him by an old sail-maker who had served forty-eight years at sea. David's adrenalin was stirred by this four-day journey to London but sadness crept in. Gustav Erikson, her owner, had recently died and his son had indicated she was for sale at the asking price of £30,000. David tried hard to find a British ship owner who would take her over as a training ship but failed to raise any interest. At length she was towed to Antwerp and was sold to the Swedes as a stationary school ship in Gothenburg. But some compensation came when he was elected to the Council of the Outward Bound Trust.

And so, without any regular employment prospect, David entered 1949 with nothing to support him and Torosay other than the operation of an unsuccessful hotel. The first manageress proved to not up to the mark and had to go; a second candidate, soon after being installed, had a series of nervous breakdowns. It began to dawn on David that he was out of his depth with his lack of experience and catering management skills. The large bedrooms, even with running water, did not make up for the lack of bathrooms and so at the end of the summer the operation was thankfully wound down. The only apparent assets were what was left over in the cellar and the building licences for essential work which would not have been available to a private house in the stringent post-war conditions. Quite how any essential work was going to be paid for was, of course, another matter. The short hotel career came to a somewhat unglorious end but it did give David moments of pleasure. He thoroughly enjoyed chatting to selected customers to all hours in the bar – albeit not to the hotel's financial advantage. His friends found it extremely difficult to force any payment on him. For the rest of his life, at far less cost, he was able indulge in these proclivities in the Craignure Inn just down the road.

10

ROMANCE, RESEARCH AND THE RAJ

1949 *to* 1950

'To the discipline, bravery and devotion to duty of the Army in India, in peace and war, I felt that I owed whatever success it was my good fortune to achieve'

– FIELD MARSHAL EARL ROBERTS: *Forty-one Years in India,* 1897

HOW EVER MUCH FUN it was, the hotel did not thrive and money or employment became essential. First of all David advertised in *The Field* 'a comfortable modernised castle, at present run as a hotel (easily convertible, if required, to conveniently run medium-sized house) with eleven acres'. This produced no takers, so he followed up an advertisement that his eye had chanced on in *The Times*. Lady Roberts, the daughter, of Field Marshal Lord Roberts, was looking for someone to write her father's biography. She specifically wanted the job to go to an up-and-coming writer who had not got a professional name. David had come to the notice of Arthur Bryant*, who recommended he should be considered. Lady Roberts liked David and he was given the task which was to keep him occupied for nearly two years.

Lord Roberts – Bobs to his soldiers – started his military career in the old East India Company's Army in 1851 and died as a serving Field-Marshal when visiting the Indian contingent in France in 1914. He had won the VC during the Mutiny in 1858; his son, who died of wounds after the Battle of Colenso in the South African war in 1899 also won the VC. By special dispensation of the Queen, Roberts was allowed to wear his son's VC on his right breast and was the only officer to serve in the Army bearing two Victoria Crosses. He had been elevated to the peerage in 1892 and the title passed, by the special remainder granted by Queen Victoria, to his daughters. The elder, Aileen, never married and the second, Edwina, married a Royal Artillery officer, Major Henry Lewin in 1914. Her son Frederick Robert Alexander Lewin should have succeeded to the title after his aunt and mother. Sadly he was killed in May 1940 in the Irish Guards – a regiment of which his father had been appointed the first Colonel when it was formed in 1900. Thus an honoured line was left without an heir.

Aileen had intended to write the biography of her father and had carefully retained his papers to this end, but her active involvements in the Forces Help Society, accompanied by a long period of ill-health, meant that

* Later Sir Arthur Bryant CH CBE; historian and author

this did not come about. Her sister, Edwina, inherited the papers when she succeeded to the title.

And so began a new experience for David. He left behind the physical challenges which had shaped his life so far and faced up to a sedentary period, calling for a mental discipline that he had only trifled with in writing his first books. The size of the problem he was confronted with, in the form of an enormous mass of papers, meant that he willingly acceded to Lady Roberts' offer that he should live with her at The Camp, Ascot for the time it took to complete the task.

Lord Roberts had been born a congenital 'magpie'. It was a mammoth task to sift through his massive collection, which consisted of:

1. All letters received from his father, school reports, youthful diaries, letters of interest from superiors, etc.
2. Every letter he received from 1878 – whether of interest or not – in 112 boxed files, alphabetically arranged.
3. All official and semi-official outgoing letters, memoranda and telegrams sent during his fifteen years of high command in India. These were printed in 13 volumes, each précised, indexed and cross-referenced. On returning to the United Kingdom in 1893 he had not such a large staff, so all such letters were copied by hand into stout exercise books.
4. Fourteen tea-chests containing miscellaneous papers, such as maps and charts, freedom of cities, and so on.
5. Twenty-three large scrap books and several bound volumes containing every speech that he had made from 1880 to 1914.

This task must have seemed just as daunting to David as setting off behind the dogs over the unknown Prince Gustav Channel not so many years before. But tackle it he did and five years later the definitive biography of Lord Roberts hit the bookshops. Lady Roberts gave her permission to destroy anything he felt was irrelevent and the remaining papers of worth were found a home in the War Office Library.

Knuckling down to this project was his main preoccupation for the months ahead but not to the exclusion of everything else.

*   *   *

Scottish country dancing remained high on the agenda for relaxation, as did keeping in touch with his old RNVR shipmates. One of these was Bill Astor who organised a dinner party at his house in Grosvenor Street before they went on to the RNVR Ball at the Dorchester. In an act of deliberate matchmaking he asked Jaquetta Digby if she would like to come as a partner to a more adventurous than usual sailor who had escaped from a prison camp as Lt. Bagerov and would be just her cup of tea. The chemistry worked.

Jaquetta was living in London with two flatmates, while she taught at a prep school at Ealing during the day. This meant that the ensuing courtship involved frequent sorties from The Camp, Ascot. But after their first assignment Jaquetta came away with no doubt in her mind that David's ambition and intention was to become a Member of Parliament. As she was to agree to be his wife before the year was over he certainly discovered something of her family and background.

The first Lord Digby was created an Irish peer when Governor of Kings County in 1620, and the family, who stemmed from Dorset, acquired Minterne in the seventeenth century from one of the Duke of Marlborough's brothers, the sons of Sir Winston Churchill. So began, tenuously, the connection with the Churchills which continues with the James family to this day.

The Digby title passed straightforwardly through sons and brothers until the 9th Baron, Edward St. Vincent inherited it from a kinsman. Edward's father was Admiral Sir Henry Digby, who had been one of Nelson's captains at Trafalgar in command of HMS *Africa* – twice finding himself alone on the poop when all around him had been killed. Fortunately he had amassed the large sum of £64,000 in prize money by the time he was 35 years old. This was a great comfort to his son Edward, when he inherited the title from his great-uncle, at the same time being disinherited from the estate, Sherborne Castle and the personal fortune. There is some dispute as to whether this was because of the behaviour of Edward's sister, Jane*, following her divorce from Lord Ellenborough, or because he believed that Edward would allow the new-fangled railway to go through the estate – which in any event it did. He was succeeded as 10th Baron by his son who also carried the memory of Nelson's victories in his name, Edward Henry Trafalgar. In 1920 Jaquetta's father, Edward Kenelm, became the 11th Baron.

He gave distinguished service in the First World War, being the youngest officer to command a battalion in action with the Coldstream Guards. He earned a DSO, and an MC and bar and in 1939 became a member of His Majesty's Bodyguard, the Honourable Gentlemen-at-Arms, before serving again at the War Office during the Second World War. He was created a Knight of the Garter in 1960. In 1919 he married Pamela Bruce, daughter of the 2nd Baron Aberdare, and in the course of time they produced three daughters and a son. His wife's interests in the services led to her becoming Chief Commander of the ATS† from 1940 to 1944. Lord Digby was devoted to his estate – and all things that go to make up rural England – so it was not surprising to find that he was Master of the Cattistock Hunt in the late twenties, that he received the Victorian Medal of Honour in Horticulture, was a founding member and Vice-President of the International Dendrology Union and President of the Royal Agriculture Society of England. The feat that probably he enjoyed as much as any was achieving the record tote daily double with a ten-shilling bet, winning £5,062 13s, by coupling *Battleship* in the Grand National with *Barbadiche* in the Bickerstaff Plate in 1938.

* Jane Digby, the subject of the biography, *A Scandalous Life*, by Mary S. Lovell.
† The Auxiliary Territorial Service, superseded by the Women's Royal Army Corps (WRAC).

His son Edward, born in 1924, was to succeed him in due course having served in the Coldstream Guards like his father. Pamela, born in 1920, married Randolph Churchill in 1939 and gave birth to Winston at Chequers in October 1940. Another link between the Churchill's and Torosay was established when her sister, Jaquetta, young Winston's aunt, married David. Pamela went on to marry Averell Harriman and as his widow was appointed to the prestigious post of United States Ambassador in Paris; she died there in 1997. Sheila, born in 1921, also married an American, Charles Moore, a businessman, and carried her father's love of horses with her to Ireland, breeding and racing thoroughbreds.

Jaquetta, born in 1928, inherited from her father a love of gardening and trees, to which in years to come she was able to give full rein at Torosay; she also followed him as a member of the International Dendrology Union. The other side of her character, pursuing the family's record of public service, came to the fore when she married and settled down in Sussex. She became a member of the Mid-Sussex Hospital Committee for about eight years before they moved to Dorset where she transferred her allegiance to the Dorset Area Health Authority. But throughout all this time her favourite charity remained the Hamilton Lodge School for Deaf Children in Brighton of which she was chairman from 1962 until 1980.

Lord Digby with his wife and daughters *Jaquetta (on the left) and Pamela. Jaquetta married David James in 1950; Pamela married Averell Harriman and died in 1997.*

David's commitment to the Roberts biography allowed him only a weekend in Mull during August. But his suit was progressing well enough with Jaquetta to return with her for five days in September, to introduce her to his family. When they got back to London plans were set afoot for David to spend the last two months of the year in Lord Roberts' old stamping grounds, Afghanistan, Pakistan and India, to soak up some of the background and familiarise himself with places with which he had become so deeply inured over the last months. The sight of a battle ground would afford him so much more authority when putting the story together, and there was the chance that he might dig out more information and material to add to what was already collected.

*   *   *

David caught a morning train from Ascot to London to join up with Jaquetta and meet her father for lunch. On the way they realised that their idea of getting married had, in David's words, 'grown out of space' and, although they considered themselves engaged, he had not formally asked her to marry him. This was rectified at noon while crossing Hyde Park Square. Lord Digby arrived 40 minutes late for lunch at Claridges, which tried their nerves a bit, but which was set right by his cordiality on hearing the news. After lunch they selected a ring at Tessiers from a number shortlisted by David and Bunny, and a yellow diamond between two white ones was chosen. Jaquetta, in turn bought David a travelling shaving kit and a St Christopher tag for his key-ring to set him on his way. Then there was a dash for the airport in Jaquetta's car.

On October 12th Lady Roberts and David left the Nissen-hutted terminal at Heathrow for Cairo, where she would stay with friends while David would fly on to India.

They set off in a very noisy York aeroplane. It was still in the days of piston engines and short hops so they stopped for a good supper on the ground at Rome at ten o'clock. David was pleasantly surprised to be able to make an extravagant phone call to Jaquetta – at the cost of 36s. for three minutes. At midnight they took off for Cairo to complete what David could only describe as a 'wonderful, wonderful day'.

So once again he was on his travels into unknown territory. For a while the graft and paperwork would be behind him and he would find himself in surroundings which, because of what he had absorbed in reading, would seem strange and familiar at the same time. The most exciting thing would be to enter this great sub-continent where the immutability of the British Raj had dissolved only some two years before. What were these people making of their new found freedom, other than indulging in a welter of bureaucracy and nostalgia?

They arrived in Cairo at 7 o'clock in the morning and, thanks to the efforts of an Embassy official, were able to shorten the protracted antics of Egyptian customs and found themselves comfortably ensconced in the Mena House Hotel by the pyramids. David was not greatly impressed with Egypt in his two days there, in spite of a visit to Tutankhamun's relics which, though impressive with their antiquity and craftsmanship, seemed to him devoid of any artistic beauty or life. The pyramids, viewed from the hotel, appeared completely incongruous, sitting at the end of a rather messy reproduction of the Great West Road. But going only a few hundred yards to the far side they were exactly what books and the imagination made them out to be, with enough sand around them to suit the most fanatical taste. For all the wonder of how the great pyramids were built, David could but shudder at the amount of suffering that went into the construction and the preoccupation with death that gave rise to them. He left Lady Roberts in Cairo and set off in an Argonaut which was a great deal more comfortable than the York. To travel in an air-conditioned, comfortable, semi-circular lounge at 17,000ft was a great step up.

They stopped at Basra for breakfast, early enough in the morning to be tolerably cool and by 10 o'clock they were off again over the Persian Gulf and across Baluchistan to arrive at Karachi at 6.30 (local time) in the evening. Customs here utterly outdid Cairo and were completely thrown by David's rifle which he was taking to use in India. Two officials played each other off admirably, taking turns to make helpful suggestions and quoting regulations to confound the other's brainwaves. The evening was drawing in, so David blew the whistle for half time and the match was postponed until Monday morning, with the offending weapon and luggage being left in bond.

David's plan was to use Pakistan as the jumping-off point to go into Afghanistan and so on the Monday started taking up the introductions he had brought with him. He began with the High Commissioner, who was not short of charm but had no suggestions to help him on his mission. This was followed up by a telephone call to the Inspector General of Special Police, a cousin of the Nawab of Pataudi*. David was immediately invited to his office where, over tea he received a lengthy discourse on the difficulties of checking police corruption, ending with an invitation to two parties. The first was at the naval base HMPS *Dilawar*, in honour of the visiting cruiser HMS *Mauritius*; the second was a Muslim wedding reception.

The naval party was a mixture of princely splendour and nostalgia. The guests included a score of Muslim girls, out of purdah in their glorious coloured clothes and with a natural carriage of dignity. They mixed under innumerable coloured fairy lights with Pakistani naval and military officers – so like their British counterparts in copying the mannerisms, speech and hairstyles of their immediate superiors. The result was that David felt more at home with them than he would have done with any American or European officer. On the far side of the parade ground in the dark some sort of display was being prepared; a salvo of rockets went off followed by a rumble of drums. Searchlights were thrown across the parade ground to dimly

* The ruler of this small Muslim state in India captained the Indian cricket team after the war; his father had played for England before the war.

illuminate the band beyond the beam. To David's amazement *The Road to the Isles* struck up and the massed pipe bands of the Baluch Regiment marched across the field, playing every bit as well as if they had come from Oban.

The Muslim wedding reception was completely different, characterised by no booze and no bride. He met some interesting people who might ease his passage to Afghanistan, among whom was the Governor of the State Bank of Pakistan. The most likeable was Colonel Mustafa, commanding officer of the Guides Cavalry, who bounded up to him and greeted him with the opening salvo 'Hello, old boy! Why did your loathsome Labour government have to send out such a swine as Mountbatten? My regiment is the Queen's Corps of Guides, founded by Peter Lumsden in 1846. I have eaten the King's salt and to him I will be true forever'. This statement rather precluded any further social conversation and after David replied that he also was true to the King's salt they parted the best of friends; somewhat bewildered he went to bed.

The next day, with the Inspector General's car at his disposal, he followed up some fruitless introductions, culminating in the inevitable cocktail party at the United Kingdom High Commission. The following morning he made use of a contact he had made there for assistance in getting his luggage released from customs, so they went to Cox and Kings office to see if there was any hope. An immense amount of bureaucratic prevarication ensued and he was assured that the most likely chance of seeing it again would be to leave it to the authorities to process it through to Delhi in due course. An appeal to the Chief Customs Officer, whom he had met at the wedding, was greeted by a terse comment that the delay was caused by the inefficiency of the agents handling the baggage. Much to David's surprise Cox and Kings rang him at 5 o'clock to say they had got the luggage through customs. Thankfully he boarded the only air-conditioned coach on the train leaving for Rawalpindi.

David's contact there was General McCay, the Chief of Staff, and after breakfast in Flashman's Hotel he took a *tonga** to GHQ, only to find that it was a military holiday and the General was away on tour. Luckily the General's wife knew all about him and asked him to move in and use her house as his advance headquarters and leave any luggage there. More to the point mail was waiting for him. As usual the day ended in a cocktail party with the Pakistan EME who were still fifty per cent British officered; ominously this led to the first, but as it turnd out only, signs of a doubtful tummy. Feeling better the next morning he went to GHQ to pay his respects to the C-in-C, General Sir Douglas Gracey. Having passed through the ADC, Captain Ameen – by far the ablest young Pakistani he had met to date – he was taken to the General who sent a long signal to Mr Gardiner, the Ambassador in Kabul, asking him to expedite David's visa and give him all the help he could.

On returning from his tour after the weekend, General McCay did David proud by presenting him with a sheaf of introductions, having arranged for

* A two-wheeled, horse-drawn vehicle

his accommodation at the Peshawar Club. A seat was reserved for him in the *dak* bus* so that he could get the most of the atmosphere of the country by travelling in daylight. Arriving at the club in the evening he was welcomed by the secretary with a telegram from Jaquetta saying that their engagement would be in that week's *Times*. A congenial evening followed with an RAF officer on leave with his wife, a Orient Airways Canadian pilot and a bottle of champagne. The following morning was filled in by Massy, the Orient pilot, taking him on a most enthralling flight in his Dakota, delivering freight to Kashmir – overshadowed by the 26,600ft Nanga Parbat at their 13,500ft. The landing at Skardu was hairy on a strip only 900ft long; the recommendations for a Dakota at that height were for a 2,000ft runway.

They got safely back to visit the Afghan Consulate that afternoon, to find no news of David's visa.

The next move was to call on Colonel French, Deputy Inspector-General of the Frontier Forces, who arranged for him to visit the Kurram Militia. Once again he caught the *dak* which took him into 'Tribal Territory' at the Frontier Constabulary Fort at Matanni and continued along the valley, thickly populated by heavily fortressed dwellings and an arms factory where even Sten guns were manufactured by hand, indistinguishable from the originals. They wound on to Kohat on a relatively modern road and then a further 60 miles to Thall through broad and fertile uplands. Just outside the city David was met by Paddy Byrne, a young officer, – the only Briton left with the Thall Scouts –who had spent four years on the Frontier, although only 24. After lunch they set off into the Kurram valley, the country he had come to see, where Lord Roberts had assembled his little force in 1878, before advancing up the valley in the first phase of the Afghan War. They climbed on up to their destination, Parachinar and got there bitterly cold at 7 o'clock in the evening. He was met by Major Peter Parr, dumped in the guest house and told that he had been invited to dinner by the Colonel and had half an hour in which to bathe and change. This gave time to light the boiler but not long enough to heat the water, so feeling somewhat jaded and scruffy he made it over to the bungalow to find himself surprisingly sipping a Martini in a dinner jacket while listening to a Prom relayed from London. After an extremely amiable dinner party, but very tired, he got to bed at midnight.

Parachinar had been deliberately chosen on strategic grounds as the site for the administrative centre of the Kurram Militia and, with its magnificent climate, was a haven to those British officers fortunate enough to serve or take leave there. In winter there was skiing and in summer some of the finest mahseer† and trout fishing as well as some of the best game shooting in Pakistan. The Militia kept law and order over the 140,000 inhabitants administered by the political agent, who saw that the tribal laws were maintained, depending on the Thall Scouts, a unit of some 1,700 men locally

* The mail bus
† *Barbus tor*, a freshwater fighting fish running to well over 50lb, often called 'the Indian salmon'.

raised but commanded by officers seconded from the Army. David was given every assistance and taken about the country to discover many of Lord Roberts' earlier locations and forts. He made his way by *dak* back to Thall and joined a convoy of Paddy Byrne's for Peshawar.

Very tired he arrived at his next port of call in front of solid wooden gates which, when opened released a substantial litter of large Baluchi nomad puppies, who removed his trousers piecemeal – treatment he had never received from his huskies. He was rescued by his hostess Margot Dent, who turned out to be a long-standing acquaintance. She and her husband John, Home Secretary of the North West Frontier Province, made David welcome and comfortable and let him relax with his mail. John was also Master of the Peshawar Vale Hunt, established in 1868 to hunt jackal, and David got a pleasant surprise when he was asked if he would like to go cub-hunting in the morning. They rose early to go by car to the meet where their horses were waiting for them. John hunted the hounds, with a Pakistani vet whip-ping-in, and there was a field of some half-dozen people among whom was a local *zemindar** on a shaggy pony and the English Revenue Commissioner. At that time of the year a third of the land was covered with sugar cane and it was almost impossible to push the jackals out. At best they could get them to go from cover to cover, rather like woodland hunting in England. They had two or three good bursts and killed a jackal and David was awarded the brush. The obstacles were all ditches and banks between irrigated fields and the main difficulty was that some of the fields were as hard as a road, while others had been watered recently, so a horse sank straight up to its hocks without any warning.

With his mind back on the business in hand, David went back to the Afghan Consultate, only to find that his visa still was not through. He unsuccessfully complained that he had been told in London that he could get a visa without delay in Peshawar. In Lord Roberts' time the Afghans were described as a suspicious and intolerably arrogant race; there did not seem to be much difference to David now. Another day was spent on the visa hunt and life was only brightened by a guest of the Dent's, a Major from the South Waziristan Scouts, who had been drunk on leave for three days. He appeared for breakfast, occasionally for lunch and rarely for dinner, but was very amusing when he did.

On November 5th, being a Saturday he was at a loose end and went to the Masonic Hall to find Lord Roberts name inscribed on the board of the Khyber Lodge as Master in 1857. This took him completely by surprise as it was the first intimation he had of his being a Freemason; it appeared in none of the voluminous records. Monday still produced no visa, which put David in a difficult situation as to know what to do. To save having to break his journey to Lahore he took advantage of a lorry going down to Rawalpindi to say his goodbyes and collect his spare luggage which he had

* land owner

left with the McCays. On return, dusty and exhausted, it was sprung on him to dine with Sir Hissamud Din, the Honorary Colonel of the Khyber Rifles, whose father was a friend of Lord Roberts. David had hopes of some fresh material at this juncture but the old man, though possessing a keen sense of humour and an even better cellar, did not seem to be well versed in matters historical. He riled against those in the Army who had given up their British decorations at the time of partition saying 'how can they be so rude to the King, who has been so kind to them?'. He was ADC to King George V, his father to King Edward VII and his great-uncle to Queen Victoria and hated the passing of the British Raj.

David decided the next day that if his visa was not through that afternoon he would cut his losses and make tracks for Delhi. At lunchtime he discovered that his visa had only just been applied for as the Afghans had never delivered Sir Douglas Gracey's original telegram. So he made the most of the rest of the day by borrowing John Dent's car and driving up the Khyber with Sir Hissamud Din.. He found the Pass not as magnificent as his imagination had pictured it, even though the road climbed up 4,000ft in less than twenty miles. He was impressed with the watch-towers of the Khyber Rifles on every commanding point up to Landi Kotal, a mile from the frontier with Afghanistan. To see these magnificent defensive positions taught David more about Roberts championing of the 'Forward Policy' than six months of reading had done, and once on the spot it seemed incredible to him that competent soldiers should have advocated remaining on the Indus. They finished back at the Mess having tea with Sir Hissamud's son who now commanded the Khyber Rifles. After a short farewell party with the Dents in Peshawar he took the train for Lahore where Adrian Reed, the Deputy High Commissioner, took charge of him. A final round of parties and he was on the plane to Delhi, curious to compare the new India with Pakistan.

David got a good welcome at Delhi airport, being met by the two ADCs of General Kalwant Singh, the Chief of the Indian General Staff. The next day he was hoping to get straight on with some work but found he would need a letter from Sardar Patel* to enable him to see the National Archives. He also discovered that everything in Delhi stopped that afternoon for five days while a Test Match was being played. He surrendered to circumstances and went off with General Kalwant to watch the cricket, before thankfully retiring for a quiet evening in his digs reading the Mutiny story for his forthcoming tour.

The next day he met Brigadier Bullock in the UK High Commissioner's Office; he had had 32 years service in India and knew a great deal about Lord Roberts. David was glad to find that the general lines that he was taking and the specific questions that he was hoping to answer in the book were those that Brigadier Bullock would have posed himself. He gave important advice which involved modifications in David's text, particularly about the causation of the Mutiny.

* The Hindu politician who masterminded the integration of Indian states – his 'basket of apples'.

Later in the day Major K.K. Singh, who had been appointed David's unofficial ADC arrived from Kashmir and immediately offered the alternatives of
polo or more cricket. David opted for the former, which turned out to be
wrong as it was only a scratch game. The next day, Sunday, was better; he fell
in with Brian Sheppard, once a clerk in the House of Commons but now seconded to the Commonwealth Relations Office, who asked him to go shooting.
Joined by the First Secretary from the American Embassy and a couple of
beaters' they went off in a jeep northwards along the Grand Trunk Road,
passing the site of the first victory against the Mutineers in 1857. They came
to an area full of sugar cane where the day's sport started and even though
partridge abounded, shooting was moderate and only five were put in the
bag. They then went to a *jheel** for some duck which flew too wide and never
gave them a shot, and in the evening drove to Naafghar, to flight duck on the
large *jheel* there. While the quality of the sport was not good and the driver
lost his way home, David enjoyed his first acquaintance with Indian bird life,
finding himself among hoopoes, cranes, rollers and green paraqueets.

Monday began in the normal sub-continental way. Sardar Patel, who was
meant to produce a letter of authorisation to the National Archives, had
failed to deliver and the car was predictably 40 minutes late to convey him
to the doctor for his first cholera injection. David was beginning to weigh up
the differences between the two countries. The Indians seemed friendly and
promised more than the Pakistanis, but there seemed to be a far greater dis-
crepancy between the promise and the performance. Lower down the scale
the bearers and drivers were certainly far less intelligent than the Pathans
who did the jobs in Pakistan.

He went to the War Office to see if his authorisation had got through;
after waiting practically the whole afternoon and reading ten day's back
numbers of *The Times* he eventually got it. It was too late to do anything, and
so he went to see the last hour of the Test Match which was still in progress.
Tuesday started with the car only 35 minutes late and David went straight
to the archives where, after all, he did not find much new. Instead he had an
irrelevant conversation with Mr Roy, the Deputy-Director, who blamed the
British bitterly for pulling out of India without any suggestions as to how, as
a matter of practical politics, they could have stayed. After another hour at
the cricket on the fifth and final day he returned to the archives to discover
that the only document that he wanted – concerning the possibility of Lord
Roberts becoming Viceroy – was the property of the Home Affairs Department. He would therefore need another letter from Sadar Patel.

The saga of vehicular incompetence reached a crescendo the following
day. He was not surprised when at 10.20 he was told that the car due at 10
o'clock was in trouble; progress would be reported at 11. At 11.20 he was
told that the car was repaired and would be round straightaway, but by
noon no car had appeared. He rang the Military Assistant to the CGS to say

* Lake or mere.

he would come round by *tonga*. Ten minutes later as he was getting into the *tonga* he was told that the car was at last on the road. So he paid off the *tonga* and waited. At 12.45 it was suggested that he should have an early lunch so that he could be picked up at 1.30; at 1.45 he was told there was no car. David then arranged for K.K., his aide, to join him at the Secretariat at 3 o'clock to submit a programme in writing for the CGS's approval. On his arrival he found that it was a half holiday and the entire place was closed. K.K. turned up, as usual half an hour late and, taxed about the morning's performance, had to admit shamefacedly that he had never been able to find the car at all; even Transport HQ did not know what had become of it. In a towering fury David pointed out that if he had been told this in the beginning he could easily have got a *tonga*.

More irritation followed when he went to BOAC to confirm the details of his air passage home, only to be told that they had changed to winter schedules and he would have to completely re-plan his journey. He ended up at the archives with only time for another 40 minutes work.

The next day dawned with forebodings about transport arrangements, although surprisingly the car arrived on time. But bureaucracy then took hold and the trip to the bank to cash a cheque took 55 minutes, a visit to the post office to send a cable took 25 minutes and finally the archives took 90 minutes to produce two volumes of the annual index. On his way back from this frustrating day he called into see General Kalwant Singh and was introduced to the Maharajah of Jaipur who – with his smoothness and charm, and his background of Harrow – lulled David into a sense of false *bonhomie*, particularly when he issued an invitation to Jaipur.

The great moment came in the afternoon when he was to visit the Ridge and various Mutiny sites in Delhi. Having kept hold of the car over lunch he made a punctual start, armed with camera, map and books. He picked up K.K., who suspiciously ordered the driver to go south instead of north and on being questioned said that they were going to see His Highness off from the airport. So they went and stood on the hot tarmac for half an hour admiring the Maharajah's Dove aeroplane and talking polo to his English doctor. The Maharajah arrived, hands were shaken all round, and then he dashed off by car for a forgotten suitcase. K.K. thought up another diversion to 'a place you simply must see old boy'. Having arrived at a decorative minaret amongst some ruins, they found no guide-book and K.K. could remember nothing about it, so the jaunt completely lost its point. Back in Delhi K.K. suddenly remembered a conference he had been ordered to attend at the War Office. David was left with a driver who was given detailed instructions, but turned out to know no English, and coming from Madras, had no idea of his way round Delhi, so they promptly got lost. With the aid of David's 1857 map they managed to find the Ridge Memorial and take a couple of photographs, but by the time they got to the Kashmir Gate it was too late for photography. David returned to his lodgings in high dudgeon.

On Friday, incompetence reached new heights. It took the Military Advisor to the CGS, K.K., the transport officer in the Quartermaster General's office and the Rail Transport Officer at Delhi station exactly three and a half hours to secure him a second class sleeper reservation to Lucknow. Among others in pursuit of a ticket, he fell in with General Russell, the British Advisor to the War Office, who promised to try and ginger things up. He paid off his digs – £22 for lodging for nine days – and with some misgivings as to what he might find at the other end, caught the train to Lucknow. To his surprise the organisation worked; his train was met and he was taken to an expensive hotel as a State guest. Only later did he discover that meant he was booked into the best hotel and left to pay for it. After breakfast a Brigadier Atel arrived and took him to meet Colonel Andrews, headmaster of the Martinière School, who had agreed to show him round the next day.

Sunday turned out to be the sort of day that David had been waiting for. After Mass he met Colonel Andrews at the Martinière, a school which had been established by a French soldier of fortune who took service in the East India company, eventually becoming Prime Minister at the Court of the King of Oudh with the honorary rank of Major-General. He died in 1800, leaving his fortune to the foundation of schools in Lyons, Calcutta and Lucknow. The school at Lucknow – which was established in his private house standing in a thousand acre park – was just getting into its stride when the Mutiny broke out. Rather than garrison the school, the boys were marched under escort to the Residency. There the fifty young lads, aged 9 to 14

The Martinière School, *Lucknow*

Sikanderbagh, *the scene of the heroic breaching of the wall by Highlanders, Dogras, Gurkhas and Sikhs.*

gained imperishable fame, the older boys holding a very exposed part of the perimeter not 50 yards from the enemy while the younger boys acted as orderlies and messengers. They were the only school in the Empire to display battle honours and LUCKNOW in letters of gold was embroidered on the school flag which flew proudly from the tower where David's tour started. This had been Sir Colin Campbell's HQ, both for the relief in November 1857 and the recapture in March 1858; from the summit of the tower the line of the advance spread out before them. The tour led to the ruined palace of the Kings of Oudh, the graves of Hodson and Mayne – who was buried by his friend Roberts in his greatcoat with his monocle still in his eye. Then on to Sikanderbagh, where marble plaques in the wall showed the exact spot of the breach which Highlanders, Dogras, Gurkhas and Sikhs raced for the honour of being first through – the prize being certain death. Next the messhouse where Sir Colin Campbell met Havelock and Outram – now the Martinière girls' school – on one of whose towers Roberts raised the flag which showed the defenders where the spearhead of relief had reached. Finally they came to the Residency, but by that time David was emotionally spent and they returned to the school for a welcome drink.

After lunch, gorged with curry David went back to the Residency – probably the most moving historical site he had ever been to. Everything stood as it did at the time when the city was recaptured. Although the Union Jack no longer flew from the tower, the site was maintained in perfect order by the Indian Army, as it should have been, because the force that held it for three months at the height of that summer was exactly half British and half Indian.

David's journey back to Delhi was distinguished by the Rail Transport Officer booking him a first class seat instead of a second class one and then putting him on the wrong train. Surprisingly, the car was there to meet him, presumably as a result of his chat with General Russell. An appointment with the Chief of Staff successfully mapped out a programme day by day – something he had been trying to induce K.K. to do from the beginning – and the car was now allocated permanently to him.

That afternoon they visited the historic Mutiny sites of Old Delhi, starting off with the Red Fort, the last place to be taken in the seige. From there they went to the Kashmir Gate and Skinners Church where the three assault columns reformed inside the City. They walked down from the Kashmir Gate to the water bastion where the breach was still extant. On seeing it only then did David realise on what a narrow front the attack had been made – and what an insignificant part of the city was in the attackers' hands that first night.

He was staying with General Kalwant Singh who had a lot of entertaining to do. No sooner had he arrived than it was time to change to go out to another cocktail party, this time at the American Embassy.

David joined K.K. and Colonel Sataravala for a day of combined business and pleasure. They drove to the village of Najafgahr, where Nicholson had defeated the mutineers trying to intercept his siege train and Roberts, very nearly killed, was mentioned in despatches. Talking to the villagers, not one of them had any idea that there had ever been a battle there. They drove on to the Colonel's favourite shooting spot where there was a wonderful *jheel* to

The Kashmir Gate, *Old Delhi.*

which he went every weekend. Stopping under a tree for lunch, they espied a big herd of chinkara* at a distance. Moving in closer, David shot a solitary doe, which had worked away from the main herd; after so little effort he did not feel elated but was mollified to learn that they were very good eating. They went on to find another vast herd about 500 yards away but the ground was so flat that they could not get near them. David took a long shot at a buck, deliberately aiming at the neck so that it would either kill or miss – he succeeded in the latter. They went back into butts round the *jheel* and David soon had a shot at some mallard and missed. Immediately the sky above the lake was swarming with duck which flew over in their thousands, most of them far too high, but David managed to get four mallard. He then walked up some wild snipe. As the evening darkened the duck started to come back in small groups and he shot three more, finishing with a solitary drake with his final cartridge. It was a great day's sport and David was struck by the variety and quantity of wild fowl, as well as getting an extra thrill from being in such unfamiliar surroundings. It seemed doubtful whether the bag compensated for all the ructions the rifle had caused with the customs in Pakistan, especially when his subsequent trip to Jaipur for *shikar*† was aborted.

Anticlimactic and boring cocktail parties followed, relieved only by the complete surprise of finding Murray de Klee, his cousin from Mull, accompanying Air Commodore Jack Slessor at one of them. They all spent the next day together touring Delhi, ending up having tea with Sir Thomas Elmhurst, Air Officer Commanding the Indian Air Force and the Rajah of Tonk (the one Muslim State in Rajasthan).

With the weekend came a visit to Jaipur and an overture of breakfasts: one before he left; one by courtesy of Indian Airlines and one on arrival, with the compliments of the Maharajah's guest master. After signing the Palace Book David visited the Museum and Zoo, and spent the evening with the Rajasthan Government's English pilot, and a doctor who was at Eton with him, who now spent his time between six months polo and gentle medicine at Jaipur, and six months 'studying' in Paris. They both warned him against having too high expectations of his visit; it was the normal practice of HH to invite people for the purpose of going on *shikar* and he was seldom known, if ever, to honour his promise. He met the Maharajah at one of the inevitable parties and he found out how right they were. He was, of course, charming and full of apologies, the grass was too long or too short, the Colonel in charge of *shikar* was away, either ill or busy. He hoped the car was satisfactory and that he would enjoy the sights, etc. etc. David, however, got into a long conversation with Rao Raja Hanut Singh, son of Sir Pertab Singh, the Health Minister for Rajasthan who asserted that his father was full of stories of Lord Roberts. But when he came to the point he was unable to remember any of them – a

* Indian gazelle
† hunting

distressingly common occurrence where memories of Lord Roberts were concerned. Four fascinating days were spent among the past glories of Jaipur. He was particularly taken by the religious village of Ganga – set in a thick, prickly jungle at the head of a gorge – which consisted of a conglomeration of dirty temples and even dirtier holy men. Up the main street there were a series of pools, rising one above the other; the lowest and largest, looking indescribably revolting, was 'the women's', the next one up was 'the men's'. Here and there were instructions printed in both Hindi and English, a most eye-catching one being, SPITTING IN THE WATER IS QUITE A BAD HABIT. The top pool, apparently, was reserved for the monkeys.

On getting back to Delhi, a trip to the Taj Mahal was arranged with an intelligent, but dissolute officer, whose sole topic of conversation was whisky. Over breakfast of porridge, fried eggs and coffee in Laurie's Hotel, David had announced he had never been to the Taj. When they got there, David was unable to take his eyes off the sheer beauty of form and construction and was appalled by the thought that in 1823 Lord William Bentinck had proposed that it be sold for the value of the marble. It even silenced his garulous companion who went white with rage at finding a party of children running round shouting in order to get the resounding echo. When they and their parents had been driven out they found themselves most reluctant to leave.

David returned to Delhi and the social round, enjoying an evening with Govind Singh, officer commanding the Governor General's Bodyguard. They produced smart cavalry escorts, as do the Household Cavalry, but were also mechanised and trained as paratroopers. Returning to the reason for his visit, permission to inspect the civil files in the Public Archives had now come through. A visit was made to find out what he could about the proposal that Lord Roberts should succeed Lord Lansdowne as Viceroy. As only too often with his researches he came away empty handed.

The highlight of the visit was on December 2nd when David, representing Lady Roberts, attended the 5th Gurkhas traditional dinner on 'Peiwar Kotal Day'. This celebrated the battle at which Roberts led the 5th Gurkhas, among other units, to defeat the Afghans, in 1878.

Accompanied by a charming Indian Officer, Major Backshi, they set off for Dehra Dun, stopping at Meerut for breakfast in a café not 200 yards from the parade ground where the Mutiny broke out some 92 years before. They arrived at the 5th Gurkha Regimental Mess for lunch where he met a hearty old gentleman of 78, full of irrelevant anecdotes about Lord Roberts. The following day he met the gentleman's wife, who was the daughter of General Hume, a contemporary of Lord Roberts; much interesting gossip of the old days ensued without producing anything particularly new. One thing she did remember was meeting the whole Roberts family at Quetta immediately after the march from Kabul to Kandahar. This could not possibly have been true as David knew that Lady Roberts and her children had gone back to England some nine months before!

The Peiwar Kotal dinner was a grand affair, with David sitting on the Colonel's right among the 40 people there. The meal was long and dull, but was enlivened by the Gurkha Depot Band and was followed by three toasts, first to the King, with *God Save the King* being played; secondly, India; and finally 'to the memory of Lord Roberts' – seventy-one years after he had led his Gurkhas up a rocky ravine to the Spingawai Kotal. The mess party went on to 2 a.m. but before David went to bed he was asked to reassure Lady Roberts how hard they were trying to keep up the honour of the Regiment and trying never to depart one inch from the traditions that meant so much. He was given two copies of the regimental history signed by every officer present, one for himself and one for Lady Roberts, also a beautifully inscribed kukri; sadly the special one that was being prepared for Lady Roberts was not ready.

This was followed by another sporting interlude, setting off to the jungle on elephant back. The shooting was testing, snap shooting at jungle fowl across very narrow rides. David found the terrain quite alien, and being warned that a leopard or even a tiger might come out in front of him, he kept one barrel loaded with LG shot, restricting his chances to the advantage of the jungle fowl. The real hazards were the other sportsmen, all shooting round the clock without regard for their neighbours. He was chided reproachfully by a next door gun for not shooting a peacock down a narrow path as it flew two feet over his head. When David pointed out his proximity, he replied, 'I could always have ducked old boy'. At 3 o'clock they came to a clearing where they found a magnificent lunch of curry, fruit and beer; after three more drives they headed for home. The total bag picked up for 12 guns was 12 jungle fowl, so David's score of 1 was well up to average.

Back in Delhi he stayed with General Kalwant Singh and his charming wife; it was with real regret he bade goodbye and set off for Pakistan again in the hope of being able to get to Afghanistan after all.

He found his way back to his friends, the Dents, at Peshawar and on the 6th December, two months after the original application, he collected his Afghan visa which had at last been authorised. He set off in the diplomatic bus – which went up to Kabul every Wednesday and back every Sunday – through the Khyber Pass and over the Landi Kotal where they were delayed about an hour while their passports were laboriously entered in a book. They had a surprisingly brief halt on the Afghan side of the frontier, rolled on to a village seven miles down on the Kabul River to another customs post where their credentials were entered in yet another book. They then proceeded along the valley of the Kabul River, through an area totally devoid of vegetation, the road being a track across the desert from which only the worst boulders had been removed; it took two and a half hours to cover the 42 miles to Jalalabad. Averaging less than ten miles per hour, passing innumerable camel caravans and gaining height, they went on and reached signs of the snowline where there was a superb view of the Hindu Kush. They then started their descent with views of wild and rugged mountains in the distance and in the gathering gloom they careered down the other side – the suicidal driver fortunately making no mistakes at corners or gradients – until they reached Butkak to find yet a third customs post. They arrived in the Embassy compound at Kabul at 8 o'clock, dog tired and sore in every joint. After absorbing two large gins and dinner David fell into bed, glad to be in Kabul at last.

At the Chancery next morning Prendergast, the military attaché provided him with a car and driver – who not only spoke English, but knew the country well – at one shilling a mile. As they motored David was able to pick up landmarks familiar to him through his reading. They motored past the Bala Hissar, an ancient fortress looking ridiculously like Edinburgh Castle, but as the Afghans were so touchy he had to take photographs of it from the moving car. They reached the battlefield of Charasia which Lord Roberts described as the most touch-and-go affair of his career. David could well believe it, for the semi-circle of hills were ideally situated for defence and extremely difficult terrain to storm. He climbed the hill nearest the road on which Sir George White gained his vc, leading the 92nd*. It was a good thirty degree slope, devoid of vegetation but with periodic outward sloping outcrops of rock which would give perfect protection for the defenders and without a blade of grass to shield the attackers. The feat was even more incredible when it is realised that this steep slope was stormed at the double at an altitude of 6,000ft. They then motored on to the western side of the position to see the hills stormed by the 72nd Highlanders† and the 5th Gurkhas and passed over the saddle into the rich Chardeh valley. David was enthralled to have seen the sites of these actions and made the most of his few days there in excursions to other sites of Roberts' engagements. Far too short of time, he found in the Embassy library a comprehensive selection of books on the Afghan Wars, including a couple of personal reminiscences that he had not read but which he sadly could only skim through.

The visit ended with a dinner party at the Embassy where the Ambassador had a long talk with David and was sympathetic and encouraging about the need for a life of Lord Roberts, and emphasised the value of seeing it all for himself. An abortive attempt was made to see round the Bala Hissar but as usual, in dealing with suspicious Afghan bureaucracy, a lot of time was taken in fobbing David off and ensuring he did not get permission to go in. His final dinner in Afghanistan was at the Ambassador's, with the most absurd of all anti-climaxes – bridge. So back via Peshawar and Karachi to home.

*   *   *

So ended a fascinating trip which added little extra to the knowledge he already had of Lord Roberts life, but put bones on the skeleton and gave him a feel for the story which he would never otherwise have acquired. He arrived back in

* The 2nd Bn Gordon Highlanders
† The 1st Bn Seaforth Highlanders

England, overjoyed to be reunited with Jaquetta. After Christmas they set off for Mull and ended the year at Torosay by celebrating their engagement.

David entered 1950 with the task of finishing off the Roberts assignment and with marriage ahead of him. The question of religion had been a matter for discussion both before and after their engagement, and Jaquetta's family was well aware that David was a Catholic while she remained a stalwart C. of E. Like all families dealing with uncomfortable matters, they hoped it would not become a major issue and assumed that Jaquetta would not change her faith for several months or years after the event. David had written to his future mother-in-law from India, assuring her that he would never bring any pressure to bear on Jaquetta to persuade her to convert. He explained that, by agreeing to marry a Catholic, she was bound as the non-Catholic partner to see a priest four times so that she could be fully informed on the Catholic view of marriage. It was these meetings with Father Christie, who was to marry them, that made her decide to change her faith.

In following David's life it is important to understand his attitude to religion at this point in his career; also to understand why he had abandoned the Protestant faith for the Catholic faith, which was so alien to the traditions and background of his forebears.

In his view the Protestant position was entirely genuine and in accordance with the British tradition of independence and tolerance and 'democratically' based, with any man's view as good as his neighbour's. But the one thing it did not do was to give a lead to people of his generation, living in an increasingly perplexing world. In the relatively short span of his lifetime he perceived that much he had been brought up to regard as immutable had crumbled. 'The British Empire was in temporary (*sic*) eclipse, the churches half empty, the ruling classes no longer ruled and the whole settled world of wealth had largely gone by the board'. Add to this the menace of Communism, the atom bomb, the prospect of a third world war and the total disappearance of those standards on which he was brought up, he felt that it was hardly surprising that he should be grasping for something more definite upon which to pin his faith for the future.

He believed he had found in the Catholic Church absolute standards and absolute certainty, going back with unbroken succession for 264 generations to St Peter. This met his need for one true teaching church – not one with a myriad of sects, based on personal interpretations, many of them manifest nonsense.

So came a testing time for David's emotions and beliefs: by displaying his hallmark of tolerance, he was able to remain true to both, without compromising either one.

Jaquetta, in her forthright way, dropped her bombshell that she intended to be received into the Catholic church before the wedding. This put the Digby family into a state of shock. They had been sure that the issue had been swept under the carpet – certainly until well after the marriage. David could not work out why it should have been acceptable to Lord Digby to give away his daughter to a Catholic husband in a Catholic Church, so she may

David and Jaquetta's wedding *at St James, Spanish Place, London.*

bear Catholic children, and yet be unable to accept that Jaquetta became a Catholic first. Right up to the end of March she was under pressure from her family to postpone the decision for at least a year – under the veiled threat of having the wedding arrangements cancelled.

Much correspondence flew to and fro. David took comfort and advice from 'dear old Lady Roberts' when writing to Lord Digby; Lady Digby also made her point to David's family. In return she received a letter from David's mother, Bridget, expressing much sympathy for her views but giving no other support. She was sorry about the distress caused by the Catholic issue at this late stage. She too had been dismayed when she heard of David's intentions to convert from the prisoner of war camp, and had begged him to wait until he got home. She thought it had been generous of the Digby's not to stand in the way of the engagement, but felt now that it was far too late to raise objections. Obviously the young couple's religion meant much to them, and David's family would be hurt if the Digby's were to boycott the wedding.

All this must have been stressful to the couple on the verge of their great adventure, but their chosen faith stood them well. The objections collapsed and they were married in a mixed religious ceremony at St James, Spanish Place, on May 20th; the reception was at the Hyde Park Hotel.

So they set up house in No. 2 Cheyne Row, given to them by David's father, Archie, as a wedding present – even though it belonged to his wife and was not his to give. An added hazard had been the removal of the sitting tenant, Field-Marshal the Viscount Slim. They started their life together with £750, and entered into a long lasting, happy and cordial relationship with their respective in-laws.

Before settling down they made the most of their honeymoon – a speeded up Grand Tour, including Paris, Italy, Austria, Germany and Denmark concluding with journey on the Rome-Stockholm Express. They stopped off at Lübeck where David was able to introduce his bride to his erstwhile captors. On a foreign exchange limit of £25 each, it was a most successful tour – helped out by staying with friends and relatives.

On getting home it came naturally that Torosay was the place from which to confirm their marriage. This they did at a nuptual Mass in 'the tin chapel' at Salen, a few miles up the coast.

I I

PUBLISHING TO POLITICS

1950 *to* 1958

'We both believe in conserving what we've got and getting honesty
within the constitution, and a free vote to Members on all matters. But
you know more of the practical difficulties than I do. I dream of fine
schemes for getting the right man in, and you see more clearly that the
best thing to do is peg away and try and make the best of what we've
got.' – LT.-COM. HICHENS, in conversation with David, 1943

WHILE STILL LIVING AT JAVA LODGE Bridget and Geoffrey started 1950, both literally and figuratively speaking trying to keep the water at bay at Torosay. Having made temporary repairs to the roof in an effort to staunch the damp, they commissioned an architect's report which was not only most unhelpful but fuelled Geoffrey's gloomy view that everything was always bound to fail. It suggested in no uncertain terms that there was little case for such a pile in the brave new world ahead and probably it would be best demolished. Surrounded with the aura of Labour post-war stringency, which contradicted the traditions and aspirations of the family, a state of complete uncertainty prevailed. This was no bad thing as it stopped a decision of any magnitude being taken.

Flailing about for some amelioration to the situation, Bridget looked round the house and saw a lot of furniture quite surplus to current and likely future requirements. Without bothering to discuss it with David, who technically owned it, she organised a sale. Much of the 'surplus' furniture had come to Torosay when her father had been forced to sell Stratford House before the First World War and could well have been of sentimental or historical value to the family. It is not known how much was raised, but even today pieces of furniture can be found in houses all around Mull which came from what was, in hindsight, a quite unnecessary sale.

Bridget then turned to the estate that had been left to her by her mother and, taking a leaf out of her book, sold further tracts of land to the Forestry Commission. Some 4-5,000 acres were sold up above Loch Don, along the River Lussa, and this second tranche once more kept the estate from sinking.

So poor old Torosay Castle still lay empty, sad and unattended, apart from a few weeks in the summer when the house was opened up for the sporting season.

David had all but finished the Roberts biography and 1950 saw another book he had masterminded and edited come on the market. This was *Wavy*

Navy, published by Harrap – a collection of articles, poems and paintings by those who had served in the RNVR, presenting a composite picture of their war. Contributors included Lt. Jack Eastern GC, Lt.-Com. Jack Ivester Lloyd DSC, Lt. Ludovic Kennedy and Lt.-Com. Peter Scott MBE DSC. David's co-editor was J. Lennox-Kerr and the proceeds were shared by the King George Fund for Sailors and the RNVR Officers Commemoration Fund. This was not only elegantly produced but sufficiently soon after the war to be a sell-out.

The new status of married life, accompanied by not inconsiderable pressure from his in-laws, made it imperative for David to find a job. Any job, however, would have to fit in with his declared intention of becoming a Member of Parliament in the not too distant future and so he pricked up his ears when a Scottish reeling friend, Adam Maitland, who worked for Eyre and Spottiswoode, suggested he had a word with Tom Burns. Burns was in the mainstream of the establishment of Catholic laity in Britain, of mixed Scottish/Basque descent, and a publisher of some repute. He had made a significant impression during the war as the press attaché to the British Embassy in Madrid, under Sir Samuel Hoare. After the war he had returned to the publishing company, Burns Oates, which had been started by his uncle but was now under different ownership, as Managing Director. He was now looking for partners who had cash. On that score David was certainly not the best candidate, but at his interviews with Tom things clicked and he went to work with a will on his father who, for the first and last time in his life helped David and staked him with £20,000 to buy his way in.

Briefly Burns Oates had got in to the hands of the publishers Hutchinson before the war and its fortunes had declined so Hutchinson had sold it in 1939 to Eyre and Spottiswoode, the Crown printers. Their publishing side put new life into it. After the war the Chairman, Oliver Crosthwaite Eyre MP, who had had a busy time in the Royal Marines during the war, took on Tom Burns as Managing Director of Burns Oates and its imprint, Hollis and Carter. Things were going well, but around 1951 Eyre and Spottiswoode offered to sell the business outright to Tom Burns at far from onerous terms. Under post-war conditions publishing was an attractive and profitable operation, particularly because of the lack of competition caused by the rationing of paper. It was at this point that David came on the scene and in his autobiography, *The Use of Memory*, Tom Burns was to write,

> 'I was greatly helped at an early stage by the advent of David James; he was an ex-RNVR officer, highly decorated for his gallantry as a remarkable escapee from Prisoner of War Camp. He was an Etonian with that touch of assurance and omni-competence which that school seems to create in its better products. He was an ardent convert, having been received into the Church in the prison camp. He was well-off and offered substantial investment in the company. We became firm friends but before long he was elected to Parliament and our interests inevitably tended to diverge.'

Tom took hold of the company and organised the whole thing into a small empire, BOW Holdings, comprising among other things bookshops; retailers of devotional articles; R & T Washbourne; a warehouse in Tottenham Court Road; *The Tablet* edited by Douglas Woodruff; the *Universe* and the *Catholic Times*. The principal directors of this group were, Douglas Woodruff, Tom Burns and David, who, while he did a certain amount of reading for the publishing side, spent most of his efforts on administration and sales activities; also all staff management, which involved successfully settling a strike in the warehouse, fell to his lot. Woodruff had been known to Burns for some time. Before the war he had lectured in various universities, had been on the editorial staff of *The Times* for some eight years, as well as having a spell on the staff of the BBC and being Deputy Chairman of Burns Oates in the thirties. He was also responsible for a number of authoritative historical books.

In selecting this company as a way ahead it was firmly in David's mind that any business he entered should allow him the time to concentrate on politics, get on the Conservative candidates list, nurse a constituency and end up as an MP. He took on the job with the determination that all this would come about. A further benefit was that the location in Victoria Street was handy for the House of Commons and would make a useful pad for late night sittings.

On the publishing side David made the most of his position and, in 1954, *Lord Roberts*, with a foreword by the Rt. Hon. L.S. Amory CH, was published by Hollis and Carter. It received over seventy enthusiastic reviews. *The Times* said 'It is unlikely to be superceded by any future writers', and Norman Scarfe of the *Birmingham Post* wrote 'I cannot think of a biography that has moved me more than this one'. Other reviews included a full page in the *Illustrated London News* and eulogies in the *Daily Telegraph* and military journals. In June 1954, Arthur Bryant wrote to Lady Roberts to say, 'It is, I consider, one of the best biographies of our century'.

In 1952 David and Jaquetta bought a house in Sussex, Townings Place at Wivelsfield Green and he started commuting to London. They soon made their commitment clear to Burns Oates by taking over the annual firm's outing from Sir Anthony Tichborne Bt of Alresford, a director under the previous ownership, who had started the tradition. From this start, fired with David's enthusiasm, stemmed a yearly pilgrimage to Lourdes which also became part of the company's traditions.

The company flourished for about ten years, by which time personality clashes between the principals started to be felt; they really came to a peak in 1967 when Douglas Woodruff retired from editing *The Tablet* and handed it over to Tom Burns. This coincided with the conclusion of the Vatican Council which ran from 1962 to 1967. With a radicalism which was not expected the Latin Mass was superceded by Mass in the vernacular – an anathema to Douglas Woodruff but the realisation of all Tom Burns' dreams. Meanwhile, although David had in common with Tom Burns a robust, anti-Communist streak, he had by then got into Parliament and had his own dreams and aspirations safely ensconsed in Westminster. A further result stemming from Vatican II was that Burns Oates, being the principle Catholic publisher in the United Kingdom, found that following the decrees substituting the use of the vernacular, they had large stocks of religious books and missals printed in Latin for which there was effectively no sales. Burns Oates was staggering on on the profits from the *Universe*, which Tom Burns thought little of. But the board of BOW had other ideas and it was decided that Burns Oates should cease publishing. The stock and contracts were sold to Herders of Freibourg who, within three years, let this famous name disappear.

Tom Burns went on to edit *The Tablet* until 1982, while David remained to manage the rump of the BOW empire until the disposal of the *Universe* was effected in 1970. Thereupon BOW. Holdings was wound up and David was out of a job. But not for long; he was returned to Parliament as the member for North Dorset in the same year.

*   *   *

When the James's moved to Sussex they brought with them Peter, who had been born in the New End Hospital, Hampstead, in April 1951. Jaquetta went back there in April 1952 to produce Patsy and again in September 1953 to have Diana. The three younger boys were all born at Townings Place: Michael in July 1955, Christopher in April 1957 and Kenelm in April 1962.

David and Jaquetta *at Townings Place, Sussex.*

David and Jaquetta with their family *at Townings Place. From left to right: Patsy, Kenelm, Christopher, Michael, Diana on the pony, and Peter.*

Soon after their arrival an advertisement for a gardener flushed out Ron Topson from Eltham in South London. He moved to Townings in 1953 and, after two months of a three-months trial period, both parties decided on permanence. Ron fetched his fiancée down from London and by 1954 they were married and settled on the farm. Four pigs started a venture which turned itself into a farm, eventually based on a thirty-sow unit producing porkers and a 3,000 battery hen unit producing eggs and rearing point-of-lay pullets for the local hatcheries. The operation was sufficiently serious for BOCM, the food compounders, to use the farm to make a promotional film about the pioneering concept, the early weaning of pigs. Soon Ron became a partner with David, and he and his wife who helped about the farm, reared their two daughters there. To complete his story, he stayed on with a farming tenancy when the James's left, which ultimately became useful when he came to retire and was able to cash in the tenancy to buy himself a house. It was a happy set up, unconfused by the Common Agricultural Policy or agricultural political correctness. Partners' meetings were conducted either in the Royal Oak at Wivelsfield or in the car on the way to Twickenham.

As well as the farm animals, on the canine side the daughter of a retired husky, Bobbie, took up residence. On a local rampage it was served by a local Labrador to produce Robert, a 'Huskador', who was born with the looks of a husky but the temperament of a Labrador. Sadly it was realised that huskies about the place were not compatible either with children or sheep and so they did not have an extensive reign.

The equestrian side was fulfilled by the children's ponies and of course David's hunters, two of which, *Transportation* and *Twelfth Night* were passed on to him by his father-in-law. Mary Marsh was employed as a groom and, by the time she came to leave, also had a good working knowledge of both hens and pigs.

Having settled in Sussex, the sight of the South Downs rising from the wooded weald, vaguely redolent of Mull, awoke his instincts as a country-man and for the chase. So he was soon regularly hunting with the Southdown Hunt, the pack made famous by Siegfried Sassoon in the first of his trilogy, *Memoirs of a Fox-Hunting Man*. On these hills enough of the gorses, banks and old turf survived the wartime ploughing to carry the romance of history. Wild remote places remained, not yet beginning to sink under the encroachment of Brighton and the coastal towns.

His first conveyance was *Transportation*, a thoroughbred grey horse bred by Lord Digby for racing, who turned out too big and so was given a home with David. He arrived in the dead of night by what was still the normal way of moving horses about: in a train at Haywards Heath station. Ron Topson, whose agricultural experience had not yet reached horses, was sent to the station and, with trepidation, he went into the railway horse-box, quite unsure of what he was to find or what to do with it when he had identified it. Fortunately the grey gave off a small glow in the dark, enough to be located and, being a gentleman who had had enough of the journey, pre-sented the right end to Ron. With great relief he was led on to the sidings ramp and home. *Transportation* and David had the same basic attitude to the hunting field – which David had clearly inherited from his mother – that one should always be going forward wherever possible and the larger and hairier the obstacles in the way the better. He had always been attracted by the competitive element in hunting, more than the venery, and relished the sheer challenge of riding a horse across big, and sometimes dangerous, country. Even so his one and only equestrian triumph was as a schoolboy back in 1935 when he won the gentleman's side-saddle competition at the Grafton Hunter Trials, clad in his mother's best habit.

Later on, after he had become a prospective candidate, he was involved in an incident out hunting when a fox went to ground on Brighton Corporation property. At the request of the tenant farmer it was dug out and despatched with a humane killer before the carcass was thrown to the hounds. The sit-ting Conservative Member of Parliament, Howard Johnson, whom David was to replace in due course, was walking on the Downs with Donald

David and Robert, *his 'Huskador'.*

Chapman, the Labour MP for Northfield and seeing this made a beeline for David, expressing his anti-hunting beliefs in no uncertain terms. He was clearly upset that his successor should have diametrically different views about what went on in the countryside to himself. In the event he whipped up the local press who published allegations that the Southdown Hunt had thrown the fox alive to the hounds. David stalwartly moved in in support of hunting both at meetings and in the Press, where the so-called rational opponents of the sport could do no better than write – sometimes anonymously which says little for the attitude of the press – 'Just read of your cruelty to a fox with members of the Southdown Hunt. You lousy, cruel, cowardly swine. You dirty skunk. I hope to God that you and the rest of the hunt fall and break your necks or die in agony.' Another nice offering was, 'It is my fervant (*sic*) desire and hope that before long you will be killed in the hunting field as a reward for your dastardly behaviour'. The incident was considered important enough to rate a leader in *The Field*.

It is a comment on the times that in David's subsequent electioneering, involving several thousand door-to-door calls and twenty-nine meetings, the subject was raised but twice and the reception to David's replies left him in no doubt as to where the sympathy of an overwhelmingly urban audience lay. After he was elected, Hollis & Carter published in 1960, *In Praise of Hunting*, which he co-edited with Wilson Stevens, the editor of *The Field*. The contributors included Reginald Paget QC, the Socialist MP; the Duke of Beaufort; Francis Pitt, an established ornithologist and lecturer on wildlife who was a Master of Foxhounds and Jimmy Edwards, the foxhunting comedian. Foxhunting was to remain the mainstay of his winter recreation so long as he lived in Sussex.

During his early time at Townings his financial situation became healthier and allowed him to become a member of Lloyds, which eventually was to underwrite the education of his children. In 1953 *Prisoner's Progress* was published in America under the name *Escaper's Progress*. To his intense pride, in October, he was summoned to Buckingham Palace to be invested with the Polar Medal, which gave him as much pleasure as his other two decorations for valour.

*   *   *

David had not got 'tall ships' out of his system and in 1955 at Easter time, he and Jaquetta set off on a pilgrimage. They went by car to see the remnants of the fleets that were still afloat and, in order to lay two ghosts at once, they went past his old POW camp at Tarmstedt. They found it looking exactly the same but somewhat less menacing, with a rustic, instead of barbed wire, fence and some excellent specimen trees planted around it. It was being used for girl refugees from behind the Iron Curtain which prompted the cynical remark that if only the Germans had put them there with him and his fellow prisoners they might have been less keen to get away. They spent the night in a largely rebuilt Hamburg and went on to Lübeck to find the *Passat* laid up, sadly looking a shambles. David persuaded a very grumpy caretaker with great difficulty to let him make a tour of inspection; needless to say he went up the foremast. He came down to complain to the caretaker that there was a crow's nest (literally) in the crosstrees. There was an explosion of fury until David produced an egg! All barriers crumbled, a bottle of schnapps was produced, and bed came rather late.

They motored via Elsinore to Hälsingborg, passing the dreaded Küllen Point where *Viking* had so nearly hit the rocks some eighteen years before, to find her lying in Gothenberg – from a distance looking in better shape than

Passat. They had stripped out all her former accommodation, which took away all the old atmosphere. On getting close, a troop of dancing girls staying in the reconstructed cabin were seen to be painting their toenails on the forehatch. This was too much for David and they left.

After staying a couple of days in Stockholm they flew on to the Aaland Islands, the home port of the Erikson fleet. After the hard winter David was thrilled to find pack-ice jammed tight against the northern coast, and old shipmates to greet him. His old captain, Captain Mörn, was having a spell ashore and he tracked down the steward to his croft; he also found the sailor with a flaming red beard – who had given the Captain a piece of his mind in East London – still painting *Pommern*'s main mast.

Tall ships remained a pre-occupation. Some months after that he went back to Denmark to take over the three-masted schooner, *Hans Eggede*, on behalf of the Outward Bound Trust's School at Burghead in Morayshire. He had been on the Outward Bound Management Committee since 1949 and was trying to arouse their interest in sail training. The take-over ceremony was simple, but moving, with the Danish flag being lowered and the blue ensign raised. In fact, from the first schnapps in the harbourmaster's office until the close of play, fourteen hours elapsed. Much of the time was devoted to lunch and innumerable toasts and David's speech in Danish, which was broadcast. He had written it in English; his Danish friends translated it into Danish and wrote it out phonetically. They had a race against the topsail schooner, *Peder Most* which they won – although being a fore-and-after it was not David's afternoon for going aloft. But it was a break before they rounded off the evening with yet more schnapps.

The *Hans Eggede*, whose name was changed to *Prince Louis*, was acquired by the Outward Bound Trust as a tender, but David was keen to nudge them towards deep-water sail training rather than having just a floating tender for a shore establishment. So, in 1956, he went with a fellow committee member, Captain Oram, to Cherbourg to take a trip aboard a Danish full rigger, *Danmark*. She was berthed immediately in front of the *QE2* and, on being invited on board the *QE2* for drinks, they found it humiliating to see that the *QE2*'s bridge was appreciably higher than the main royal of *Danmark*. They crossed the channel to Weymouth, with *Prince Louis* under full sail, making about 8 knots. Both Joe Oram and David found they still had the ability to go aloft up to the main royal and then make their way out to the end of the bowsprit to see all 21 sails pulling to perfection. Sadly the trip did not achieve what they had sought since they were not able to convince their colleagues that they needed a self-contained floating Outward Bound School rather than a tender.

His interest in sailing awarded him the consolation of being appointed a Trustee of the National Maritime Museum from 1954 to 1965. It sharpened his appreciation of the historical and aesthetic aspects of what he had enjoyed on and off for so many years. Otherwise the sea knew him not, since once started in square-sail – and deep water at that – neither inshore sailing nor steam exerted the same fascination. This in no way denigrates the ocean racers or Cape Horn yachtsmen who have run risks David would never have contemplated; it is just that it is *different*. Later on, in 1976, when politics ceased to exert their grasp, he satisfied his yearning by regularly attending the Annual Congresses of the A.I.C.H. (Amicale Internationale Cap Hourniers).

The Outward Bound Trust was set up to provide, for boys from all walks of life between the ages of 16 and 19, short term character training courses both on land and sea. Schools had been set up to achieve this as far apart as London, Germany, Malaya, Kenya and West Africa. When David was appointed to the Executive Committee in 1954 he was the youngest member to serve. In 1957 Routledge Kegan & Paul published a book of articles by distinguished people with interests in the development of the Trust, edited by David, much on the lines that he had edited *Wavy Navy*. Among the contributors were Kurt Hahn who had founded Gordonstoun; Spencer Summers, a steel industrialist MP from Wales; Alan Villiers DSC, who had served in the RNVR and square-rigged ships, and taken the replica *Mayflower* to the USA in 1957; Field Marshal Sir Gerald Templer, the CIGS, and Earl Mountbatten, the First Sea Lord.

*   *   *

One of the most fateful encounters of his time on the Council of the Trust was crossing paths with Victor Feather*. David had arranged for the *Danmark* to call at Dover and take a group of Council Members out for a day trip. Among those who came was Feather, Assistant Secretary of the TUC and their representative on the Trust. He and David took to each other and, incongruously, had a long chat on the forecastle head about the creeping penetration of Communism into some trade unions. Before leaving the ship they exchanged addresses and Feather promised to send him a copy of his booklet, *How do the Communists Work?*, which he had published in 1953.

David was a committee member of Common Cause, a non-party organisation that sought to oppose totalitarianism in all forms, but particularly Communism, which at that time presented the principle threat. He became chairman in 1957 and dropped Feather a line to say that Common Cause would always be at his service. The response was remarkably quick; within days Feather rang up and asked if he could call on David in his office. His call was as urgent as his voice sounded during the subsequent meeting. He was clearly desperately worried about the way affairs were going in the ETU, where the Communists under Foulkes and Haxell[†], by ballot-rigging and

---

* Trade union leader who became General Secretary of the TUC in 1969. He was created a Life Peer in 1974.

[†] Frank Foulkes was the Communist President of the ETU and Frank Haxell its Communist Secretary. They were found guilty of ballot-rigging in 1961.

other devices, were rapidly getting a stronghold which, according to Feather, could put the whole of British industry at peril.

In his experience there was only one man who had the stature and toughness to thwart their designs and that was Les Cannon, an ex-Communist who had seen the light as a result of the Russian invasion of Hungary in the previous year. Times were not easy for Cannon. He had lost his job as head of the ETU Educational Centre and was making a living at his trade, which limited his ability to travel, speak and organise. It was having a serious effect on his family life for both reasons of morale and money. Feather was determined to sustain Cannon and enable him to continue his fight. This meant underwriting Les Cannon's domestic life, which was the real reason for his approach. David gave Feather and Cannon lunch at the Travellers' Club, liked what he saw and promised help. He approached people he knew in business and organised a weekly subsistence allowance of £10 a week, – a not inconsiderable sum for those days – to underwrite the Cannon domestic budget. This was paid to Mrs Cannon via a solicitor's account and David's farm account. Victor Feather's biography, published in 1973, was to state 'it was neither the only nor the biggest outside contribution to the campaign, but it came at a critical moment. The payments continued for about eighteen months.'

David took no further part in this battle but was delighted when, in 1961, Foulkes and Haxell lost their case in the High Court and disappeared from public gaze forever. Being an ardent anti-Communist, David took the greatest pleasure in having this small walk-on part in the Communist Party's biggest set-back since the war's end. Later on, at Les Cannon's death in 1970, Vic Feather wrote to David:

'It was very good of you to write about Les Cannon He always appreciated, as I do, the very valuable and practical assistance which you provided at a very difficult time – which in fact became historic so far as the union was concerned'.

This incident was later to have repercussions on David's political life.

As the decade rolled on he achieved his over-riding ambition, which was to be adopted as a Conservative candidate. In September 1957, the Kemptown Division, Brighton obliged, after an outspoken adoption speech. This was in the face of considerable opposition, mainly stimulated by the Labour side, for being a Roman Catholic, from his predecessor who closed ranks with the Labour candidate in condemning his field sports activities, and for being educated at Eton. David countered this by defending Eton to the hilt, and the record of so many Etonians over the years, but agreed that there were some bad old Etonians; for example the Labour ministers Dalton and Strachey. From there on his main pre-occupation was nursing his constituency and making preparations for his political career.

◉ *Meanwhile what had been happening to Torosay? While the recently married James's were concentrating on moving into Townings, the first of two strokes of luck struck which were to bring Torosay back to life.*

It transpired that the inhabitants of Soay, an island off the west coast of Skye had decided that all that was left for them was to evacuate the island. Their living was at stake on such an infertile island, exacerbated by the decline of their mainstay, the lobster population. The school was closing, there was no medical attention and regular ferry services were to be withdrawn. Their misfortune, however, was Torosay's gain, and a getting together of the Scottish Department of Agriculture in Edinburgh with Bridget resulted in the purchase of Java Lodge and 200 acres as a haven for the 27 dispossessed islanders. They were welcomed to their new home at Craignure by Lord Home, the Secretary of State for Scotland, in 1953 and the proceeds enabled the Millers to take up permanent residence in the Castle.

The money was used firstly to make Torosay habitable by concentrating on their living quarters in the west end. The 'lairds suite', which Olive Guthrie had continued to live in on the ground floor, was turned into a manageable kitchen, leading into a reasonably sized dining room, which in turn led through to the existing unchanged light and spacious drawing room. Above this, on the first floor, was a self-contained suite of two rooms and a bathroom which were independent from the rest of the first floor bedrooms. The main landing, off which were the principal bedrooms which had all been given washbasins during David's short life as an hotel manager, were opened for visitors during the summer months and the stalking season.

Things looked quite settled when this was completed in 1953, but in 1954, when Geoffrey and Bridget had taken up residence, they realised that in spite of their attempts to make good the roof after the war, there was still a pervading problem of damp. Twenty or more containers, varying in size from sardine tins to saucepans, were installed in the attics and the old staff bedrooms, to catch the drips and a daily routine of emptying them had to be set up. As Geoffrey had morosely declared a few years before when the hotel was advertised with 'running water', it did not specifically state that most of the water was running down the walls. A report now declared unequivocally that the roof was 'nail sick'. Thus the voracious jaws of decay opened their mouths once again and further sales of the estate were looked for to satisfy the hungry monster.

The farm, lying between Loch Don and Duart Castle on the Gorten peninsular, found a happy home with Nina Porter who, with her doctor husband, an ardent fisherman, became welcome neighbours and firm friends. Their daughter, Sylvia, struck by the island's magic, recorded it on canvas to the perpetual joy of those lucky enough to own one of her pictures. Other plots of ground were sold, such as a site on Druim Mor, a grassy hill emerging out of the parkland woods to the north of the house, to the GPO as a telephone exchange. It seems quite unnecessary in retrospect to have given up the few square yards of land for such a paltry sum of £38, but on the other hand it shows how close to the bone the estate was running. It was some ten years before the re-roofing was finished, by a gang of slaters who daily visited the Castle from Oban when the weather was clement enough. It was always an unexplained mystery to guests when they heard in the morning that somebody would have to go to the boat to 'meet the slaters', and yet no new guests had arrived at the dinner table when they returned from stalking. It was only after visiting for two or three years that inquisitiveness was satisfied by daringly putting the question, 'were the Slaters coming again this year?'

The second stroke of good luck occurred in 1955 when Geoffrey, much to his surprise, inherited a considerable sum of money from his Australian second cousin, Esmé Miller. He was not close to the family, having left Australia in his youth and spent most of his life living a dilettante existence in France and Italy. This good fortune was not lost on Torosay and Geoffrey, the adopted Mulleach and Guthrie consort, proceeded to pay generously for his contentment by restoring and creating features in the gardens, not only with financial help but also with his physical effort. One of Geoffrey's sisters generously said that, although they were not included in the inheritance, they felt that Esmé surely would have approved of all that Geoffrey had used it for in restoring and enhancing such an 'historic home'.

Geoffrey went resolutely and enthusiastically about any project that he thought up, often making it harder by setting about it the longest way. But many of his visions and hopes were defeated by Mull mañana as well. Locally he became part of the wider scheme of things, being appointed a Church Warden and elected a member of the Argyll County Council. From this plank he assumed the position of Convener of Roads on Mull and soon an enthusiastic quarry man persuaded him that Mull's highway future depended on 'doing it yourself' with its own mobile crusher. Over the months and years this was seen, – like the skeleton of a dinosaur – at various roadside sites until it came to rest rusting and decaying in the site opposite Pennygowan church ruin, which over the centuries had suffered from the fairies removing its roof.

The first mark he made on the garden was to plant an arboretum of Australian eucalypts between the south fence and the Eas Mor burn – a touch of nostalgia – which flourished in the warming influence of the Gulf Stream.

Torosay was occupied and alive again. Its centenary was celebrated in 1958 by a ceilidh for the family and locals. Among them was Geordie Duncan who, with his father, had worked on the estate for four generations under Arbuthnot, Murray, Olive and Bridget Guthrie – a span of very many years. Geordie received an MBE for being a long-lasting and effective thorn on the flesh of the council and, later, David made his visit to London for the investiture, a justifiable excuse for a further party. Dancing went on to the early hours to the music of Bobby Macleod's Band and ended with a toast to the Castle.

⚜ *Torosay ended its first century holding fast to the Guthries and with the Guthries now deeply committed to the Castle.*

Back in Sussex, nursing his constituency, David gained the confidence of his Association and the electors. The Association had become bedraggled and rudderless until the advent of Councillor Sam Taylor as Chairman. He set about transforming a bankrupt and leaderless body, with the assistance of a lively young man, David Peel, the new and energetic agent. When the election was called for 8th October 1959, there was still a serious element of doubt whether the Conservative Association recovery was enough to hold the constituency.

The opposition concentrated on what they thought were David's weak links; Eton, religion and field sports – largely aided by the views of his predecessor. He was under fire for being a Catholic and pro-hunting, with Lewis Cohen, his Labour opponent – who, forsaking his Rolls Royce for his bicycle on his campaign trail – accusing him of seeking votes on religious grounds.

His manifesto was typically forthright and, among others, embraced the following points:

Dislike of all forms of extremism, Communism in particular.
Britain was not always wrong as claimed by the other side, e.g. over South Africa or Cyprus.
Opposition to the break up of family life and easier divorce.
Opposition to the state monopoly of education.
The government should attack slums, increase family allowances and improve hospitals, education and schools – where there was a poor Socialist record.
No party had a monopoly of religion but 'Marxist materialism of the Left is a threat in direct proportion to its vigilance'.

He had a tough time at the hustings with Labour hecklers from Sussex University doing their best to prevent him getting a hearing. But, after a doughty fight, he took the seat with a majority of 5,743, an increase of 500.

So he was returned to Parliament, fulfilling the last of his tutor Hubert Hartley's predictions: 'He would make a good MP with his quick, acute mind'. Thus he joined the ranks of seven of his direct forbears who sat in Westminster, amassing 131 years of parliamentary service over the previous 156 years. The most recent were his father, Archibald James; his great grandfather, John Henry James and his maternal grandfather, Murray Guthrie. Furthermore his great, great grandmother, Minnie Seymour was the adopted (some say natural) daughter of Mrs Fitzherbert, the morganatic wife of the Prince Regent, which gave him links with Brighthelmston and the Royal Pavilion, going back to the end of the eighteenth century. He was tipped by *The Sunday Times*, along with Margaret Thatcher, 'as one to be watched' and had achieved his great ambition. Everything lay in front of him.

12

WESTMINSTER:
THE WILDERNESS AND BACK

1959 *to* 1979

There never was a scandalous tale without some foundation.

RICHARD SHERIDAN (*The School for Scandal*)

DAVID SETTLED INTO PARLIAMENTARY LIFE like a duck to water and his natural companionability soon had him making himself known to newcomers
from both sides of the House. It turned out to be a distinguished intake
including Margaret Thatcher, Christopher Chattaway, Geoffrey Johnson
Smith, Jeremy Thorpe and Judith Hart. Although his feelings were akin to
those he had experienced in his first term at school, he found it exciting. He
enjoyed being part of the establishment and intended using its rules to make
his mark and to convey his ideas and beliefs – which were not always conventional. Although he was not very close to his father he was glad to
enhance his reputation with him, by following in his footsteps and con-
tributing to the continuity of service by both sides of his family.

His maiden speech – the first hurdle which comes to all newly elected
MPs – he tackled with a great deal of trepidation. Typically, while revelling
in being part of the establishment, he straight away moved from the
accepted conventions and having drawn a ballot for a member's motion,
instead of delivering a demure, short and uncontroversial speech dwelling
on the marvels of his constituency, he chose to combine the motion with his
maiden appearance. After managing a neat tribute to Prinny's Brighton – in
spite of the fact that there was not a yard of canal in the constituency – he
went on to move a motion welcoming the Bowes Committee of Enquiry Report
on Internal Waterways. He exhorted the Government to take more action as
little was recommended, in spite of the sharp deterioration in the state of the
canals. He was effusively supported by Robert Grant Ferris* who said, 'To
make a maiden speech at any time is a difficult undertaking and one which
produces the inevitable butterflies in inordinate quantities'. He went on to
stress the problems of making a speech on an unfamiliar subject which
needed much research and 'in submitting it to the House in such a convincing way is almost unique in our parliamentary history. I congratulate my

---

* Robert Grant Ferris MP was a member of a leading English Roman Catholic family – a hunting squirearchy to whom politics were a duty rather than a career. He was created Lord
Harrington in 1974.

Hon. Friend – whose great qualities I have had abundant chance to appreciate in private life – very much indeed upon the fine speech which he has made.' Canals were to be the subject of his own maiden speech when he was elevated to the peerage in 1974. David received compliments also from outside the House. Peter Scott wrote 'However the Government may stall, the debate must have shaken them'. The Press gauged the speech, 'a huge success including charm, information, form, erudition and history, leavened with pastoral and comical asides (but not too much)'.

During the summer of 1960, having found his feet in Westminster, he used his influence as an MP to forward his ambitions for sail-training for the young which he had tried to launch through the Outward Bound Trust. This had not gone as he wanted it so he convened a meeting in the House of like-minded people, which stimulated the creation of the Sail Training Association. Sadly his later illness put paid to him being of further service to the cause, but he was proud to have given the movement its initial boost.

The 'new boy' period was quite behind him by the end of the summer recess. But in October, after his Mull holiday, he was dealt a bitter blow – he was struck down with cerebral meningococcal encephalitis. This was the first really frightening set-back he had experienced; illness of this magnitude was an adventure that had never come his way. His temperature rose to 104° and he became delirious. Jaquetta nursed him at home but the retreat of meningitis led to a post-viral depression, accompanied by disturbing illusions, panic attacks and phobias. The main illusion that kept recurring was that he had murdered one of his ship-mates by failing to rescue him from the water when taken prisoner of war and that he should go to the police station to give himself up. Jaquetta, who had bravely nursed him through the meningitis at home, had the added burden of standing by and steering him through the uncharted maze of mental ill health, and encouraging him to seek specialist help. After a fort-night or so of treatment by sedation in a London hospital, he returned home for Christmas, after which his specialist persuaded him to have ECT (electroconvulsive therapy) with its so often miraculous results. It was common knowledge that he had been ill but the seriousness and the mental side of the illness was known only to a few, including his constituency chairman Sam Taylor, who gave his unstinting support with the 'cover-up'. David, in retrospect, referred to 'the agonies of a post-viral depression' being alleviated by 'the blessed relief of electroconvulsive therapy'.

As a consequence 1961 did not start with hopes as high as expected, but he was given the 'green light' by the doctors and gradually got back to work, subject to a 10 p.m. curfew for six months. By then the Whips had been made aware of the position and showed their understanding. While he had emerged from his illness with his spirits seemingly undaunted, it clearly started to take its toll on his physical stamina, and imperceptibly began to cloud his judgement as he advanced into middle age. He was lucky to come out of such an appalling illness alive – and as it turned out with no recurrence in the years to come, against the doctors' prediction. However, his head was noticeably more susceptible to alcohol and by 1971, when Jaquetta noticed deterioration after merely drinking barley-water, an allergy to barley was confirmed; this he largely resolved by switching from grain to the grape.

To all intents and purposes his recovery was complete by the autumn visit to Mull and the Torosay Game Book shows he was back to his physical form on the hill; stalking the author into his first Mull stag in August. Each time he went back, he found the gardens taking the old familiar pre-war shape. His mother and stepfather, by dint of hard work, were taming banks and crumbling walls of undergrowth and brambles, opening up pathways, clearing streams and even planting afresh in the borders round the terraces of the castle – as well as shrubs and trees in the domain.

Probably the greatest event in 1960 was to welcome Mull into the twentieth century with the inauguration of a grass runway 'airport' at Salen. Duncan Campbell, a local farmer, on being given a 'promotional' ride in a small single-engined plane, commented, 'I canna' see the sense. You'll no get many sheep in these things'. The adjacent hotel saw great riches ahead and the Roads Department, presumably under the guidance of its convener Geoffrey Miller, constructed the only quarter of a mile stretch of dual carriageway on the island by the entrance of the hotel and the airfield; it remains 'unimproved' to this day. A scheduled service was inaugurated by Loganair, and the Royal Bank of Scotland appeared weekly with its flying bank. The hotel chickens soon took possession of the fire engine and the sheep continued to graze undisturbed except by the scheduled arrivals. These have become less frequent over the years, to leave the access to Mull fundamentally and rightfully in the hands of the almighty McBraynes.

By the end of 1961 David was back in his stride in the House and found himself Vice-Chairman of the Labour Committee and Secretary of the Foreign Affairs Committee of Conservative backbenchers. These were the first steps on the lower rungs of the political ladder.

On the domestic front, at Townings, Jaquetta was delighted to welcome Birgetta Mörn, the daughter of David's captain of the *Viking* – conceived when David was on *Viking*. She had come over to stay with them for a year to learn English and, in return, helping with the burgeoning problem of the children. She was followed by Britt-Marie, the daughter of Borje Borenius, the leading seaman of David's watch. Their charm and the way that they fitted in with the family so easily invoked in David a feeling of nostalgia, such a poignant feature of all sail-going seamen.

*   *   *

His parliamentary career was proceeding more or less conventionally, when in 1961 David was approached by two well-known naturalists, Richard Fitter, who was on the Council of the Fauna Preservation Society, and Peter Scott*, appealing for his help in promoting, at Westminster, a serious investigation into the Loch Ness phenomena. David declined, telling them that he entered the House to make a reputation and not to destroy one. They both lent heavily on him and persuaded him to read Constance Whyte's book *More than a Legend* before making his decision. He reluctantly agreed to do so with much cynicism, caused by the rash of mysterious sightings following the construction of the new loch-side road in 1933–4 and extravagently reported by the media. David found her book – based on careful cross-examination and analysis of eye-witness accounts – persuasive. He stayed at the guest house of the Benedictine Abbey at Fort Augustus for a few days and took the trouble to meet some of the people who had sighted the 'monster' recently, finding them all to be surprisingly convincing. From this point he became sufficiently intrigued to encapsulate all the evidence to date and present it in an article in the Christmas issue of *The Field* in 1961. In this he questioned how one could doubt the veracity of 3,000 people, coming from all walks of life, and brand them all as fools or liars.

The outcome was that his sense of romantic adventure and exploration – coupled with curiosity – persuaded him to take a lead with Constance Whyte, Richard Fitter and Peter Scott in forming the Loch Ness Phenomena Investigation Bureau. Among the independent enthusiasts scanning the loch at the time was Tim Dinsdale who shot some remarkable footage of a sighting he had in April 1960, the first motion film of a sighting. He was hoping to show it to scientists privately but the Press got hold of it in advance, much to his disappointment, and the BBC showed it on their *Panorama* programme. At about the same time Dr Denys Tucker, a Principal Scientific Officer at the British Museum (Natural History), and a team of thirty Oxford and Cambridge graduates embarked on a scientific survey of fish in Loch Ness to try and determine whether it was ecologically capable of supporting a colony of large animals. Tucker himself had championed the cause for some years but when he told the authorities he was going to do this as a holiday task he was immediately warned off by his principals. But the survey went ahead under the command of a graduate, Peter Baker, who was eventually to become a professor of zoology at Exeter. It seemed to David

---

* Sir Peter Scott CBE DSO 1908–89 was the son of Scott of the Antarctic. He had served in the RNVR Coastal Forces with David. Wildfowler, painter, Olympic yachtsman, he became Vice-President of the World Wildlife Fund and was the founder of the Severn Wildlife Trust.

that it was 'quite evident that a massive case was going by default, simply because the already available evidence had not been sufficiently widely disseminated, particularly to those people who are best qualified to form a judgement, namely the professional zoologists'.

In April 1961, in face of complete indifference from the British Museum (Natural History), a meeting was convened under the chairmanship of Peter Scott at Burlington House. It was attended by five leading biologists from Oxford and Cambridge universities and the London Zoo who took the available evidence and recommended there was a prima-facie case for investigation, worthy of consideration by the Royal Society. Nothing could happen because there were no funds. But it was enough for David to get the bit between his teeth and in March 1962 the Bureau for Investigating the Loch Ness Monster Phenomena Limited was formally incorporated as a charity, the directors being David James, Constance Whyte, Peter Scott and Richard Fitter. It was to act as a clearing house for information, as well as promoting active research; in the unlikely occurrence of any profits arising, these were to go to the World Wildlife Fund and the Council for Nature.

The next move followed David's persuasive enthusiasm at a lunch with the directors of Associated Television (ATV). Norman Collins,* a pioneer of television, was Deputy Chairman and offered to pay for some active research. Following David's hunch that the species may well be nocturnal, he paid for the installation and manning of two searchlights – with a range of six miles – loaned by the War Office, to operate on the loch every night for a fortnight in October 1962. This effort added only one sighting to the list, with the RAF's Central Reconaissance Establishment verifying that about eight feet of something was visible and it 'was not a wave effect but that it had some solidarity, is dark in tone and glistens'.

To view the evidence which was consistently trickling in, an independent committee was set up, chaired by Adrian Head, a barrister who subsequently became a judge. It consisted of a marine biologist and two naturalists (including the author) none of whom were connected with the Bureau. Their task was to consider the mass of sightings in the past but in particular to concentrate on those of the last eighteen months. The committee's findings were 'that there is some unidentified animate object in Loch Ness which if it be a mammal, amphibian, reptile, fish or mollusc of any known order is of such a size as to be worthy of careful scientific examination and identification'. ATV then ran a twenty-minute programme entitled, *Report on the Loch Ness Monster*. It had little impact on the public or Press other than the *Inverness Courier* which headlined, 'There is a Monster in Loch Ness – Expeditions findings accepted by experts – Highlanders vindicated'. This is just what the Bureau had hoped for, but the timing was unfortunate and the story was swamped by more world-shaking news – the Cuban missile crisis.

* Norman Collins, author of *London Belongs to Me*. He was Controller of BBC TV after the war, before moving to Independent TV.

But the concept of an annual expedition grew and a permanent site was established at Achnahannet in 1965. From May to October cover was maintained from two camera sites, each consisting of a 35mm cine with a 36in lens and two still cameras with 20in lenses. By then Norman Collins had become chairman of the Bureau and ATV supplied both financial and practical help.

Up to now David's enthusiasm had not conflicted with his day-to-day work as a politician and slotted in easily on a trip from London to Mull. It satisfied his enjoyment of *bonhomie* among people from all walks of life and echoed his days of exploration. As a Council member of the Outward Bound Trust his aims dovetailed into those he was incidentally achieving with the Bureau. It provided opportunities for the young, or people of slender means, to indulge in a healthy expedition fantasy with the supreme prize of perhaps being 'the one to see it'.

It was such a background that prompted Nicholas Witchell, as a schoolboy, to set off for the Highlands. Having been entranced by the subject as a boy and made it a school project for which he got a minor prize; nothing more happened,

> until I was 16 and looking for somewhere to spend the summer camping holiday with two school friends. I remembered Loch Ness and suggested it; my friends agreed. It would not simply be a camping holiday we decided but an expedition – so I wrote off to every local company I could think of to try and enlist some sponsorship. Several months and one much-prized crate of baked beans later we found ourselves in a field a few miles south of the loch-side village of Dores. For two weeks I watched obsessively, saw absolutely nothing but began to talk to some of the people who lived their lives by the loch. It was these straightforward accounts of eyewitnesses, most especially the local farmers, who were set apart from the tourist industry, which persuaded me that the Loch Ness story was more than a mirage.
>
> In 1972 during a year off between school and university I took myself back to Loch Ness and built a wooden hut high in a field overlooking Urquhart Castle and the bay beside it. I lived alone in it for five months. I had a large 35mm cine camera and a powerful telephoto lens loaned to me by the Loch Ness Investigation Bureau and a still camera and lens of my own.

Just like David a decade before, something urged him to take up the cudgels to try and get a proper inquiry established, and he was to write in his book:

> 'No men took up the challenge with greater vigour in the 60s and 70s than David James and Tim Dinsdale. David it was who cajoled his naval and exploring chums to join his fledgling Investigation Bureau and spend their summer holidays keeping watch on the surface of the loch. It was slightly eccentric and extremely British: an adventure that was shared by baronets in their country tweeds who had once done wartime watches with David aboard Royal Navy motor torpedo boats and young people

who were only too eager in the 60s to rub up against the accepted wisdoms of the day and if possible to stick a large pin in them. Loch Ness was a lark but with a serious purpose, spearheaded by a resourceful group of enthusiasts for whom half the fun was conjuring up experiments with a minimum of equipment. At their head was David James, a man who had marched out of a German prison camp in a celebrated wartime escape, who had explored some of the least welcoming corners of the globe on foot and by sailing ship and when those adventures had run out had gone into Parliament and in search of a legend.

One of David's eccentric Irish cousins – also a cousin to Winston Churchill – who had settled in Mull, also got himself in on the act. Lionel Leslie, brother of the equally eccentric baronet Sir Shane Leslie, had walked through the Himalayas, across north-east Burma and into China in the 1920s before getting a commission in the Queens Own Cameron Highlanders and serving for four years in India. He then moved on to live with the Masai in Kenya for a year on his way to join an expedition in Labrador. He was stopped from joining the Foreign Legion in Morocco by malaria, so ended up living in an artist's garret in Paris, studying sculpture. After serving with his old regiment in the 1939 war, he finally settled with his wife at Grass Point on Mull to write poetry, sculpt and serve teas to tourists on boat trips from Oban – while regaling them with his tales.

The Loch Ness Investigation: *the expedition headquarters at Achnahannet.*

1964 was the year of David's bitter parliamentary defeat, described later in this chapter. The existence of the Loch Ness enterprise gave him a place to nurse his wounds and employ his energies while trying to rectify the injustices of politics.

But in 1965 and 1966 the sun shone on the Loch Ness project. David submitted Tim Dinsdale's film for evaluation to the RAF's Joint Air Reconnaissance and Intelligence Centre (JARIC), which was an internationally respected photographic and film analytical authority. Their analyses gave authority to the interpretation of photographs and confirmed the respectability of the exploration. Also an inquisitive American tourist was found hanging around the expedition headquarters for several days, asking more intelligent questions than usual, so the leader at the time referred him to David in London. He turned out to be Professor Roy Mackal, a Research Professor of Biochemistry at the University of Chicago who had independently decided there was something unusual in Loch Ness and felt that the Bureau was exactly the instrument he was looking for to try to solve the mystery. He was quickly co-opted on to the Board and returned to the USA to try and raise funds. Much to his surprise, for all the wealth in Chicago and his standing in the academic world, he had door after door slammed in his face, which did not surprise his English partners who were quite used to that sort of treatment. At his

Loch Ness: *David and Jaquetta watching filming at Achnahannet.*

The camera platform.

request, with the approval and support of Norman Collins, David went over and addressed the Chicago Adventurers Club whose remit was to mount field expeditions all over the world. He extracted from them a welcome $5,000, as well as more than welcome volunteers.

The permanent camp and the display there were now attracting paying visitors – rising from 1,000 to 25,000 in a single year – and in 1967 the interest with the public grew to such an extent that the Highlands and Islands Development Board produced a grant of £1,000 in recognition of the services to the Tourist Industry in Scotland. This was followed by a superb donation of $20,000 from Field Enterprises Educational Corporation of Chicago, who published the *World Book Encyclopedia*. This meant that, at its peak, the expedition's equipment had risen to twelve caravans based at Achnahannet and five Bedford vans, painted to a uniform colour, which patrolled the loch ensuring seventy per cent coverage of the surface. All the camera equipment had been upgraded accordingly. Sightings recorded on camera were sent for interpretation to JARIC who sadly were never able to reach a firm interpretation, for example:

no definite statement can be made on the origin of these disturbed areas, although the statement made by Mr James that no shipping had been in the area certainly leads one to the possibility of a solid object breaking the water's surface. The combination of relatively long-range and low-resolution colour film makes detailed interpretation impossible.

On the film can be seen a wash and wake pattern not obviously associated with any surface object. It is not possible to detect the shape or nature of the object causing the disturbance, though varying optical enlargements up to ×38 have been used. From time to time there is an impression of some object at the head of the disturbance as if the object was momentarily breaking the surface though mainly submerged.

The third sequence shows something like a vertical head and neck leaving the water and leaving a V-shaped wake; on the evidence it seems unlikely to be a bird but no suggestions can be offered of a suitable alternative solution.

In 1968 the way was clear for David to enter politics again and the running of the Bureau largely passed out of his hands. Field Enterprises sponsored a large expedition in 1979, including a mini-submarine and sonar search, which was unfortunately rocked by a hoax. Also Vickers Oceanic *Pisces* submersible was undergoing trials in the loch and made unidentified sonar contacts. Regrettably a Walt Disney film crew arrived that year to make a semi-serious production, *Man, Mysteries and Monsters*, which did nothing to elevate the debate.

By 1970, with David back in Parliament, Tim Dinsdale had taken over directing the surface watching at Loch Ness with Bob Love in charge of the underwater scanning. David, of course, continued a non-executive interest in the activity he had helped to launch. But the Bureau was wound up for lack of funds following their inability to get planning permission to remain on the site. Nevertheless enthusiasts of some stature kept the search alive as is so ably set out in Nicholas Witchell's book, *The Loch Ness Story*. No one has yet succeeded in proving that Nessie does exist but, at least, by the early 1990s the zoologists from institutions such as the Natural History Museum had climbed down from their ivory towers and joined a privately funded research project called Project Urquhart to gather information about the biology of the loch. At long last the objective which David and others set in the sixties, for the loch to be taken seriously by professional scientists, is starting to be realised in the nineties.

Put into perspective, this episode of David's life cannot be seen to be the obsession it was portrayed to be by some of his political contemporaries as the reason for his lack of parliamentary preferment. Rather, it was just a continuation of a life which embraced curiosity, adventure, enjoyment of the out of the ordinary, and companionship which coincided with a period giving his mind relief from the more distressing aspects when he was cast out in 1964. It was then that he became most active at Loch Ness which gave way to serious politics when he was re-elected in 1970. Surely it is plain to see that this interest was not enough to turn away the Conservative voters of North Dorset from selecting him as their candidate in 1968.

Elspeth Huxley* when she was writing the biography of Peter Scott perceptively wrote to Jaquetta saying:

> I didn't know that Peter and your husband knew each other in the Navy in the war and that it was Peter who first involved him in Nessie. Both of them were very brave to come out in the open as they did, knowing that ridicule would follow. This may well have damaged your husband's chances of holding office, though his independence of mind might also have been an impediment.

*   *   *

In the context of the early sixties, the Loch Ness Monster enterprise seemed little more out of the ordinary for an MP than Edward Heath racing his ocean-going yachts. David's career was progressing well; so much so that he was noticed by the BBC and selected to be a victim of *This is Your Life*. One February morning, arriving at Victoria Station on the 8.54 from Haywards Heath, he was accosted at the barrier by Eamon Andrews and reacted with a deleted expletive. On the show that evening Eamon introduced him as a 'walking adventure story' and confronted him with a gathering of characters from his earlier life. Outside his family, they included, Archie McColl, the retired Torosay stalker; Captain Uno Mørn of the *Viking*; John Barker, an able seaman who was one of the crew of the MGB when it was sunk; John Wells, a civilian master tailor who became Lord Mayor of Westminster, who sewed on his Bulgarian Navy shoulder flashes in prison camp; and Paul Shädrich the German policeman who recaptured him at Lübeck. The programme was signed off by Eamon Andrews in the language of the time:

> David James, this book salutes a vivid figure of the present era whose zestful spirit recalls the gay (*sic*) adventures of the past and sets a bright example to those whose future lies in the New Elizabethan Age.

His political life continued smoothly with the Whitsun recess spent on a parliamentary delegation to Spain. He had not been there since before the war when, with his father, he was targeted and shot at by both sides. Parliamentary affairs were over-shadowed by the long drawn out agony of the Profumo Affair which emotionally scarred many MPs, particularly on the Conservative benches – not least David as he and John Profumo had been at Oxford together. It led to the resignation of Macmillan and the appointment of Alec Douglas-Home of whom David was a devoted follower. Macmillan had been struck down with prostate trouble during the party

---

* Elspeth Huxley CBE, Kenyan born novelist, author of *The Flame Trees of Thika*.

conference in October and sent a message via Douglas-Home, to say he could not carry the burden into the next election. Douglas-Home was chosen by the Party and reluctantly gave up his peerage and the Foreign Office and bravely set about winning back Conservative morale, knowing he had only a year before the next election. He was found a constituency in Scotland and David went up to help and to heckle Willie Rushton who was standing against him as an independent in what Douglas-Home described as 'A campaign which was turned into an unprecedented circus by the multitude of journalists who had joined the caravan . . .'.

Soon after this David found himself in the same train compartment as Harold Macmillan on their way to a Summer Fields reunion. Conversationally he asked Macmillan what he considered was the most desperate moment in his life. Macmillan replied that it was when he was in King Edward VII Hospital for Officers 'and two men in white coats came in and removed the scrambler phone from under my bed'.

*　　*　　*

In 1964 Bridget and Geoffrey decided to convert the pantries, kitchens and serving quarters at the east end of Torosay Castle into a more compact and comfortable 'semi detached residence' with its own front door. So the opportunity was taken, with the rare occurrence of having contractors on the island building the long awaited pier at Craignure, to create Little Torosay. While being separate, it was still part of the castle and was to be their home for the rest of their lives. The main part of the castle was now lived in only during the summer months and the stalking season. To help recoup expenses the sleeping quarters that Bridget and Geoffrey had vacated were let off to visitors as the West End Flat, as were the Garden Flat leading from the lower ground floor on to the terraces and other estate cottages. Something of the old pre-war atmosphere was returning, with the children enjoying the glorious surroundings for their summer holidays, and David generously including many of his friends and relations in the autumn's sporting activities.

As the years went by – while David did not see the end of his political career as imminent – he was beginning to realise more and more strongly that Torosay would be the home in which he would end his days.

Political life went on its way but pressure increased with the run-up to an election. His trip of the year was in the interest of forwarding East-West relationships in view of the efforts Khrushchev was seeming to make to dismantle the Cold War. He joined an all-party delegation to Moscow, which including Denis Healey. He felt he had travelled in time rather than space when he observed the Edwardian bourgeois décor of the TU 124 jet and the brass knobs and antimacassars of the Metropole Hotel. David rubbed shoulders with Ilya Ehrenburg, the revolutionary writer and, much to his delight, a visit to the Bolshoi Ballet was arranged to see the *Sleeping Beauty*.

October was to become the turning point in David's career when all his hopes were to be dashed by electoral defeat. Nevertheless he hung on obstinately and grimly till he was adopted again in 1968; but his ambitions had been shattered and his heart and mind were really beginning to yearn for his home, Torosay.

*   *   *

Before recounting the drama of October 1964, the state of the Kemptown Division over the years leading up to the election needs to be described. It will then be seen that David could hardly be said to have gone into the fray with the support of a firm organisation behind him. When he was adopted the Association had been through a series of crises in a matter of months, getting through three chairmen and two agents, as well as leaving itself bankrupt. Sam Taylor was then appointed Chairman and when his term had run its course, he left an election-winning machine with a well earned MBE. Sadly internal bickering returned within twelve months, so unfortunately the rot was not out of the system. With the departure of the much liked agent, David Peel, for health reasons, David's only consistent contact with the Division was through its President, Harold Myerscough. He took every precaution not to take sides in the ceaseless rows within the Executive Committee.

Around the time of the election, a new area agent, Arthur Banks, appeared on the horizon. The constituency itself still lacked adequate structure; in David's view there was a shortage of 'officers'. Those members who commuted to London lacked any sense of local involvement, but there was a magnificent band of 'NCOs' who had local commitment but, unfortunately, did not often see eye to eye with each other. He identified some Conservative trade unionists as his most stalwart allies.

As was bound to happen, dissatisfaction spread to such a degree that Sam Taylor – now an active vice-president – faced up to the area chairman, the Hon. Mrs Sylvia Fletcher-Moulton at a Disraeli Club cocktail party and pointed out that the absence of the agent and other important constituency officers at the party was symptomatic of the inertia and the general state of affairs within the Division. Unless drastic changes were made the constituency could well be lost by the Tories. This not unnaturally got back to Arthur Banks, the area agent, who from then on set his hand against Sam Taylor and, as it turned out, apparently David. Banks persuaded the area chairman to call on David to deliver his complaint about poor Sam Taylor, in particular that he was driving out the constituency agent, who by then had had enough and had decided to leave for more congenial employment. Then Banks followed up with a call to David to tell him that he was about to lose his agent through the capacity for intrigue and disloyalty of Sam Taylor, 'the wickedest man he had ever met'. David, having been on holiday, was quite unaware of the background of this outburst and vigorously rebutted his implications. But Banks would not accept that after six years in the constituency David might be a better judge than he after merely two or three flying visits.

Regrettably it seemed that the Division's affairs had reverted to the back-biting and chaos they were in before Sam Taylor pulled them together in 1957. An emergency meeting of the Executive was called to appoint a new agent, without the Chairman – and more significantly without David who was held up in London by a parliamentary whip. Banks took the lead, and untruthfully saying there were no alternatives, steam-rollered the Executive to appoint a Donald Arthur as agent without disclosing any of his known defects. These defects included the fact that he failed to be accepted as a Conservative candidate (and subsequently was found to hold a grudge about it), and that he had a record for drinking which had showed up during his appointment as a temporary assistant agent at the Orpington by-election in 1959, which the Conservatives lost to the Liberals. Banks called on David in his London office the day after the meeting to inform him of the appointment, emphasising that Arthur had been only seconded to the Division by Central Office, who were to pay him for the period up to the election – again giving David no inkling of his unsatisfactory past. It was a 'take it or leave it' situation and in view of the possibility of an election being called as early as March or April, David felt he had little alternative other than to accept the situation.

David took an early opportunity to invite his new agent to stay at Townings Place in April and could not but help noticing his uncouth behaviour as a guest. In particular his manners at table were appalling; he piled his plate high with mountains of food and, on being offered a cigarette from a box, took one and quite openly pocketed a further dozen. David, as was his nature gave the newcomer the benefit of the doubt, failing to deduce anything sinister. Arthur indulged in plausible conversation about his anti-Communist work for IRIS, an off-shoot of Common Cause, which David had chaired in the days he had helped Vic Feather. He projected himself as a double-agent, boasting of his Communist contacts and flaunted his expensive tastes which he claimed were invariably met by Central Office funds. He pulled the wool over David's eyes right up to the election, distracting him from firm action by deliberately making hashes of times and places of meetings. A typical example was to persuade David not to bring his father with his car on election day, on the grounds of his age and that he already had a surfeit of cars laid on. Other cars were sent away too; in fact as many as fifty from other constituencies as far away as Littlehampton were told they were not required. As it was to turn out just one more car working for Kemptown would probably have secured victory.

Then came the October 15th election and David lost the seat for the Conservatives with 22,301 votes – 12.7 per cent down, but less of a swing than adjacent constituencies. He was tantalisingly beaten by his Labour opponent, Dennis Hobden, by only seven votes after seven recounts.

In the preceding weeks David had trusted Arthur's advice to maintain his holiday arrangements to visit Mull on August 28th, breaking the holiday to come down for a mass meeting addressed by Sir Keith Joseph. He came back to the constituency for his final official engagement as an MP on 23rd September. The dissolution was on 25th September and he was adopted on the 29th. David had naively ignored warning signs and his instincts that all was not well. The Press scenting something, persistently pestered Ron Topson at the farm as to David's whereabouts, while responses emanating from Arthur could only be described as bromidic.

Once back in the constituency David's mind was completely focused on the hustings. His real ordeal started at the count when Arthur's true colours became obvious. Things started to look uncomfortable when a recount had to be called because, with Labour ahead, some 200 votes were found to be missing. On the second recount David was ahead by 25 votes which put him in. Then, to everyone's astonishment, Arthur called for a further recount.

This could have been a grave error arising from his excessive intake of alcohol; but the whole of Arthur's behaviour seems to point to his determination to ensure that David lost his seat. Whether this fundamental disloyalty sprang from some collusive bargain with Banks – who now resented David's candidacy – or from some deeper undisclosed Communist affiliation we shall never know, since both are dead. The deeply worrying question remains, if Arthur wanted to make an opening for the inclusion of a significant number of additional Labour votes, where did they come from, how had they been uncounted so far, and how did Arthur know of their existence?

The horrors then started to mount, at the end of what in retrospect had been a gruelling, single-handed campaign. The agony was drawn out from 10 p.m. to 2.40 a.m. with a total of four recounts. Arthur, getting progressively drunker and more obnoxious, abused the returning officer in front of 200 constituents, trying to hit David over the head with an empty whisky bottle, while hanging on drunkenly round his neck. He had to be forcibly evicted and taken home, and the next morning was still too far gone to reappear on the scene. This left David with no professional advice – not that Arthur's would have been of any account – but it is probable that had he had good advice from a competent agent during the first counts, when Arthur was drunk, or the last two when he was absent, the seat need not have been conceded. David had to face the final act on his own with only Jaquetta unswervingly supporting him. It seemed an age before the final recounts were completed and David had to swallow the bitter cup of defeat.

The Monday after the polling day David had seen Paul Bryan, the Vice-Chairman in charge of candidates at Central Office. He refused to accept David's offer to resign and encouraged him to apply immediately for readoption, clearly quite unaware that barriers were being erected against this. He then called on the Director General at Central Office to discuss whether to petition against the result and the agent's behaviour naturally came under discussion. The Director General agreed with David that it was best to do nothing as it was unlikely to regain the seat and Arthur's performance, if exposed to an open court, could only do harm to the Party. Then David, insisting that Banks should be present, reported on Arthur's drunkeness and inefficiency and urged that his loyalty should be probed.

These conversations were obviously considered confidential by David; he went straight off to Mull for a few days to lick his wounds. He was, therefore, shattered to get news from Brighton that Arthur was openly bruiting about this confidential meeting at Central Office, at which he, of course had not been present. He either learnt of it from somebody at Central Office – which was most improbable – or from Banks, who had decided to defend his own position by involving Arthur. David's request to the Director General for Arthur's immediate removal was totally ignored, and on his return south he found a letter from a solicitor, threatening him with a writ for defamation, purporting to be on the instructions of Arthur. Back in Brighton David was well received at the 'Disraeli Club' cocktail party – ironically planned as a victory celebration – and the question of his not being chosen again entered no one's head. David momentarily drew some crumbs of comfort.

But the next blow was not long in coming; on November 4th, at the first Divisional Executive, from which David was excluded, Banks whitewashed Arthur and no motion from the floor for David's renomination was accepted. Two letters hostile to David were read out but over a hundred in support, from people of all walks of life, were never mentioned. This meeting was followed the next day by a thoroughly mendacious report in the local press which had come plainly from a leak from Arthur. Banks, being faced with this by David, did nothing to refute it.

When the ritual dance of another Executive meeting was repeated fourteen days later, David could hardly be blamed for deciding he had had enough and that he would try elsewhere – so he submitted his resignation. This had the effect of Banks rounding on his erstwhile lackey, Arthur, and ousting him, giving rise to the obvious suspicion that once Arthur had levered David out, he had outgrown his utility. This also confirmed that Arthur was employed and answerable to Central Office, rather than to the constituency – contradicting the Party Chairman's views, expressed to David, that Arthur's conduct was a local matter, one in which Central Office could not intervene. The Conservative establishment was running for cover.

Over Christmas and the New Year there were appeals from David's supporters to make him change his mind, but he remained understandingly reluctant. However, pressure from the officers from one of the wards did induce him to re-enter the lists but he was neither short-listed nor interviewed.

Looking for relaxation he joined his mother, Bridget, in Switzerland for a skiing holiday in the hopes of recalling happier memories. Unknown to him a Divisional Executive Committee took place while he was away. Indignation over his treatment finally exploded and the Chairman had to accept resolutions placing David on the list of candidates, for consideration by the entire association. His supporters were so relieved that they naively concurred with the proposal for a meeting in February at the Dome in Brighton. Doubtless by Arthur's machinations the result was rigged by the issue of tickets to members recruited after the official cut-off date. Arthur, who was officially on sick leave, had distributed cards to former Young Conservatives from Worthing, who were identified sitting together at the back of the hall. George Cowan, of Brighton and Hove District Conservative Trade Unionists, discovered irregularities in cards issued against a list supplied by Arthur. David's ally, Sam Taylor – now a senior Vice-President – along with a senior Vice-Chairman, being alerted to the situation, tried to inspect the books in the offices but were barred by Banks, even though he had no jurisdiction to do so. Serious warnings from Harold Myerscough, the local Party Chairman, and George Cowan were sent to Edward Du Cann, the Party Chairman, who had probably arrived on the scene too late to unravel the web of intrigue.

In spite of believing the meeting to be rigged by Arthur and his cronies, David attended so as not to disappoint his supporters and thus witnessed the loss of his nomination.

He had taken legal advice which urged him to take Banks and Arthur to court on the same type of criminal conspiracy charge that had succeeded against Byrne and Haxell in the matter of communist infiltration into the ETU. He had decided against; it would not regain the seat for him and would deny his innocent successor any chance of doing so. He still hoped that, by putting the party first, the serious matters would receive proper investigation in private.

It soon became obvious to David that behind all the uncomfortable goings-on lay a smear campaign which Banks and Arthur had been nurturing for some time, with the object of getting him out. The secondary, and equally important, objective was to leave them clear of blame for any failure by placing it firmly on David's doorstep.

The lie on which the case against David rested was simple – he had neglected his constituency. While it can be convincingly demonstrated that this was not so, as a smear propagated by Arthur and then broadcast by Banks, the lie served its purpose. It was a technique lifted from the communists, whose principles and tactics were well known to David since he gave help to Victor Feather over the ETU matter, before he got into Parliament.

Sometimes the local journalist tells a franker truth, free of innuendo, than the studied comments of interested parties. Perhaps that was the case when the leader in the Brighton local newspaper, the *Argus*, in December 1964 proclaimed,

> Ever since the shock Socialist victory which ousted Mr James from his seat the local Tory party workers have sought to find a scapegoat, one man around whose neck they could hang their joint shame. It now seems clear that the scapegoat they have chosen is David James himself.

From the moment his defeat was known he has been subjected to a prolonged campaign of pinpricks, the total effect of which has been a virtual crucifixion.

Behind closed doors in Kemptown Tories met and muttered. When news of their doings reached the outside world they protested their innocence and justified their actions by explaining that they were merely following the party rule book.

Rules or no rules, however, few defeated Conservative MPs could have survived the series of snubs and humiliations which were handed to David James by his once close supporters. His only course of dignified action was to resign.

Any stick, it would appear, has been good enough for the Kemp Town Conservatives to beat Mr James with. His Loch Ness Monster trek and his fox-hunting have all counted against him in the grim days of reckoning. That the single Socialist success should have deposed one of the county's youngest and most enterprising Conservative MPs was unfortunate enough. There are other Divisions in the area where the blow could more justly have fallen. But that the Tories of Kemp Town should deliberately consolidate the fuss by their actions in the past few weeks is even more unfair to Mr James.

He has served his constituency loyally and well. His defeat was due as much to the wound down state of his party's organisation as anything else.

In November, David, trying to find another seat, received advice from Lord Margadale who had in his House of Commons days been Chairman of the 1922 Committee:

'I appreciate only too well how deeply distressed you are by this whole sordid business and can more than understand your anxiety to get it sorted out. However, I am bound to say I am absolutely certain that it is in your own best interest not to pursue it further at the moment but to seek readoption elsewhere. Once you have been successful, as I have no doubt you will be, you can then take up the whole thing very strongly with Central Office without there being any suggestion of bitterness or desire for revenge on your part. Please do not think I am trying to hush things up, I really do feel that it is in your own best interests to ignore this for the time being.'

From this the inference was that the Conservative Party did not wish to have the background to the loss of the seat bruited about in public, and that David's efforts to expose things could be neutralised by persuading him to search for another constituency. He did try for some but innuendos were being spread and he was not successful.

The campaign led to a permanent rupture with his father who heard and believed the smear which emanated from Arthur Banks on the morrow of the election result, that 'James deserved all that was coming to him since he never visited his constituency'.

Soon David was being taken to task in Pratt's Club by Selwyn Lloyd, and at the same time Jaquetta, attending the consecration of a Catholic church, was upbraided by the Bishop of Arundel and Shoreham for allowing her husband to ruin a promising political career by his slackness. For David, who had been brought up with a background of service traditions, it was as damning as being accused of 'failing to lay his ship alongside and engage the enemy'.

Before the election campaign, reports critical of David had emanated from Central Office, presumably calculated to sow the seeds for a ready explanation of a possible defeat. The first of these reports took David to the Chief Whips Office where he was reproached for constituency neglect, which he could but deny. The second was in August, when the Party Chairman was told that David only proposed to mount a one-week campaign; this resulted in a warning letter from the Chief Whip. In fact an election blueprint had been agreed the previous January, postulating a Monday as D-minus-18 for the adoption meeting, and the Royal Pavilion at Brighton had been provisionally booked for the only two possible dates.

The essence of a good whispering campaign is that the victim should be unaware of it and certainly not know its source until too late. In David's case all of the known facts strongly indicate that only a premeditated, carefully thought out and resolutely executed campaign could have led everybody whose view was relevant to believe facts precisely the opposite of those that had occurred. Had David been confronted with a direct charge it would have been possible for him to show that the rumours were as baseless as they were damaging. In the 1963–4 parliamentary session leading up to the election, David missed one Friday surgery by going up to support Alec Douglas-Home at his by-election, and another because he went to Moscow in his role as the Secretary of the Foreign Affairs Committee. After introducing Arthur in April, the only weekly surgeries he missed until the House rose in July were two trips abroad on Foreign Affairs Committee business and the Whitsun Recess. He also fitted in eight or nine branch AGMs, as well as the Divisional AGM, and, living so close to the constituency, offered his constituents a 24-hour service. Jaquetta was, of course, deeply involved in constituency affairs as Chairman of the Women's Advisory Committee and had other local charitable interests. Fifteen years later Denis Hobden, his late antagonist but now the Mayor of Brighton, confirmed to David in a letter that the damaging slur came from Conservative sources and not from the other side.

The evidence is strong that Donald Arthur lost David his seat, either by incompetence or, far more likely, by design. For whatever reason, it was enough to cause considerable embarrassment to the Party's bureaucracy and, in particular, to the area agent Arthur Banks who was clearly condoning

Arthur's shortcoming as a cover-up vital to his own reputation. Decisions were taken, without the normal consultation with the Executive Committee, which excluded David from renomination. The unanswered query is what motivated Arthur?

Arthur's background was that, coming from Wales, and having been a merchant seaman, he became a trade union convener at Cowley and turned from poacher to gamekeeper when he joined the Tory Party professionally as a probationary Trades Union Pool Organiser while taking his Agent's preliminary examinations. He was then made Trade Union Area Organiser for the South East and attempted, but failed, to get on the Conservative candidates list – which Central Office failed to disclose to Kemp Town 'as it would have been improper to do so', when they imposed him on the constituency.

In 1962 he was seconded to IRIS, the anti-Communist satellite of Common Cause at the request of Jack Tanner, the head of the AEU, to help out with the records. Soon MI5 gave them a tip-off of some sort and Arthur was dumped; Vic Feather continued to press the security services to investigate him but without success. It was here that Arthur became aware of David's role in cleaning up the ETU and was admirably placed to pass it on, if he had Communist affiliations. David's role with the ETU was originally known only to Vic Feather and the Special Branch, but it had become public in Feather's biography. In his cups, when he had become David's agent, Arthur boasted of knowing all about it and claimed to have close ties with the Communists, working for counter-intelligence.

The link between Arthur's suspected Communist connection and the result in Kemp Town becomes apparent when in the year after the election he appeared at a seminar run by the Trotskyist weekly, *The Week* – not surprisingly a little worse for drink. He also spoke at a Brighton Federation of Socialist Youth meeting, where he was credited with adding four new members to the Labour Party. During the election Arthur, against all the rules, set David up to speak at a meeting outside the constituency at Sussex University; there he became a target of the militants, who had him on their hit list.

Superimpose on this background his behaviour in abstracting at least £300 contributed to the Fighting Fund, disseminating lies about David's availability in the constituency, dissuading supporters from voting for him, and turning away cars – let alone his drunken behaviour at the polls – then a probable reason emerges for his calling for a recount with his member home and dry. May he not have been trying to earn rewards from elsewhere for his treachery?

The effect on David was a feeling of devastation, dismay and particularly anger, at the incomprehensibility of being completely deserted by 'lady luck'. Jaquetta too had her fingers crossed as she remembered the doctor's warning that his depression could be triggered off again at any stressful moment – but thankfully the ECT treatment remained effective.

He persevered like a terrier to get the matter taken seriously by Central

Office. Their embarrassment at losing Kemptown was acute and none of his erstwhile colleagues could, or would, help. Luckily he still had a job with Burns Oates to keep his mind ticking over; this also had the inestimable advantage of giving him a London base. He never stopped 'worrying the bone' – which was beginning to irritate Central Office – neither did he stop applying for constituencies. There had been little he could do but hope that Central Office would carry out an investigation as the Party Chairman had promised, or that MI5, to whom he had sent a copy of his file, would become involved. Fortunately there were challenges on the domestic front at Torosay on which he was glad to be able to spend more of his time.

He had been in the wilderness for three years when, in April 1968, a Mr Nolan, refusing to say who he was on the telephone, asked for an appointment. He turned out to be a Detective Sergeant from the Special Branch and after a three-hour interview announced that David's report had been thoroughly investigated and found correct and, among other things, Arthur had been working in collusion with the Hungarian embassy. Central Office would be informed accordingly.

It was six fraught weeks later that David found himself up before a Selection Committee for North Dorset where the very first question, predictably, was, 'had he neglected his previous constituency?' He replied that there was, of course, no truth in the allegation, which had been broadcast by a double-agent. This was an electric moment; at the request of the Chairman the area agent rang Central Office who confirmed his story and consequently he secured adoption.

It seemed to David that he was now fully vindicated but in practice this was not the case. When he returned to Westminster he had to endure many snide comments from so-called friends, invoking slackness and the Loch Ness Monster and he realised that he had left the House as a young man with a future but returned to it as an ageing man with a past.

On David's adoption, following the Special Branch report, he replaced Sir Richard Glynn, the sitting MP who was standing down. David and Jaquetta sadly sold Townings Place, after sixteen happy years of bringing the family up there – to Ron Topson's advantage, leaving him the sole tenant of the farming activity. They followed their political star and bought Malabar House in their new constituency.

Straight away they set about nursing the constituency and had little trouble in getting the confidence of the voters. David was elected, increasing the Conservative majority from 5515 to 16376, in June 1970 and rejoined the House of Commons under the leadership of Edward Heath.

On his return to politics David found high on the agenda of domestic politics was Ireland and the IRA; he decided to take an eccentric position and declared himself as a Catholic Unionist. He recalled his maternal Irish ancestory in putting forward the case which he eloquently floated during the life of the Parliament.

He made three trips to Northern Ireland during this time and was thanked in February 1972 by Edward Heath, the Prime Minister, and Reginald Maudling for a 'thoughtful' report. In November 1973 he made a speech invoking his Catholicism and pleading for the Catholic Church in Ireland, both north and south, to help lessen the tension between the two communities by making a breakthrough and relaxing the almost Victorian rigours which applied before Vatican II. Parents should be entitled to follow their consciences over marriage, education and religious upbringing.

Another sortie was with a Labour MP, Edward Milne to Swaziland and Mauritius to assess the effects of the EEC on the Commonwealth Sugar Agreement. What came out of this other than the opportunity of gaming in the casino in Swaziland is not known. The achievement he rated highest in his time as member for North Dorset was chairing the Standing Committee on the Thames Barrage and subsequently seeing it brought to fruition. During this Parliament the truth dawned on him that, while being deeply wedded to the Conservative principles, there was no chance of getting preferment, nor being offered a position in Government; at last he was a truly independent MP

After the March 1974 election when Ted Heath succumbed to Harold Wilson, David was returned with a smaller majority of 6,883 – in spite of the fact that his support went up by nearly 2,000. His political life in opposition remained just as full. While Northern Ireland remained his main pre-occupation, he sponsored a Private Member's Bill on the use of seatbelts and one to extend British Summer Time by five weeks which reached its second reading. Another matter in which he took great interest was the Public Lending Right Bill and, being on the Standing Committee, he took over A.P. Herbert's* mantle with tremendous activity behind the scenes. This Bill was to give authors the right to payments in respect of loans of their works from public libraries and David's publishing experience provided the required expertise.

On Northern Ireland he pressed the Protestants to assert their independence – his proposed solutions were tending to become more off-beat. Later in 1974 he made a substantial and much interrupted speech in the House, making the point to the Protestants that 'home rule was not Rome rule', although it might seem so to them. If Ulster were to have a degree of independence they might well find the power-sharing problems would vanish. He went on to talk of the border which he felt should be rationalised to become 100 miles shorter, with 50 fewer road crossings and pointless footpaths abolished. It would then have geographical validity as well as reflecting ethnic differences and would certainly make the security aspect easier for both Belfast and Dublin.

While his judgements may have been becoming suspect, it did not detract either from his loyalty to the Party or his personal bravery. By June or July

---

* Sir A.P. Herbert 1890–1971. Playwright, author and barrister. Independent MP for Oxford University, Chairman of Society of Authors and the British Copyright Council.

1974 he was so strongly convinced that the Conservatives would never get back to power without a change of leadership that he stuck his neck out. As usual he was patently honest and told both Edward Heath, the Party Leader, and the Chief Whip what he was about to do. He wrote to Lord Carrington, the Party Chairman, and 120 of his colleagues pressing his point, with his room-mate, Sir Julian Ridsdale helping him tally up the score.

His criticisms were based on the premise that although the policies were unquestionably right, Heath 'lacked the political sense of timing and ability to project himself on the all important TV screen to present his policies to the best advantage'. Also the Party was acquiring a hard-faced image. In talking to a broad cross-section of MPs there seemed little support for a change in Heath's leadership but there was recognition for the need for change in the style of leadership and the manner in which it was presented. This was an eerie time for David; miraculously, security held and the media got no inkling of what was going on. There were no official reactions either, as the Chief Whip had courageously decided that his office should stand aside until a credible alternative had emerged. However, David pushed his luck too far at some point and suddenly, after ten years, Kemptown was flung in his teeth and the bile rose in his throat as this everlasting political hurt was paraded again.

In 1975 David, risking his political future – and even more to the point his status in his constituency – defied the North Dorset Executive Committee, who had voted 70 to 30 in favour of Ted Heath. He voted for Margaret Thatcher to take on the leadership in the firm belief that he could, 'see no justification for a man of independent mind and without (political) personal ambitions, unless he has the guts to stick his neck out for what he profoundly believes to be in the interests of our still great country'.

Harold Wilson was replaced by Jim Callaghan in 1976. David retained his seat, but by then, his parliamentary ambitions having been shot away, his mind was progressively turning to sharing the rest of his life with Torosay, and matters political were of fading interest. He had organised a dinner of the Conservative 1959 Club, when 27 of the original 1959 intake of Tory MPs attended with Dennis and Margaret Thatcher to mark her election to the leadership of the Party. But by October 1976 he had decided he had had enough and wrote to her to say he was not going on after the next election. She replied, 'I am very sorry you will not be with us in Westminster. Since we both entered the House I have always valued your counsel and advice'. The election came in May 1979. Margaret Thatcher got home and Torosay claimed David.

13

TOROSAY – HOME AT LAST

1964 to 1986

*This is whence I came and where I ever return and my
real life's work has been restoring a semi-ruin to its
former glory, giving pleasure to thousands and bringing
jobs into the hauntingly beautiful area I love.* – DAVID JAMES

THROUGHOUT ALL THESE YEARS, David's determination was to return to Torosay, complete its reincarnation and ensure its future. His mother who owned the estate, his step-father who tenanted the home farm – and also put time and effort into regenerating the garden – and David himself who owned the house and garden made a formidable team. They were united in the objective, but not unsurprisingly at times, at loggerheads about the methods.

With the addition of Kenny MacKinnon, a partner in the Oban solicitors, D.M. MacKinnon & Co. the three became the first trustees, in 1964, of the Craignure Trust, a discretionary trust made in favour of David's four sons. Omitted from the Trust was Little Torosay which, while it remained under David's ownership, was to be Bridget and Geoffrey's home for their lifetime. Whatever course of action was to be chosen to safeguard Torosay, a long haul beckoned. The first idea pursued was an approach by Geoffrey in 1969 to the National Trust for Scotland. The negotiations ground their weary way, the core of the matter being whether the family could endow the estate with money and if so how much. David and his mother, having no further disposable funds, the ever generous Geoffrey stepped in and offered to set it up with £30,000. This was not enough, even when consideration was given to making over only the gardens to the Trust, and the negotiations grew more and more desultory until they finally broke down in 1976.

In the meanwhile Geoffrey single-mindedly went on with the garden, paying the gardener's wages – one against the pre-war strength of six. He discovered some marble pillars lying in the farm workshop, which had lain fallow since the last century when Murray Guthrie brought in the statues from Italy, and with them created a colonnade in the walled garden in 1968. The colonnade ends in a rotunda, tucked into the corner of the original wall, which houses a classical group bought by Geoffrey; it now carries his memorial plaque. He rebuilt the collapsed lower terrace in 1975 from the pile of brambles and rubble, which had become a centrally placed home for ravenous rabbits. In the face of scepticism and mild disapproval, he constructed the Japanese garden in 1980. He generously and lavishly planted in

Torosay Castle *from the Lion Terrace.*

the gardens, but his skill at siting shrubs and trees did not live up to his aspirations. However, some specimens given a home, either not too close together, nor too shady or too boggy, have grown on to contribute to the enchantment of the garden. One of the lucky survivors was the *Embothrium* planted with pride just off the statue walk in the early 1960s. Geoffrey was doing his pre-breakfast patrol to surprise the rabbits who had left the crumbling fastness of the lower terrace when early morning tea was rudely interrupted by the sound of gunfire. Geoffrey appeared for breakfast unusually dejected; he had found bigger game, in the shape of a hare, munching his

Embothrium. Bang! – the hare had survived but the *Embothrium* appeared mortally wounded. Nevertheless, with tender, loving care administered by the colonel, a misshapen *Embothrium* survived for thirty years.

In 1973 Strutt & Parker were called in by the trustees to produce a report on the future. The brief was 'to inspect the estate and to carry out a land use survey and to recommend a policy for the estate in the future'. The conclusions were general but wide ranging on the possibilities of development around Craignure and Loch Don; the use of woodlands either by leasehold or excambion* of land, involving the Forestry Commission, and the prospects of opening the house and gardens to the public. One recommendation was that before this last idea could be contemplated attention would have to be given to the structure of the house with a careful look at the woodwork, stonework, plumbing and wiring to put the castle 'in a permanent state of repair'.

After due dithering by the trustees, David intervened positively from his home in Dorset and the decision was taken to open to the public. Geoffrey, fighting a predictable rear-guard action, thought it would be a hopeless operation. While the gardens were not officially open to the public, an honesty box and sign had been up on the gate for some years saying: 'Visitors Welcome', yet they had never collected more than £30 a year! How could it be a success? With memories of previous practice, the trustees agreed that the money required to repair the roof and the gables of the castle should be found by the sale of a third tranche of land to the Forestry Commission. So three generations, grandmother, mother and son, had ensured survival by nibbling away at parts of the estate in order to save the core.

🙲 *There now was a will and determination to start the long journey to make Torosay a future home for the family by building it up as an attraction to welcome the public. From now on David's impetus in life was towards this end.*

A second report, commissioned a year later, advised the trustees 'on the physical and financial feasibility of opening Torosay Castle and gardens to the public on a commercial basis with a view to an application being made to the Highlands and Islands Development Board for financial assistance'. A detailed blueprint emerged, setting out in principle what would be needed in the way of staff facilities, attractions, alterations and marketing to get a going concern established which would meet the requirements for the HIDB to consider grant aid. The scheme called for capital costs of over £66,000, on which it was estimated an operating surplus, on the basis of 30,000 visitors a year, of just under £2,000 could be made before interest. The receipts (based on a charge of 30p admission), were estimated at £11,500 against an expenditure of £9,500, so it was a somewhat slim prospect. But with faith rather than finance, starting with sales to the Forestry Commision, and prospects of sales of sites and access for telecommunication masts, there was deemed to be enough in the pipeline to begin work.

* Scottish legal term describing exchange of lands

It was now vital to attract and retain the interest of the HIDB and so in 1975 the Council for Historic Buildings of the Scottish Development Department was inveigled to make a visit. They quickly noted that the trustees were busy making the fabric wind and watertight and structurally sound and gave signs of getting enmeshed by their unsolicited criticisms and advice. They stressed that care should be taken when repointing the stonework so that the style matched the original. They were critical of other matters such as Geoffrey leaving out some original features on the retaining terrace wall which he had rebuilt out of his own pocket. He did not receive this too kindly. Thankfully the outcome was that the report was looked upon favourably by the Scottish Building Council and the HIDB who came through with generous grants. Their grounds for doing so were that while the house represented a reasonable example of Bryce's architecture, there were many similar if less grandiose examples – but when the gardens by Lorimer were added it represented a matchless feature. They also felt it would be worthwhile in due course to include the farm square, built between 1780 and 1800 – before the house – in the restoration scheme.

David had always stuck to the line, which Strutt & Parker emphasised, that the castle, far from being the biggest drain on resources, was the principal asset, if restored and opened to the public. From then on David, from Dorset, moved faster than either his mother or step-father and stimulated, what for Mull, was instant action to get things moving. Once more the scaffolding went up, the slaters returned. the foundations were underpinned and the gable ends and tower were rebuilt.

He quickly latched on to an approach by Graham Ellis, a railway enthusiast, and entered negotiations to build a narrow gauge railway from the old 'Stevenson' pier through the policies* to a terminus at the Torosay slip. The Estate was to provide the land and access, as well as £5,000 worth of civil engineering work, while Ellis and his partners would provide stock and equipment to the tune of £20,000. With the minimum amount of hiccups, the Mull and West Highland Narrow Gauge Railway Company Ltd got under way and Scotland's first island passenger railway was opened by Chris Green, the General Manager of ScotRail, in October 1984. This $10^{1}/_{4}$ inch gauge track runs for one and a quarter miles and carries eleven Mull-built coaches, drawn by two diesel and three steam locomotives; one of these, the *Victoria* built in Sheffield, and based on the Puffing Billy Railway engines running in Australia, is the largest tank locomotive built in this gauge. The Tarmstedt passing loop is named from the narrow gauge station in Germany through which David passed on his two escapes. The contribution the railway has made to Torosay can be measured by the 25,000–30,000 passengers a year making this novel approach from the Oban ferry at Craignure to the Castle.

Alex McFadyen, who joined as gardener in 1975, was a past master in persuading the contractors who were upgrading the road from Craignure to Iona

* Scottish legal term to describe private lands belonging to a building.

past the drive gates to lend their equipment to shortcut a lot of backbreaking heavy work landscaping the gardens. The success of this was such that when the contractors finished, the trustees then persuaded themselves to buy a digger and dumper – to be justified initially by the railway work – so long as 'a complete record of the time when both the digger and dumper are in use is kept'. Alex stayed as the mainstay in the gardens for nearly twenty years.

By 1971 the estate was able to afford a stalker again and the sporting side started to show more potential. The long established forestry fences were deteriorating as the trees grew, giving access to a secure and quiet haven and good feeding for stags instead of banishing them to the hilltops during the summer months. These beasts emerged from their fastness as the rutting season approached, and the quantity and quality of deer increased so that, in October 1973, David and the author each shot a heavy bodied Royal* fairly low down on the hill. Two Royals in one season, let alone in one week, had not been claimed since August 1914. Alas, within days the papers carried the headline, 'Israelis drive into Egypt'. The fighting stayed local but the financial repurcussions were grim; the price of petrol went into orbit with ensuing disasterous economic turmoil. Nevertheless, ignoring international problems, game began to make a significant contribution to Torosay's funds.

Over the next ten years the number of visitors rose steadily from two thousand people paying 5s. each to nearly 30,000 paying over £1 a head. David – with the end of his parliamentary career in sight – had set in motion the regeneration of his beloved castle in which he soon intended to live permanently. There was still much work to be done but he was still at an age when his energy was unflagging.

*   *   *

Back in Dorset, the James's, with the family having flown the nest and the decision made to leave Parliament, realised that Malabar House was far too big. In 1977 they moved into a smaller house called 'The Haven' which they renamed 'Viking House'.

After leaving Westminster in 1979, David took his family on his last quasi-political tour to Israel with the British Conservative Friends of Israel. To both David and Jaquetta, with their deep Christian convictions, this was an heaven-sent opportunity to see the Holy Land. The tour embraced Jerusalem, Bethlehem, Gallilee and Nazareth – where they planted commemorative trees in the Churchill Forest. The political aspects included a visit to the Golan Heights, then still a hotspot, Gaza and the Knesset where they met Menachem Begin, the Prime Minister, and Moshe Dayan the Foreign Minister.

*   *   *

Although David's main task now was to concentrate on the refurbishment of Torosay, and its future presentation, he found he had time to spare and

* A mature stag carrying twelve points on its antlers.

started research on his autobiography. He was exercised as to what form the book should take and it came to him when he found a copy of Dr Axel Munthe's *The Story of San Michele* in the library with the inscription, 'To Olive from her old friend the author' on the fly-leaf. On the title-page was a photograph of Munthe with the equally aged King of Sweden; this brought back memories of David's meeting with Munthe in his 'grace and favour' apartment in Stockholm in 1944 when the old man was in his nineties and David was on his way home from prisoner-of-war camp. The link with the days in 1922 when Munthe had stayed at Torosay as Olive Guthrie's guest made David read the book again and inspired him to hope that his own disparate activities could similarly be linked by the permanence of Torosay. But he doubted whether he had the skill to do it as appealingly as achieved by the old doctor. Anyhow the decision was made that *The Story of San Michele* was to be the model for his autobiography.

In theory this was to be his employment during the five winter months when the castle was closed, plus whatever time he could snatch in between. He began in fits and starts by bringing together work he had done on the family history over the years, and drafted out the chapters leading up to the

Torosay Castle *nestling in its domain.*

war. Taking it further he uncovered the political files which had accumulated during the 1964 débâcle, until he was re-elected by North Dorset. This
reopened the old wounds, and in his mind one of the primary objects of the
book became to expose the wrong done to him, rather than recounting it as
an unfortunate incident during an otherwise interesting life. During the
years left to him he was unable to shake off this burden, although he did not
willingly discuss it nor lumber any of his friends with it. But the mass of correspondence, which continued well into the eighties, belied the fact that it
was a thing of the past. He was so engaged in worrying this stale bone that
no further effective work was ever done on the autobiography.

In January 1981 he approached Harold Evans, the editor of the *Sunday
Times*, with this episode, intimating that he intended to present it as merely a
chapter in his book, but had been unable to obtain from Central Office any
clarification of events. 'This story deserves greater in depth treatment than I
could ever give it and also a higher degree of objectivity than I could hope to
achieve since I don't want to do anybody an injustice.' His motives for want-
ing the story told were that, having been run out of public life by a commu-
nist-inspired rumour, he felt justified in seeing the record put straight and in
causing an enquiry to be set up by Central Office. The *Sunday Times* started
investigations at a cracking pace through their 'Insight' team and all seemed
to be well on the way to confirm David's story. Donald Arthur, who subsequently did, was located drunk in a disreputable bar in Swansea (5ft 4in high
and 20 stone in weight, with health most suspect), and admitted being willing to descend to any depths of venality if the price was right; moreover the
communist connections seemed to stack up. But therafter, whether it was a
change of personnel or policy, the *Sunday Times* appeared to lose interest. It
also failed to return to David the voluminous files he had loaned them for
many months. After vituperative correspondence, lasting until late 1982,
they called a halt to the investigation, claiming that Arthur's lawyers had
advised that there was a binding undertaking given by David that he would
not repeat the allegations he had made in 1964.

All that can be found is a holding letter from David's solicitors in 1964
asking Arthur's solicitors for more information and that 'pending receiving
this information and being able to consider it with our client he authorises
them to give an undertaking not to discuss it'. There is no evidence of any
follow-up, nor can any further correspondence be found.

David, getting more thwarted, aired his dilemma among his cronies and
contacts, the most influential in terms of advice being Lord Home of the
Hirsel. Having bumped into him in Sloane Street and sounded him out,
David followed it up with a four-page letter requesting advice from a moral
and political point of view as to how far he should go in incorporating the
saga in his memoirs – as a warning that communism was still a lethal conspiracy, and because of the importance of exposing the blocking tactics that
had been continuously used by Central Office. Other friends, including a

County Court Judge and an ex-Deputy Director of MI5, felt it should be pursued – not to mention Norman Collins, a friend who had shared that view as long ago as 1964.

Lord Home's reply came in a charming handwritten letter which put the whole thing in perspective and should have closed the issue.

My Dear David

I should not clutter up a good and interesting book with the Agent trouble. I think that the reaction would be that you and the local Conservatives must have been very naive to allow Arthur to muck up your affairs to such a degree.

The other trouble is that the story is so involved and virtually impossible to simplify.

Anyhow most of the contemporary witnesses would say that they could not remember. At the time I certainly cannot recall if anyone told me, presumably not, as the events you describe were taking place right up to the election. Anyhow I think people would be bored (a weekend is a long time in politics) and the impact would be minimal.

As I said earlier your life is so interesting that it ought not be cluttered up with this. Have a good summer in Mull.

Yours
Alec.

So the saga of the 1964 election should have been put to bed, albeit unresolved. But the hurt rumbled on with David and coupled with his concentration on Torosay and his impending final illness, meant that he failed to complete – let alone start properly – what should have been his best book.

Whatever Lord Home advised, the incident has been given space in this book because the event and consequences bit so deeply into David's mind that it is a sad but essential part of what otherwise is a happy story. He could, over the years, suppress some bitterness but could never come to terms with the lack of justice and the want of any positive support by any of his contempories. It clearly drained his health but by clinging to Torosay and his profound religious beliefs, he invoked both hope and faith in that order right to the end; charity was never in doubt.

*   *   *

Reverting to happier things, while he was still in Parliament he found that he had the leisure to start going to the annual conferences of the Amicale Internationale Cap Hourniers,* a French organisation, set up in St Malo before the war. After the war it embraced fourteen member countries, with strict rules on qualifications for individual membership. The first congress he attended in 1976 in Marieham coincided with the political Whitsun recess. David wallowed in the vigorous dancing and lusty singing by several hundred

* International Association of Cape Horners

Bridget Miller, *David James' mother, was the 3rd Laird of Torosay. She inherited the estate from her mother, Olive Guthrie, in 1945. The portraits of Bridget and Geoffrey were painted by Sancho Carlos.*

Lt.-Col. Geoffrey Miller, *Bridget's second husband, was responsible for restoring and creating new features in the gardens at Torosay, including the colonnade, the lower terrace and the Japanese garden.*

nostalgic, ageing men, and gave a dinner for his *Viking* shipmates. Captain Mörn, assuming his old role of Master, flatly put his foot down to the inclusion of old 'Redbeard' (now Greybeard) who still occupied his sober moments painting *Pommern's* masts – a sort of Scandinavian one-man Forth Bridge project.

Westminster interfered with the Helsinki congress in 1977 but a year later it was held at Greenwich so there was no difficulty in singing shanties at 9 p.m. and being in the Division Lobby an hour later. A particularly good *Viking* contingent was there with wives – including Junie Clark from the USA. Bridget, his mother, who had got him involved in the first place was also there. With her was old friend Dorothy Laird, a passenger with her back in 1935, and who had interviewed David in Stockholm after his escape from the prisoner of war camp.

The 1979 congress was held in Adelaide, and no one was expected to appear from Britain. But the Government fell in time for David to propose the adoption of his successor before making last minute arrangements to fly out. This was a time full of memories when they visited Port Victoria and the bar of the Wauraltree Hotel. Forty-two years before, as apprentices, they had all sneaked out of the bar when Captain Mörn came in – but now they entered together arm in arm to see the same faded pictures of sailing ships. Although the nudes were now in full colour, nothing had changed except the pianist thumped out *The Sting* whereas his predecessor played *In the Mood*. They threw a wreath in the sea and moved on to a cemetery to honour a German boy who had fallen from aloft in the barque *Pridwell* in 1936. Throughout the tour they were accompanied by two Australian pipers in full Highland dress who at this point broke into *Deutschland Über Alles*, a march not well suited to being played as a lament. The incongruity of it all made it near impossible for David to stifle his mirth, while the German friends had tears streaming down their cheeks.

So the congresses rolled on, returning to St Malo in 1980 – as was the custom in every fifth year. But, like the 'Ten Little Nigger Boys' members decreased year by year. To an extent they were wallowing in the nostalgia of friendships created in the past that had endured, but David tried to remind himself it was not the end. What of the splendid yachtsmen of the day: Chichester, Rose, Clare Francis, Chay Blyth and the like? A further ray of hope was that a five-masted barque had been designed for the wool trade with an engine to cope in restricted waters and calm belts. She could be the precursor of many, with the shortage of fossil fuel. In fact the days of commercial full-rigged sail were over, but David's optimism was in some way rewarded by the achievements of the Jubilee Sailing Trust. In 1986 it started operating the three-masted ship, *Lord Nelson*, designed to enable disabled people of all ages to get to sea.

David confidently booked his atttendance to the conference to be held in Sydney in 1988. In the meanwhile, to keep the love affair with sail alive, he set out on a 'modest voyage' in November 1985 in the Caribbean Sea aboard the brigantine *Romance*. She was built of wood for the Baltic trade after the war and was also strengthened for ice to go to Greenland. In 1965 Alan Villiers converted her to an 1840-rig to star with Julie Andrews in Michener's film *Hawaii* and several others. The current owner, Captain Arthur Kimberley, and his wife, with a crew of four pre-college Americans, ran the ship in the old style, starting with scrubbing down the decks at 6 a.m. and acknowledging orders with the time honoured, 'Aye, aye Sir'. They cruised the islands by instinct rather than by bearings – which was just as well as the skipper had lost the sight of his right eye. David met the only other passenger Chad Gilpatrick, an old Balliol friend and Rhodes scholar with whom he had sailed in the Mediterranean for the two months before the war. They had a marvellous, relaxed and uncomplicated cruise, although sadly the trade winds deserted them. The biggest problem turned out to be the management of currencies on their landfalls; the French islands needed francs; the Dutch guilders; the Commonwealth islands dollars (not at par with the US); and the Virgin Islands US dollars. It was not an exciting voyage but one of peace and recollection and still one of gentle discovery of places, people and practices around the islands –but it was also one where signs of his impending illness began to show.

*   *   *

In 1983 Viking House was sold and farewell was said to Dorset and the political past. Taking its place was Torosay Castle which became home at last – benefiting from the return of much of the furniture which had been liberated on the James' marriage thirty-three years before.

David's efforts from now on were concentrated on bringing Torosay back to its former glory – to be enjoyed not only by his own circle of family and friends but shared with a wider public. There was to be no delegating in this task. Bridget and Geoffrey were well into their eighties and only just giving up their annual outings; trekking through the Himalayas – Bridget in her gumboots to get as near the Everest Base Camp as possible – to making an early trip to the Seychelles before the islands were 'discovered'; or beating Pol Pot to the temples of Angkor before they were desecrated – as well as their routine visits to Australia. David took control of the estate but there was little he could do about improving the agricultural arrangements with Geoffrey still tenant of the Home Farm and at this point not wishing to upset the tenants on the hill and other farms. Instead he concentrated on his beloved castle and gardens. While not being a practical or sustained gardener himself he revelled in owning the garden which was being maintained and improved by the efforts of others! Jaquetta's love of plants and trees was at last given a chance – though in the early days only by tactful manipulation of Geoffrey and Bridget did her influence and management start to take effect. David's sense of family history was given full rein and he wrote every caption and notice and planned the appearance of every room in the castle to be opened to the public. Staffing of the tea room and shop was taken care of by Jaquetta and both liked nothing more than waylaying visitors either in the house or in the garden – a most effective and unsophisticated PR effort. Word went about and built up the number of visitors, many of whom from abroad passed on the good news of Torosay, or from home returned year after year.

Although David had given up excursions to the hill after he took his last stag in Scallastle corrie in September 1975, he still wanted news of the hill and the health of his deer. The pull of the tide, bringing migrating sea-trout under the Loch Don bridge, was ever strong and pulled him there too. It was his favourite spot and he brought thirteen fish to his net during the summer and autumn of 1984. The previous year it was thirty two but civilization was starting to take a toll of this wonderful fish, whose number was fast declining. But the hills behind, the ever changing light, the stags roaring in October and the flighting wildfowl were there to give the illusion of eternity.

A melancholy coincidence occurred in the same week during 1983 when Castle Guthrie was sold and the contents dispersed after 500 years, and the other Guthrie home, Craigie near Dundee, already in the hands of the local authority, was demolished. This left the Guthries without a clan seat and the Americans, with probably a greater sense of clanship that the natives in Scotland, felt this loss and appealed to David to consider Torosay as their new one. No commitment was made but it remains an issue for David's son and successor, Christopher, to contemplate. With his sense of history David assumed the additional name of Guthrie, hoping that his family might follow. He consolidated this by quartering the arms of James and Guthrie of Craigie and matriculating the arms of Guthrie-James at the office of the Lord Lyon King of Arms in Edinburgh. His closeness to his mother and Gran'Ol, his grandmother, gave the Guthries the edge over the James' and it was bearing their name that he proudly went towards the end of his life.

David's health was failing for his fundamental physical strength became undermined by cancer of the lung. But he never hesitated in his endeavours to see to the castle's survival. Work was continuing to put it in a permanent state of repair. The garden was expanding and in the five years from 1980 to 1985 the number of visitors rose from around 15,500 to nearly 30,000 a year. Dramatically, as David grew weaker – his defiance failing to recognise it – his will power went on leading Torosay through a state of resurgence. He had made provision for his children who were up and away; by mutual consent, Christopher was chosen to benefit from the discretionary trust.

Only by a visit to the gardens can anyone experience the magic of the layout and the maturity of the trees and shrubs, underpinned by progressive planting over the years. David spotted the essentials of the past to be restored and his final years were given to such details and directions. Meanwhile Jaquetta soldiered on with day-to-day practicalities, while nobly nursing and favouring him as his illness made him braver and more obstinate. The end came where he wanted it, at Torosay – at home. The light of dawn rose over Torosay while the dusk closed over David.

It was his faith that carried him through the last difficult days. He knew the end was near and that was that. Two months before he died David and Jaquetta returned to their beloved Lourdes. Among the party was his old colleague Kevin Ney from the Burns Oates days who, over a still mutually enjoyed drink, asked David 'Don't you have any doubts?' David replied 'No, but if I had it would be the biggest con ever known to mankind.'

David died at the right time for him – with his romantic hopes for the world dying with him. There was to be no great resurrection of sail. The Antarctic wilderness was despoiled with the junk of civilisation, and the huskies were moved out as being an alien species – their places taken by petrol-driven, polluting sledges. Within the next two years David was followed by his mother and step-father but this did not leave Torosay bereft. He had left everything in place to restore Torosay, and he was not let down by his son, Christopher who, untried, bravely took up the cudgels, being well embued with the family's sense of service and history – and his father's stubbornness – to safeguard the future for Torosay.

Torosay proves that the continuity of great values must mean something to people of today, starved of uniqueness, excellence, constancy and elegance. The efforts of Christopher and his mother, Jaquetta, ensure that Torosay, alive and welcoming and arrayed in its former glory, is an example to the future and a tribute to the past.

David died on 15th December 1986 and his ashes joined his grandfather at the cross by the Torosay slip. In February 1987 representatives from all his activities and achievements met for a service of thanksgiving and a requiem mass in the crypt chapel of the Palace of Westminster.

The cross *by the Torosay slip, painted by Sylvia Macartney.*

INDEX